GNOME 3 Application Development Beginner's Guide

Step-by-step practical guide to get to grips with GNOME application development

Mohammad Anwari

PACKT PUBLISHING

open source*
community experience distilled

BIRMINGHAM - MUMBAI

GNOME 3 Application Development Beginner's Guide

First published: February 2013

Production Reference: 1080213

Published by Packt Publishing Ltd.
Livery Place
35 Livery Street
Birmingham B3 2PB, UK.

ISBN 978-1-84951-942-7

www.packtpub.com

Cover Image by Duraid Fatouhi (duraidfatouhi@yahoo.com)

Credits

<table>
<tr><td>

Author

Mohammad Anwari

Reviewers

Dhi Aurrahman

Joaquim Rocha

Acquisition Editor

Mary Jasmine

Lead Technical Editor

Ankita Shashi

Technical Editors

Charmaine Pereira

Dominic Pereira

Copy Editors

Laxmi Subramanian

Aditya Nair

Alfida Paiva

Ruta Waghmare

Insiya Morbiwala

</td><td>

Project Coordinator

Abhishek Kori

Proofreader

Mario Cecere

Indexer

Tejal Soni

Graphics

Aditi Gajjar

Production Coordinator

Aparna Bhagat

Cover Work

Aparna Bhagat

</td></tr>
</table>

About the Author

Mohammad Anwari is a software hacker from Indonesia with more than 13 years of experience in software development. He has been working with Linux-based systems, applications in GNOME, and Qt platforms. The projects he has worked on range from the development of constrained devices and desktop applications, to high traffic server systems and applications.

He worked for his own startup company during the dotcom era before moving to Finland to work for Nokia/MeeGo. Now he's back in Indonesia, regaining his entrepreneurship by establishing a new startup company that focuses on Node.js and Linux-based projects. In his free time, he serves as an executive director for BlankOn, one of the biggest open source projects in Indonesia.

In the past, he has published a couple of books on Linux in the Indonesian language.

This book would have been impossible to write without the great and continuous support from my family: Rini, Alif, and Abil.

About the Reviewers

Dhi Aurrahman is a Project Manager at Labtek Indie, where he leads the development of custom-tailored interactive applications for various installations and platforms. Prior to this, he worked on various projects based on real-time computer vision systems with Samsung Electronics in South Korea. He has proven skills in C++ programming; application development using Qt for various platforms, including desktop and mobile; and JavaScript programming. Dhi has done his B.Sc in Computational Physics from Bandung Institute of Technology, Indonesia, and his M.Eng in Computer Engineering, focused on computer vision and machine learning, from Chonnam National University, South Korea.

Joaquim Rocha is a Portuguese software developer with an M.Sc. degree in Computer Science. He has over six years of experience in developing graphical user interfaces and has been involved in a number of Free Software projects.

He is also a member of the GNOME Foundation and is the author of the most complete OCR application, OCRFeeder, which was developed for the GNOME desktop.

As part of his work for the Free Software consultancy Igalia, Joaquim has created the world's first Free Software skeleton-tracking library, completely written with GNOME technologies.

www.PacktPub.com

Support files, eBooks, discount offers and more

You might want to visit `www.PacktPub.com` for support files and downloads related to your book.

Did you know that Packt offers eBook versions of every book published, with PDF and ePub files available? You can upgrade to the eBook version at `www.PacktPub.com` and as a print book customer, you are entitled to a discount on the eBook copy. Get in touch with us at `service@packtpub.com` for more details.

At `www.PacktPub.com`, you can also read a collection of free technical articles, sign up for a range of free newsletters and receive exclusive discounts and offers on Packt books and eBooks.

`http://PacktLib.PacktPub.com`

Do you need instant solutions to your IT questions? PacktLib is Packt's online digital book library. Here, you can access, read and search across Packt's entire library of books.

Why Subscribe?

- Fully searchable across every book published by Packt
- Copy and paste, print and bookmark content
- On demand and accessible via web browser

Free Access for Packt account holders

If you have an account with Packt at `www.PacktPub.com`, you can use this to access PacktLib today and view nine entirely free books. Simply use your login credentials for immediate access.

Table of Contents

Preface

This book is about developing GNOME 3 applications with the Vala and JavaScript programming languages. It guides you to build GTK+, Clutter, and HTML5 applications on the GNOME 3 platform. It covers GNOME 3 specific subsystems such as data access, multimedia, networking, and filesystem. It also covers good software engineering practices such as localization and testing.

What this book covers

Chapter 1, Installing GNOME 3 and SDK, discusses installing GNOME 3 and the Software Development Kit in some popular Linux distributions.

Chapter 2, Preparing Our Weapons, talks about the basic usage of the Integrated Development Environment and User Interface Designer used in this book: Anjuta and Glade. This chapter also touches on the development reference tool – Devhelp.

Chapter 3, Programming Languages, covers the basics of Vala and programming JavaScript with Seed. This chapter will be the foundation to understand the following chapters if you are yet not familiar with Vala and JavaScript.

Chapter 4, Using GNOME Core Libraries, guides you to exploit the commonly used features of the GNOME core libraries.

Chapter 5, Building Graphical User Interface Applications explains the steps of building GUI applications with GTK+ and Clutter.

Chapter 6, Creating Widgets, explains how to create GTK+ widgets from scratch. This chapter also talks about extending and customizing widgets.

Chapter 7, Having Fun with Multimedia, contains lots of information on GStreamer. It covers both playing multimedia stream and applying filters to the stream.

Chapter 8, Playing with Data, explains presenting data with the TreeView API family. While showing the data presentation, it also talks about getting data from Evolution Data Server.

Chapter 9, Deploying HTML5 Applications with GNOME, explains how to embed WebKit into a GTK+ application. It also talks about the JavaScriptCore library, which makes it possible to get the JavaScript running in WebKit to talk with the backend system written in Vala.

Chapter 10, Desktop Integration, discusses about creating applications that integrate nicely with the GNOME 3 desktop. It talks about D-Bus, session management, keyring, launcher, and notification services.

Chapter 11, Making Our Applications Go International, discusses about internationalization and localization in GNOME 3 applications. It also provides a proposal of the localization process as a bonus.

Chapter 12, Quality Made Easy, talks about performing unit testing and stubbing. This covers both testing GTK+ and non-GUI applications.

Chapter 13, Exciting Projects, offers two exciting projects to build a web browser and a Twitter client. It covers many aspects learned in the preceding chapters and uses them in these two projects.

What you need for this book

This book requires a basic level of object-oriented programming. Prior experience with Vala or JavaScript will make your experience more enjoyable. In order to follow the book, you must install the latest version of Fedora, openSUSE, Ubuntu, or (preferably) any Debian-based Linux distribution.

Who this book is for

This book is suitable for software developers who target GNOME 3 as one of the deployment platforms. This book is also beneficial for developers who want to create multiplatform applications, as many of the GNOME 3 libraries are also available in Linux, OSX, and Windows.

Conventions

In this book, you will find several headings appearing frequently.

To give clear instructions of how to complete a procedure or task, we use:

Time for action – heading

1. Action 1
2. Action 2
3. Action 3

Instructions often need some extra explanation so that they make sense, so they are followed with:

What just happened?

This heading explains the working of tasks or instructions that you have just completed.

You will also find some other learning aids in the book, including:

Pop quiz – heading

These are short multiple-choice questions intended to help you test your own understanding.

Have a go hero – heading

These are practical challenges and give you ideas for experimenting with what you have learned.

You will also find a number of styles of text that distinguish between different kinds of information. Here are some examples of these styles, and an explanation of their meaning.

Code words in text are shown as follows: "Modify `configure.ac` to include WebKitGTK+ into the project."

A block of code is set as follows:

```
using GLib;
using Gtk;
using WebKit;

public class Main : WebView
{
  public Main ()
  {
load_html_string("<h1>Hello</h1>","/");
  }
```

```
    static int main (string[] args)
    {
Gtk.init (ref args);
varwebView = new Main ();
var window = new Gtk.Window();
window.add(webView);
window.show_all ();

Gtk.main ();

    return 0;
    }
}
```

Any command-line input or output is written as follows:

```
LANGUAGE=id LC_ALL=id_ID.utf8 src/hello-i18n
```

New terms and **important words** are shown in bold. Words that you see on the screen, in menus or dialog boxes for example, appear in the text like this: "Click **Continue**, finish the setup of **GTranslator** and go ahead and open the `id.po` file using its menu."

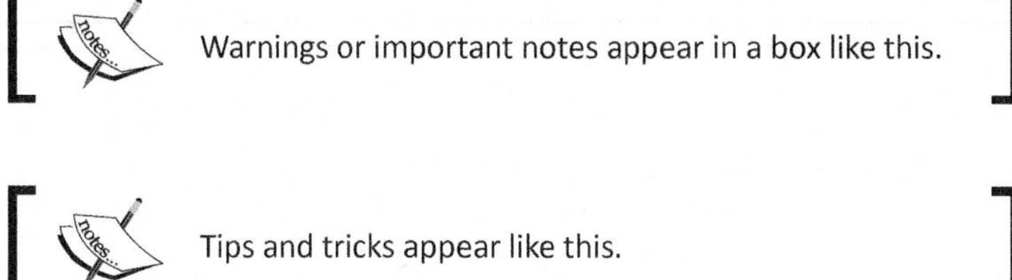

Warnings or important notes appear in a box like this.

Tips and tricks appear like this.

Reader feedback

Feedback from our readers is always welcome. Let us know what you think about this book—what you liked or may have disliked. Reader feedback is important for us to develop titles that you really get the most out of.

To send us general feedback, simply send an e-mail to `feedback@packtpub.com`, and mention the book title through the subject of your message.

If there is a topic that you have expertise in and you are interested in either writing or contributing to a book, see our author guide on `www.packtpub.com/authors`.

Customer support

Now that you are the proud owner of a Packt book, we have a number of things to help you to get the most from your purchase.

Downloading the example code

You can download the example code files for all Packt books you have purchased from your account at `http://www.packtpub.com`. If you purchased this book elsewhere, you can visit `http://www.packtpub.com/support` and register to have the files e-mailed directly to you.

Errata

Although we have taken every care to ensure the accuracy of our content, mistakes do happen. If you find a mistake in one of our books—maybe a mistake in the text or the code—we would be grateful if you would report this to us. By doing so, you can save other readers from frustration and help us improve subsequent versions of this book. If you find any errata, please report them by visiting `http://www.packtpub.com/submit-errata`, selecting your book, clicking on the **errata submission form** link, and entering the details of your errata. Once your errata are verified, your submission will be accepted and the errata will be uploaded to our website, or added to any list of existing errata, under the Errata section of that title.

Piracy

Piracy of copyright material on the Internet is an ongoing problem across all media. At Packt, we take the protection of our copyright and licenses very seriously. If you come across any illegal copies of our works, in any form, on the Internet, please provide us with the location address or website name immediately so that we can pursue a remedy.

Please contact us at `copyright@packtpub.com` with a link to the suspected pirated material.

We appreciate your help in protecting our authors, and our ability to bring you valuable content.

Questions

You can contact us at `questions@packtpub.com` if you are having a problem with any aspect of the book, and we will do our best to address it.

1

Installing GNOME 3 and SDK

GNOME 3 is the latest and greatest version of GNOME since it was released for the first time in 1999. GNOME 3 delivers a breakthrough desktop user experience compared to its previous versions. While providing smooth user interface with fluid animations, it uses a different metaphor of how a modern desktop would work by introducing GNOME Shell as its new user experience (UX). However, the traditional user experience still persists as a fallback whenever the hardware configuration is not supported.

GNOME is known for its simplicity and has been chosen as the default desktop environment in many popular Linux distributions. It is also one of the **first free types of software** that has user interface guidelines, hence securing itself as usable and user friendly.

During its evolution, the architecture also changed and was extended, making it one of the most advanced freely available desktops in the world. With that, it requires more and more advanced technology to be available in the system to be able to maximize the usage of the hardware and at the same time give users an enjoyable time when using computers.

Before we go any further, a proper installation of GNOME as well as the development environment should be available in our computer. And as a starter, we will talk about the installation in a few popular Linux distributions. Specifically, we will cover these topics in this chapter:

- Understanding the system requirements
- The basic GNOME 3 architecture that we will cover in this book
- Installing GNOME 3 and the SDK on various Linux distributions

So let's get started.

System requirements

GNOME 3 provides two sets of **User Experience** (**UX**) that target different types of installed hardware—**GNOME Shell** and **GNOME Panel/Fallback**. These two UX have different requirements, but they share the basic ones:

- 800 MHz CPU power (at least 1 GHz for optimal performance)
- 512 MB of RAM (at least 1 GB for optimal performance)
- More than 2 GB of available hard drive storage (more, if you want to install more applications)

The GNOME Shell

This is the latest addition in GNOME 3, and provides slick user experience. This UX requires 3D acceleration through an OpenGL-capable video card properly installed in your system. On a safer note, most of the video cards from Intel, ATI, and nvidia brands would work nicely.

However, even though you know that you have a video card that is capable of doing OpenGL, make sure that your video card is really activated with the proper drivers, otherwise the system will not let you use this UX.

You can check whether your video card would work with this UX by checking the **h-node page at** `http://www.h-node.org/videocards/catalogue/en` and check whether it has the **works with 3D acceleration** verdict stated there.

GNOME Panel/Fallback

This is the good old GNOME desktop, which provides a basic and less attractive user experience. The system will fall back into this UX whenever it cannot activate the OpenGL. This UX is similar to the older versions of GNOME, but the user interface is modified a bit so that it will look similar to a state of GNOME Shell user interface. For example, the main UI is totally different but the lock screen is pretty similar in both.

Fortunately, only a few parts of this book will make use of the GNOME Shell UX in great depth, so we can safely work with GNOME Panel/Fallback UX in order to follow this book.

Development requirements

As we are doing software development on top of these requirements, obviously we will need more computing power, RAM, and storage. Fulfilling at least the following requirements would make our development time enjoyable:

- Multicore 2 GHz CPU
- 4 GB of RAM
- 500 GB of hard drive storage, preferably SSD

The good news is that we can easily develop GNOME 3 applications using virtualization. By installing the Linux distributions in virtual machines, we can switch between them and tackle the issues found there so that we can make sure that our applications will be built smoothly in GNOME 3 regardless of the distributions. In case of GNOME Shell, you need to make sure that you have enabled the 3D acceleration option in your favorite virtual machine program.

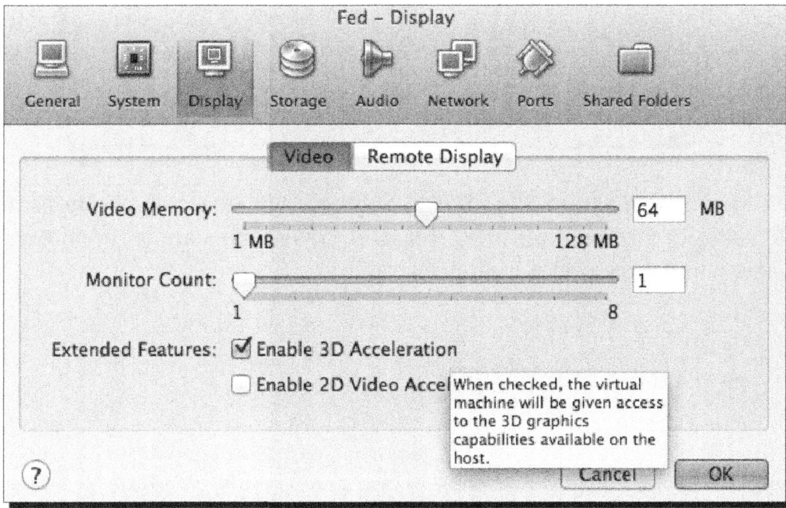

For example, in **VirtualBox**, we can go to the **Settings** dialog of a virtual machine, click on the **Display** option, and then tick on the **Enable 3D Acceleration** option. Remember, though, that you will not be able to activate this option if your host machine is not capable of doing 3D acceleration by itself.

GNOME 3 desktop architecture

When talking about GNOME 3, usually many people refer only to the GNOME Shell. This is incorrect. GNOME Shell is just a part of the whole GNOME desktop architecture. It can be replaced (as in the case of GNOME Panel/Fallback UX) or even removed.

In fact, GNOME is more than GNOME Shell. It provides the infrastructure of the applications so they can talk to the system, render text nicely, flow the animation, read data, and so on. We need to understand the architecture better before starting any development. This would help us to know which parts need to be installed, too. Let's start with looking at the following simplified GNOME architecture diagram:

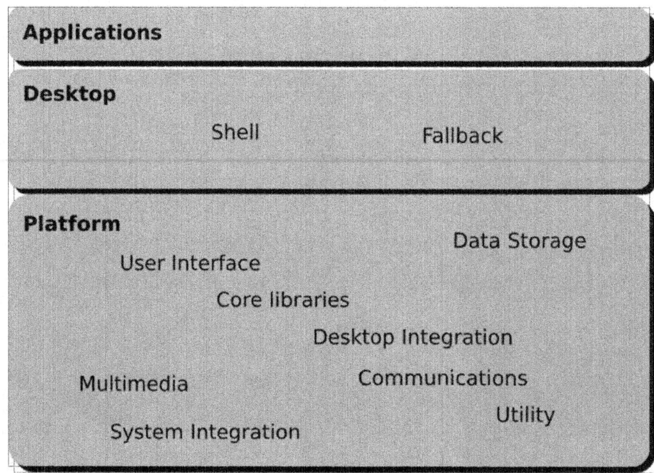

As we can see from the diagram, the GNOME Shell, along with the applications, sits on top of the GNOME platform architecture stack. This book covers the platform architecture and will touch on some parts of the upper layer.

> The GNOME platform reference can be studied in more depth in the GNOME developer website, `http://developer.gnome.org`.

The following are the specific components of the GNOME platform that we will cover in this book:

- **Core libraries**: These are the lowest interface in the architecture. It includes the following:
    - **GObject**: This is the object system in GNOME. It is the GNOME's object-oriented programming approach with the C language.
    - **GLib**: This is a general purpose library that contains the infrastructure used by all the parts in the architecture.
    - **GIO**: This is a virtual filesystem library that provides access to files, volumes, and drives in an abstracted manner.

- ◆ **User interface libraries**: This is the toolkit for building graphical applications, and includes:

  - ❑ **GTK+**: Historically named as the **GIMP toolkit**, this is the default toolkit to build graphical applications in GNOME. It provides a set of widgets and tools.

  - ❑ **Cairo**: This is a library that helps us draw on the canvas. It is mainly used for creating new widgets or extending the existing ones.

  - ❑ **Pango**: This is a library that helps us to do text rendering.

  - ❑ **ATK**: This is the accessibility toolkit. It provides ways to offer a good experience for special users of GNOME that have different needs.

  - ❑ **Clutter**: This is a toolkit that is used for creating applications with rich and fluid animations. This requires OpenGL.

  - ❑ **WebKit**: This is the web toolkit. It provides full-featured engines capable of displaying HTML5 documents.

- ◆ **Multimedia libraries**: Provides playing and authoring multimedia files, and includes:

  - ❑ **GStreamer**: This is a powerful multimedia library

- ◆ **Data storage**: Provides libraries of accessing data:

  - ❑ **Evolution Data Storage (EDS)**: This contains **libebook** and **libecal**, and provides access to the address book and the calendar managed in your Evolution.

We will also use several tools in this book; they are as follows:

- ◆ **seed**: This is a JavaScript interpreter in the GNOME world. We will use this when we develop our GNOME application scripts. We will have seed automatically installed when installing the GNOME Shell, so we will not see this explicitly later when we do the installation.

- ◆ **vala**: This is an emerging object-oriented programming language, mainly used for developing GNOME applications.

- ◆ **Anjuta**: This is an integrated development environment software for GNOME.

- ◆ **Glade**: This is a graphical application layout designer for GTK+.

- ◆ **Gtranslator**: This is a tool for translating our application user interface to local languages.

- ◆ **Devhelp**: This is a reference lookup tool; really handy when developing applications.

Note that the actual package names of these parts are not standardized, so you will find that the package names are slightly different from the preceding list. These will be specifically covered in each section.

GNOME and the SDK

We will go through installing GNOME and the **Software Development Kit (SDK)** in our favorite Linux distribution. A few popular distributions are covered. However, we are not going to talk about installing any of these distributions, so it is expected that we already have it up and running. We just need to install several additional packages to get the GNOME and the SDK.

You can directly go ahead to the section discussing your distribution without bothering to read the other distribution's installation descriptions. And if your distribution is not listed here, no need to be worried, just pick the closest distribution variant and adjust the package names as we will use the search function in the distributions when we are installing. Now let's pull our sleeves up and jump right into the action.

Time for action – installing GNOME and SDK in Fedora 17

Fedora 17 uses GNOME 3 by default, so our focus here is to install the SDK. To install packages in Fedora 17, we are going to use the **Add/Remove Software** tool. This is how we do it:

1. Click on the **Activities** button on upper-left corner of the screen.
2. Click on the **Applications** button.
3. Click on the **Add/Remove Software** button.

4. The following tool shows up:

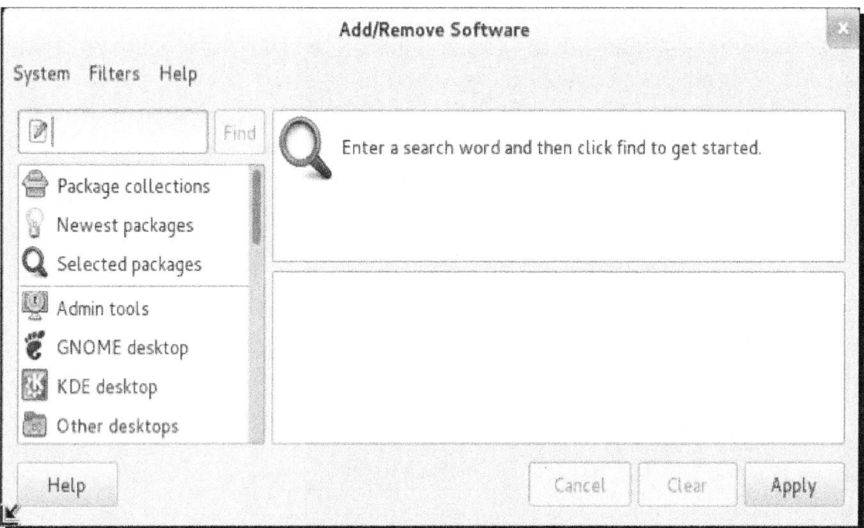

What just happened?

The **Add/Remove Software** tool shows the database of Fedora 17 packages that we can browse and select. The left-hand side of the screen displays a search textbox, and below it we can see the collection packages. The collection package is a group of packages that serve similar functionalities. On the upper-left corner we can see the place where the search results or the contents of a collection will be displayed, and below it we can see the description box of a selected package we choose in the above area.

The SDK comes in the form of so-called development packages. In Fedora, the development packages use `-devel` as its postfix on their names. The actual libraries are inside the package without the `-devel` postfix and they are by default installed when the `devel` packages are installed. For example, GLib is available inside the `glib2` package and the supporting development package is available in the `glib2-devel` package. Whenever the `glib2-devel` package is installed, the `glib2` package is automatically installed.

> The development package means that it contains header files and other files needed only when you do development, but not needed when you are only running it.

So let's start finding them.

Marking packages to be installed

Before a package can be installed with this tool, it must be marked for installation. Head on to the search box and type `glib2-devel`. Click on the **Find** button and we will see the search results. It should be a couple of lines with one of them showing the `glib2-devel` string followed by a long version number (`glib2-devel-2.32.1-1.fc17`, in my case). Tick on the checkbox to its left. We should see that the tool stamps the icon with a big plus sign, meaning that it is marked for installation. If you don't see a checkbox, it is already installed.

The following table provides a mapping between the package names in Fedora 17 and the GNOME components described in the architecture section earlier. We also want to install the documentation packages (the names are inconsistently postfixed with `-doc` or `-docs`). We also will install the tools and basic development packages that we are going to use throughout this book. So let's go ahead with marking these packages in the tool by searching and ticking the checkbox.

Subsystem	Package names
Core libraries	`glib2-devel` (GIO and GObject are already inside this package)
User interface libraries	`gtk3-devel`
	`gtk3-devel-docs`
	`cairo-devel`
	`pango-devel`
	`atk-devel`
	`clutter-devel`
	`clutter-doc`
	`webkitgtk3-devel`
	`webkitgtk3-doc`
Multimedia libraries	`gstreamer-devel`
	`gstreamer-devel-docs`
Data storage	`evolution-data-server-devel`
	`evolution-data-server-doc`
Tools and basic development packages	`vala`
	`vala-doc`
	`vala-tools`
	`anjuta`
	`glade` (don't mix up with `glade3`!)
	`glade-libs`
	`gtranslator`
	`devhelp`

Ready to install the packages

After we mark the packages, we are ready to install them. Just click on the **Apply** button at the bottom of the screen. We will get a dialog popping up and asking whether we want to install additional packages required by the packages we selected previously. Make a nod gesture to agree by clicking on the **Continue** button. Then enter the root password and relax for a while as the tool will download and install all the packages into the system. After everything is installed, we will get a new window, as shown in the next screenshot, that displays that there are newly installed applications that we can run; let's keep this dialog for the next chapter.

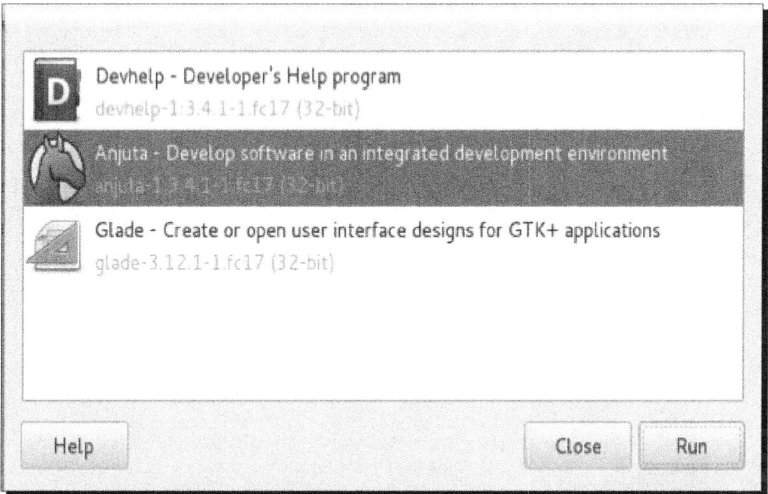

Time for action – installing GNOME and SDK in openSUSE 12

openSUSE 12 ships GNOME by default, so we don't need to worry about it and can just concentrate on getting the SDK installed. To manage applications, openSUSE provides the **Yet another Setup Tool (YaST)** tool. Follow these steps to install the SDK in openSUSE 12:

1. Click on the **Activities** button on the upper-left corner of the screen.
2. Click on the **Applications** button.
3. Click on **YaST** (or type `YaST` in the text field).
4. **YaST** is now opened; to continue, click on the **Software Management** icon.

5. After a while taken for contacting the servers and refreshing the package database, it is ready to use. This is how it will appear:

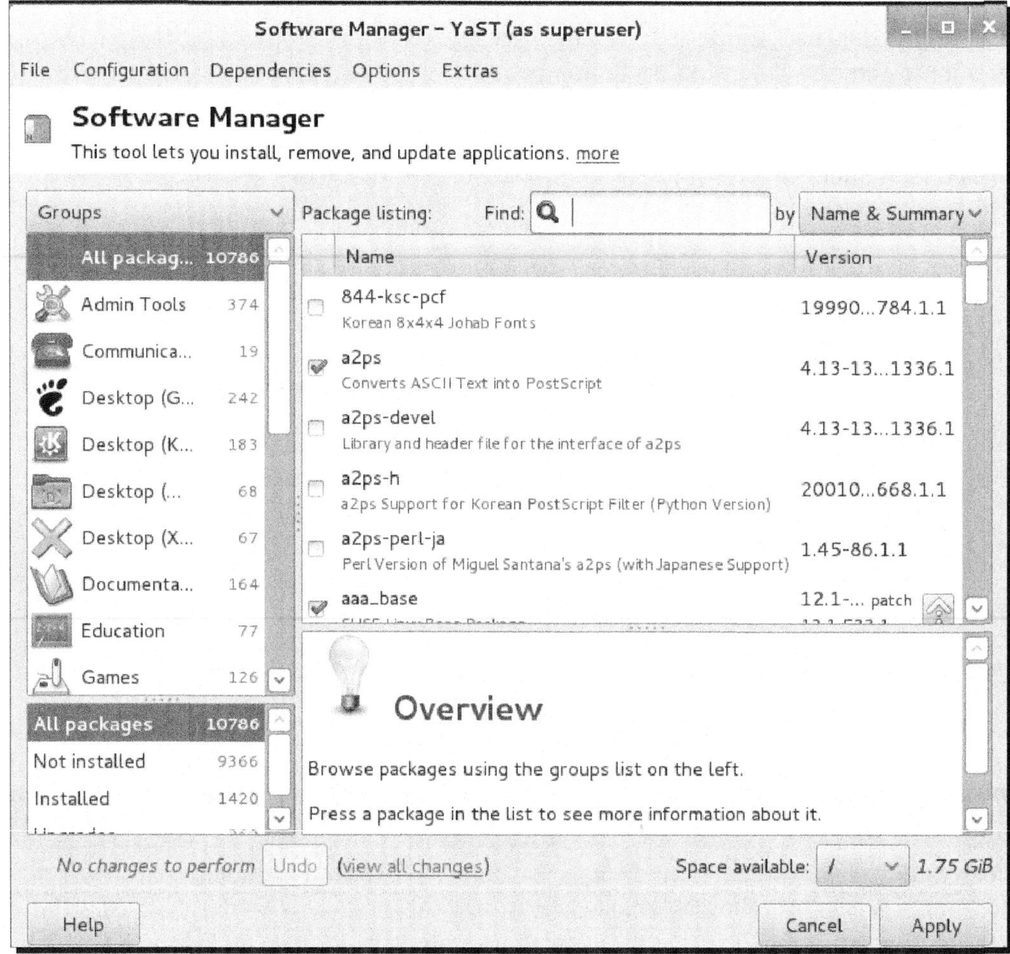

What just happened?

YaST is a collection of system management tools in openSUSE, and **Software Manager** is one of the tools. As the name suggests, we will use this tool to install the GNOME SDK. As you can see, the tool has two main columns, with each column having two sections each. The left-hand side column shows package categories whereas the right-hand side column shows the content of the selected categories (or the search results) and the description of the package. We will use this tool only by using the search functionality and not touching the categories to the left.

Similar to the **Add/Remove Software** tool in Fedora, **YaST** uses a mark-and-install paradigm, meaning we need to mark a software before installing it. With this concept, we can first select the software we want and then make the final move by just pressing a button to get the selections installed. Let's do it.

Marking SDK packages

SDK are scattered in many different development packages. Similar to Fedora, which uses the RPM package management system, the development package names are postfixed with `-devel`, and the corresponding library will get automatically installed when the development package is installed.

The following table provides a mapping between the openSUSE package names and the GNOME components described in the architecture section earlier. We can go ahead and type these names (one at a time) in the search box and tick a checkbox situated to the left of the search results entry. By ticking this checkbox, it means that the package is put into an installing queue. If you see that the checkbox is already ticked, it means the package is already installed.

Subsystem	Package names
Core libraries	`glib2-devel` (GIO and GObject are already inside this package)
User interface libraries	`gtk3-devel`
	`gtk3-devel-docs`
	`libseed-gtk3-devel`
	`cairo-devel`
	`pango-devel`
	`atk-devel`
	`clutter-devel`
	`libwebkitgtk3-devel`
Multimedia libraries	`gstreamer-0_10-devel`
	`gstreamer-0_10-doc`
	`gstreamer-0_10-fluendo-mp3`
Data storage	`evolution-data-server-devel`
	`evolution-data-server-doc`
Tools and basic development packages	`vala`
	`anjuta`
	`glade` (don't mix up with `glade3`!)
	`gtranslator`
	`devhelp`

Starting the installation

After marking the packages, let's now hit the **Apply** button to start the installation. Let's wait a while until all the packages are installed; after this, we are good to go to the next chapter.

Time for action – installing GNOME and SDK in Debian Testing

Debian Testing (also called **Wheezy**) uses GNOME 3 as its default desktop, so our focus now is to get the SDK installed. Same as Fedora, Debian Testing uses the **Add/Remove Software** tool to do the package management. So let's get started by running the tool:

1. Click on the **Activities** button on the upper-left corner of the screen.

2. Click on the **Applications** button.

3. Click on the **Add/Remove Software** button.

4. The following tool shows up:

What just happened?

The **Add/Remove Software** tool is a mark-and-install package management tool. It means that before doing any real installation, we are given a chance to select the packages we want to install. The installation is postponed until the time we provide confirmation by pressing the **Apply** button. With this installation style, we can keep browsing the packages without getting bothered by the installation process.

As you can see in the previous screenshot, the tool has two main columns. The left-hand side column shows the search box and the package categories. The right-hand side column shows the search results (or the category contents), and below it there is a box showing the package description.

Marking SDK packages

The SDK packages come in many development packages. The development packages contain the header and all the supporting files required during compilation and linking. It is not necessary for them to be installed when we just need to run the applications linked to a library.

These packages are named with the `lib` prefix and the `-dev` postfix. They have internal dependencies to the actual library needed by the applications; so whenever we install a development package, the package containing the actual library goes with it automatically.

Here is a map of the Debian packages and GNOME components described in the architecture section. Let's type the names of the packages into the search box and mark them for installation.

Subsystem	Package names
Core libraries	`libglib2.0-dev` 9 (GIO and GObject are already inside this package)
	`libglib2.0-doc`
User interface libraries	`libgtk-3-dev`
	`libgtk-3-doc`
	`libcairo2-dev`
	`libcairo2-doc`
	`libpango1.0-dev`
	`libpango1.0-doc`
	`libatk1.0-dev`
	`libatk1.0-doc`
	`libclutter-1.0-dev`
	`libclutter-1.0-doc`
	`libwebkitgtk-3.0-dev`
	`libwebkitgtk-3.0-doc`
Multimedia libraries	`libgstreamer0.10-dev`
Data storage	`libecal1.2-dev`
Tools and basic development packages	`valac-0.16`
	`anjuta`
	`glade`
	`gtranslator`
	`devhelp`

Applying the installation

After marking the packages, let's now hit the **Apply** button to start the installation. Let's sit back and relax. Wait a while until all the packages are installed. After that, we are clear to go to the next chapter.

Time for action – installing GNOME and SDK in Ubuntu 12.04

Ubuntu ships with its own desktop, called **Unity**. Our focus here is to install the GNOME 3 desktop as well as the SDK with the **Ubuntu Software Center** tool; let's see how this is done:

1. Click on the **Ubuntu Software Center** icon on the left-hand side of the screen. The next screenshot shows this tool.

2. Click within the search box and type `gnome-shell`.

3. Click on the **Install** button of the first search result.

4. GNOME Shell is installed.

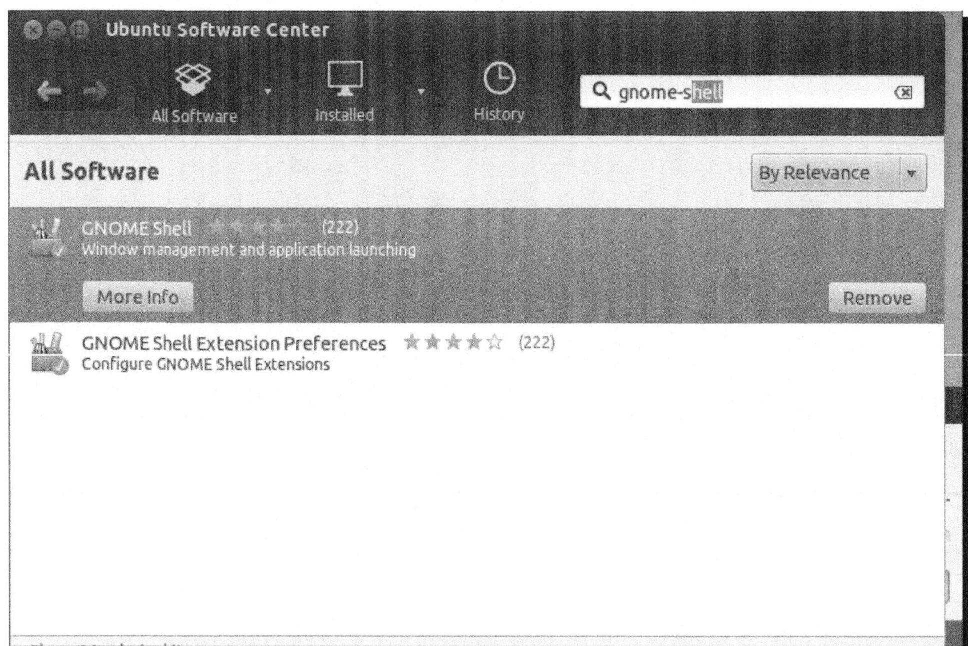

What just happened?

What we have done is install the GNOME Shell desktop. Because the GNOME Panel is also coupled with the GNOME Shell in form of package dependencies specified internally, we will get both the UXs installed.

The **Ubuntu Software Center** tool doesn't use the mark-and-install paradigm, so we need to do installation on every search result. The installation process is done in the background, but unfortunately we can't search while installing. However, if some other package that we want to install appears on the same result page, we can click on the **Install** button to queue it in the installation process.

Continue installing the SDK

Ubuntu gets its root from Debian, hence the package naming system is the same. Let's see the mapping of the Ubuntu package names and GNOME components in the Debian section explained earlier. Get all the packages mentioned in the map installed one by one.

After all of the packages are installed, we are ready to go to the next chapter!

Summary

We learned a lot in this chapter about system requirements, basic architecture, and installing GNOME and the SDK. Specifically, we learned that GNOME 3 provides two UXs. We understood their system requirements for running as well as for developing on top of them. Also, we learned a small tip for getting it to work in a virtualization environment. We discussed the basic GNOME desktop architecture and the description of each of the components inside it, along with the tools that we are going to use in this book.

We also now know where certain GNOME components sit in the architecture diagram. We also know the tools we are going to use and how they are packaged in popular Linux distributions. We also learned how to install them. The advantage of this is that it will give us insight into how Linux distributions ship the system.

This is a good start for us to learn how to develop applications on top of GNOME 3. The next step is to prepare our development tools. We are going to learn how to use them and touch on a little bit of Vala, one of the programming languages we will use in this book.

2

Preparing Our Weapons

One of the great factors that contributes to a successful software project is familiarity with the tools used in the project. The tools we are using in this book can be considered as our weapons. If we use them correctly, not only could they take down our targets (which is the software we are creating) nicely, but we could also save time by using them efficiently. Otherwise, they could backfire and hurt us.

In this chapter, we want to master the main tools that we are going to use throughout the book. They are the **Integrated Development Environment (IDE)** called Anjuta, the user interface layout designer called Glade, and the development reference browser called Devhelp. These tools are a great help for beginners, and even if we become experts after finishing this book, we would still benefit from using them.

As a quick outline for this chapter, we will take a look at these topics:

- Creating a project in Anjuta
- The IDE layout
- Source code navigation and manipulation
- Managing project building
- Using mockup to design application layout using Glade
- Reading reference books with Devhelp

So let's start!

Firing up Anjuta

We are going to use Anjuta in this chapter. Let's do that by invoking Anjuta by navigating to **Activities | Anjuta** in GNOME Shell or **Applications | Programming | Anjuta** in GNOME Panel.

Time for action – creating a new Vala project

We are going to create a simple Vala project to warm up. We will use this project to go through the features of Anjuta. So here we go:

1. In Anjuta's main screen click on **Create a new project**.

2. In the dialog box that appears, click on the **Vala** tab.

3. Click on the **GTK+ (Simple)** option and then click on **Continue**.

4. Fill in the project information dialog, type `hello-world` in the **Project Name** field, and fill the rest with your own preference and click on **Continue**.

5. Leave the next few questions as they are (except if you really want to make changes, for example, to the path of the project). Make sure that the **Use GtkBuilder for user interface** checkbox is ticked. Click on **Continue.**

6. If you are happy with the information shown in the confirmation dialog, hit **Apply.**

7. A new project has now been created, as shown in the following screenshot:

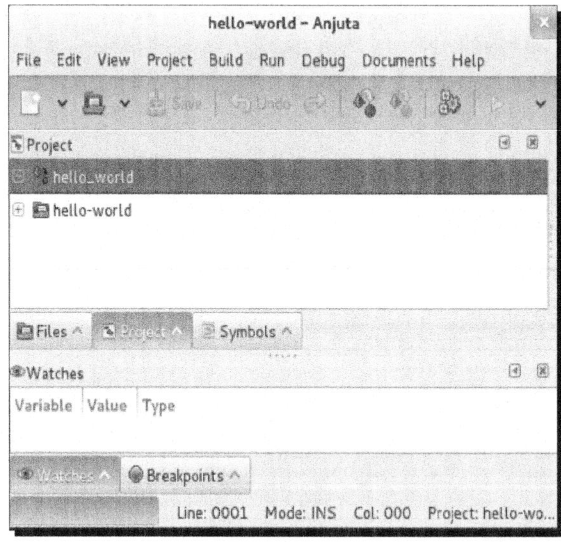

What just happened?

In Anjuta, we will create a project that is a container of all the files and resources that collectively make a software. We will add source codes, files, images, and so on, which are required for project building and deployment. What we have just done is that we have created a simple GTK+ project using the Vala programming language. Don't worry if you don't know what Vala is at this point and the code presented here does not make sense to you, because you are going to learn about it after this chapter.

The wizard that we just ran created a set of files, including generated source code and a user interface. These files can be considered as templates, and we will make changes to these files when we do the development.

As an IDE, Anjuta is quite full featured. It has a source code and general files' editor, a debugger, and Glade, a user interface layout designer. If you are familiar with other IDEs, you may find the view a bit different; so let's dissect this further.

The IDE layout

The layout of the IDE is quite simple and is composed of a toolbar, an editor, and arrangeable docks. The toolbar is quite straightforward and is a familiar element. It is a shortcut of certain functions, such as file and editing operation, project running and building, and debugging operations.

There are two kinds of editors in Anjuta. The source code editor and Glade, the user interface editor. Let's talk about the first one.

Like other advanced source code editors, Anjuta provides quite a powerful editor. The notable features are:

- **Line numbering**: You see the line number on the left side of the editor. The line number on the current line is emboldened so it is easy for us to know where we are.

- **Syntax highlighting**: The tokens in source code are colored so we can easily distinguish variables, classes, comments, and so on.

- **Code completion**: Anjuta provides decent code completion. A candidate list of class members or methods are displayed when we type an object instance.

Docks are a set of tools that contain specific functions. We can decide whether we want to show or hide the docks by toggling them individually in the **View** menu. Let's see a quick introduction of each dock.

Bookmarks

This tool enables us to bookmark places inside the files that we are editing. When our source code becomes larger and more complex, this tool would come in handy. Whenever we edit more than one file and they are cross referenced with each other, we can go back and forth between the files quickly by just clicking on the bookmark entry.

Files

This tool lists all the files in the project. It is a quick view of the files inside the project folder. If we want to edit the file, we just need to double-click on the file we are interested in, and the editor will pop up.

Project

This tool acts as our view to the project. It categorically lists the contents of the project. We can easily see which files are user interface files, which files are source code, and so on. A double-click on the project item would either bring up the editor (for the user interface layout files or the source code) or a dialog (for other project items). Here we can control Anjuta and many aspects of the project items, such as the installation path, compiler switches, and so on.

Symbols

This tool shows all the symbols inside our project. The **File**, **Project**, and **Search** tabs represent the scope of the symbol that we are interested in. When we double-click on the symbol, the editor will immediately go to the line where the symbol resides.

Watches

This is a debugger tool that shows the values of all the variables that we are interested in. If you are a "debugging-by-doing-printf" person, you may find that this tool is better. Unfortunately, this tool only works when we develop with the C language. However, we can still use this with C code that is generated from Vala.

Breakpoints

This is also a debugger tool that manages the breakpoints. Breakpoints are places in the source code that we want to pause at when we run the program. Breakpoints and Watches are really useful and powerful tools that will make our life easier. It's the same with the Watches dock; this tool only works when we develop with the C language.

Messages

This dock displays the compiler's, linker's, and other build tools' messages. This dock is activated when we start building a project.

Terminal

This dock embeds a terminal shell. We can invoke commands to the shell directly. This dock is activated when we have built a project successfully.

Navigation between tabs

The editor is capable of editing multiple files at the same time. The files we are editing are displayed in tabs, and we can easily switch between them.

Time for action – navigating between tabs

Let's try to open a couple of files from our project and see how we can navigate between the files. One scenario we can imagine is that we are editing a complex project and one file depends on the other, so editing one file would require us to change the other file.

1. Click on the **View** menu and make sure that the **Files** dock is active.

2. Click on the **Files** dock and navigate through the list until you find **src/**.

3. Expand the list by clicking on the plus button.

4. Double-click on **hello_world.vala**.

5. Double-click on **config.vapi**.

6. Now we have two files open, and we can switch between these tabs by pressing the *Alt + 1* and *Alt + 2* combination keys on the keyboard. If you open more files, go ahead with using *Alt + 3*, *Alt + 4*, and so on to navigate.

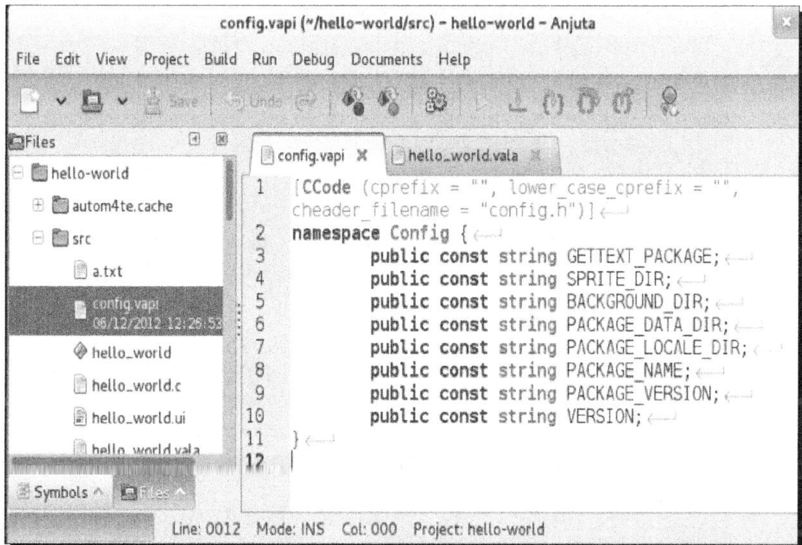

What just happened?

Whenever we open a file, Anjuta will put it inside a tab. Tabs are quite useful during development involving many files. Usually, we will open more than one file at the same time. The feature discussed here makes it easier for us to switch between these files.

Comment block

Anjuta provides a quick way to enclose a block of text in the source code into a comment block. It can also do the opposite and remove the comment markers from a block of text. Imagine that we have a block of code that we are doubtful of or of which we want to see the effect when they are commented out. This functionality helps us comment and uncomment them, especially when the block is large.

Time for action – commenting/uncommenting a block

We can follow these steps to learn how to comment/uncomment blocks of text:

1. Open the `hello_world.vala` file or activate it from our previous activity.
2. In the source code text, search for the following two lines:

   ```
   using Glib;
   using Gtk:
   ```

3. Highlight these two lines with your mouse cursor.
4. Activate the **Edit** menu and choose **Comment/Uncomment**.
5. The text will be commented out. See the **/* */** pairs enclosing the selected text? They have automatically been created by this command.

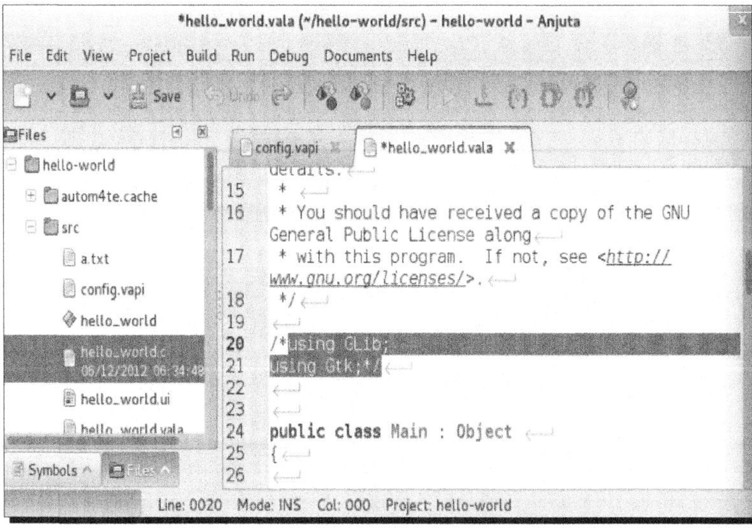

What just happened?

Anjuta wraps the text selection block with a C-style comment. It puts the **/*** characters in front of the text and ***/** at the end. This means that this trick will also be applicable to our Vala and JavaScript projects later on.

Have a go hero – uncommenting the block

Now try to uncomment the block by repeating the previous steps. We have to do this *now*, otherwise our next activity will not work!

Time for action – running the program for the first time

As we have not yet changed anything in the project (You have uncommented the text in the previous section, right?), let's try to run it.

1. Click on the **Run** menu and choose **Execute**.

2. A pop-up dialog will open; let's go ahead and click on the **Execute** button without making any changes.

3. Wait for a moment while Anjuta builds the program.

4. An empty window pops up on the screen like in the following screenshot:

Congratulations! This is one small milestone for us!

What just happened?

What we see now is a small grayish window without anything in it. That is because we have not yet added anything to it. Actually, the window itself was added by the **Create a new project** wizard that we started earlier. The wizard created a class called `Main` inside the `hello_world.vala` file. Inside it we see the following snippet:

```
var builder = new Builder ();
builder.add_from_file (UI_FILE);
builder.connect_signals (this);
```

This code opens the `hello-world.ui` file and loads it into memory. But before we load the file, we have these lines that we defined earlier in the source code:

```
/*
 *Uncomment this line when you are done testing and building a tarball
 * or installing
 */
// const string UI_FILE = Config.PACKAGE_DATA_DIR + "/" + "hello_
world.ui";
const string UI_FILE = "src/hello_world.ui";
```

This means that the `UI_FILE` file mentioned previously comes from `src/hello_world.ui`, which is inside our project directory. The comment placed there seems suspicious, but that is actually required to remove the comment on the first line of code and comment out the last line, because the `hello_world.ui` file's location during deployment is not inside the `src/` subdirectory anymore.

```
var window = builder.get_object ("window" as Window;
window.show_all ();
```

And, this code finds the `window` instance from the `hello-world.ui` definition and then displays it on the screen.

The point here is that the program uses a separate file, which is `hello-world.ui`, as the UI layout definition and displays the content on the screen. This means that we do not create the widgets manually in the code.

When we start the execution of the program, Anjuta first saves the project, builds the executable binary by compiling the source code, and then runs it. The whole build process is visible in the **Messages** dock. For compiled languages, such as Vala that we are using now, the build is made up of two steps, namely the `configure` step and the make step. These two steps are shown in the **Messages** dock in tabs.

The build status in each step is shown as an icon in the respective build step tab. We can see whether the build is failing by looking at this icon. When everything is OK, we can see the green tick icon.

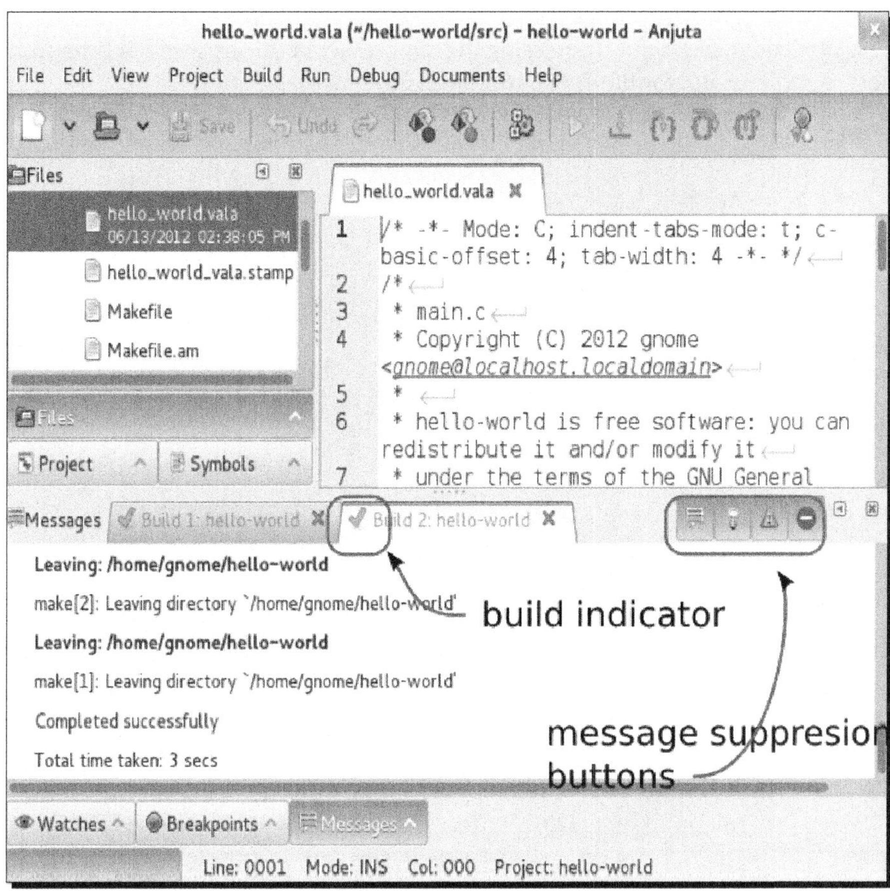

By default, Anjuta shows the output of the build process inside the tab. However, you can suppress the output by pressing the message suppression toggle buttons. These buttons are used to show or hide normal information, warnings, and error messages. Sometimes it is quite useful just to hide all the messages except the error and warning messages so we can focus on what is wrong and not get confused because of other messages being received from the build tools.

Make an error and see how it works

Go ahead and modify the source code, for example, by typing `I'm an error` on top of most of the code in the `hello_world.vala` file. Save it and try running it again. You will find that the build is broken as shown by the build indicator icon. Let's try to suppress the messages presented by Anjuta by pressing the suppression buttons one at a time. You will find these buttons useful for filtering out unnecessary messages.

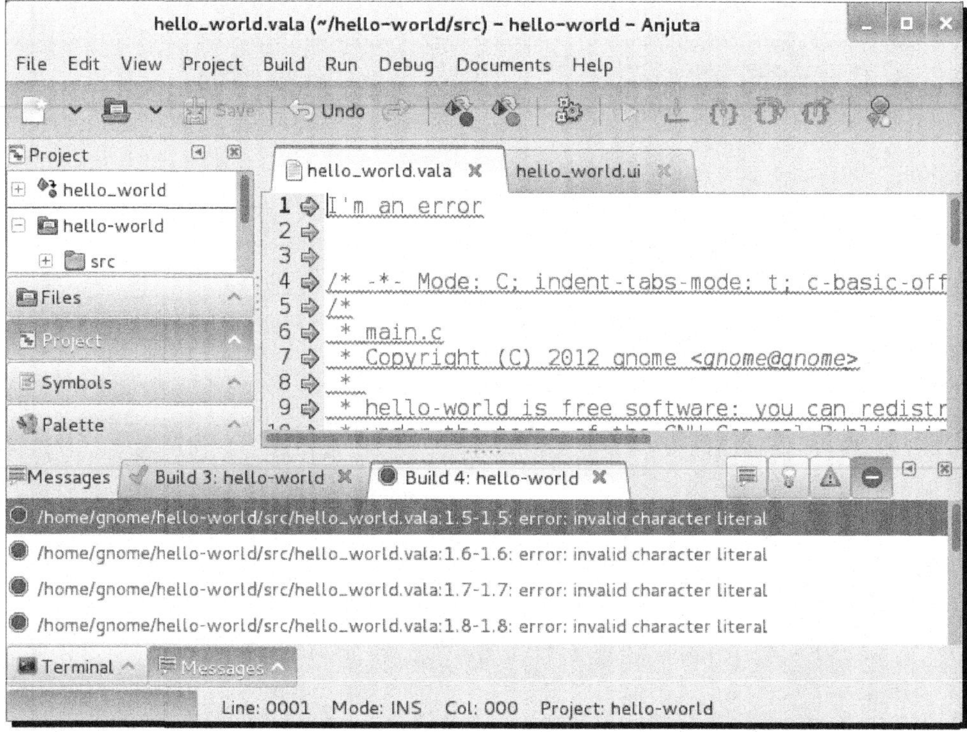

Now let's try to disable all messages except the error messages. When you see the error, try double-clicking it.

Do you see what happens? Yes, the editor immediately shows you the place where the error occurred.

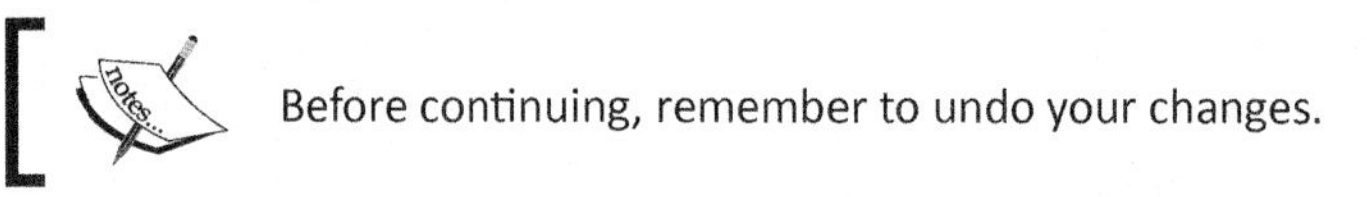
Before continuing, remember to undo your changes.

Editing UI

In Anjuta, we can edit not only the source code but also the UI. Earlier, we saw only a plain window with nothing in it. It is now time to make some progress.

Time for action – editing UI

Let's now try to edit the user interface:

1. Activate the **Project** dock and click on the **hello_world** folder.

2. After it has been expanded, further expand the **src** folder.

3. Expand the **ui** object further.

4. There is a **hello_world.ui** item listed there; double-click it.

5. The user interface editor is opened.

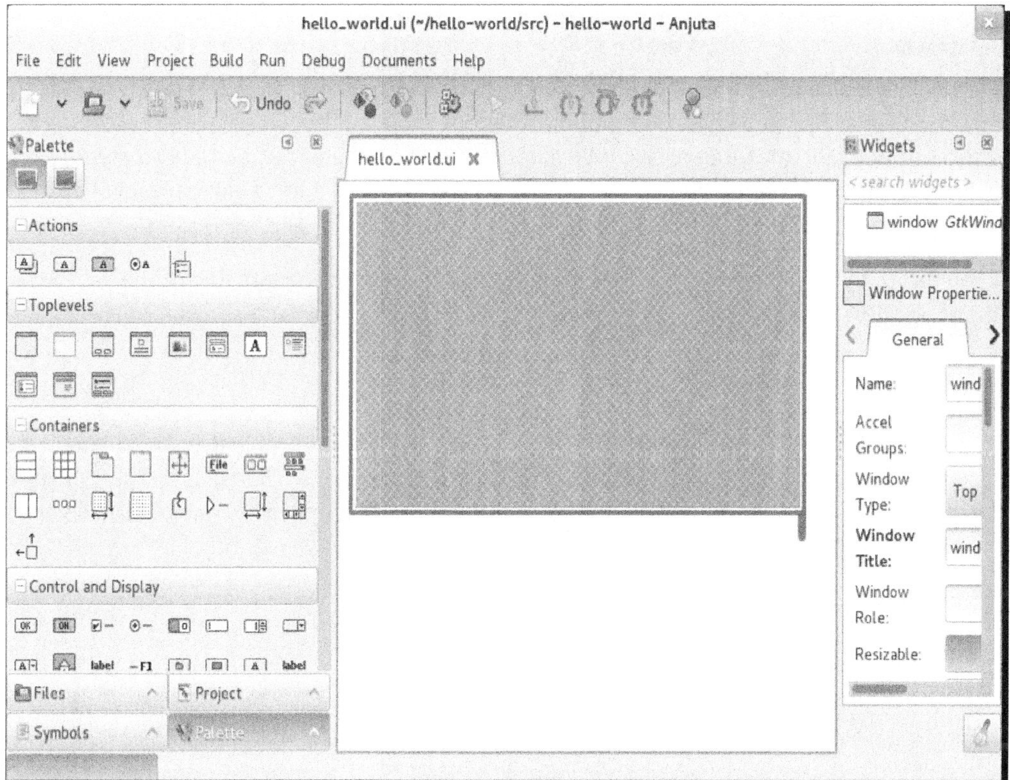

If your Linux distribution pops up a dialog mentioning that the `hello_world.ui` file requires GTK+ Version 2, no need to worry. This is harmless so just go ahead; these messages will go away once you save it. This happens because the initial code generator invoked by **New application wizard** wrongly put the Version 2 definition inside the `hello_world.ui` file. When we save it later, this definition is replaced with Version 3.

What just happened?

The user interface editor is Glade and it is embedded inside Anjuta. This is a desirable feature as it ensures that Anjuta is fully integrated. We will find the exact same editor if we run it individually from the GNOME system menu.

Glade provides two additional docks to Anjuta. Let's look at them now.

Palette

This dock contains selectable GTK+ stock widgets as well as third-party widgets. We can choose these available widgets and put it inside our project. The widgets are represented with icons and laid out categorically. We can show or hide the widgets inside a category just by clicking on the category name. The widget name is visible by hovering our mouse over the widget icon.

If you haven't changed the layout, this dock usually resides on the left side of the Anjuta window.

Widgets

This dock has two parts, namely the widget tree and the widget properties. The widget tree shows the hierarchy of the widgets, and by clicking on a widget in the tree, the properties of the selected widget are shown in the widget properties. If you haven't changed the layout, this dock usually resides on the right side of the Anjuta window.

Let's now try using these tools.

Downloading the example code

You can download the example code fi les for all Packt books you have purchased from your account at http://www.packtpub.com . If you purchased this book elsewhere, you can visit http://www.packtpub.com/support and register to have the fi les e-mailed directly to you.

Time for action – adding a label and a button

We are going to follow a UI mockup as our guideline when editing the UI layout. A **mockup** is a rough design of the UI and is usually created by the application designers. This mockup is then proposed to the development team to be implemented. Now let's consider this mockup:

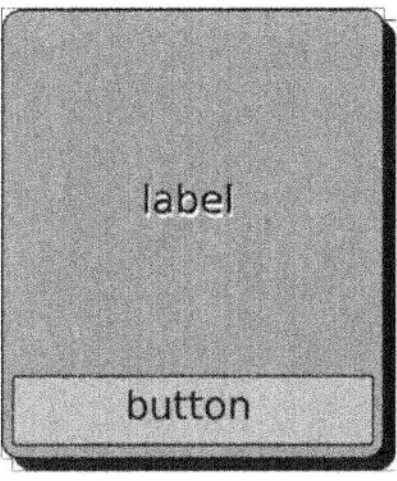

Based on the mockup, we see that two widgets, a label and a button, are required. The label is laid out on top of the button. Now we are going to put these widgets inside our window. Follow these steps to do it:

1. In the **Palette** dock, find the **Container** category.

2. Choose **Box** by clicking on the box icon (remember that we can find the **Box** object by hovering over the icon list).

3. Click on the **window** object, which was created by Anjuta, in the center.

4. A dialog will pop up and ask how many items are preserved inside the box. Type 2 for the label and button.

5. The box would be inserted on the **window** object, even though it is hardly noticeable, but we can see that the window is now split into two parts.

6. Inspect **Box Properties** on the right-hand side. In the **Orientation** option, make sure we have the **Vertical** value; if the value is **Horizontal**, change it.

7. From the mockup, we can see that the label is at the top and the button is at the bottom.

8. Find the **label** widget in the **Control and Display** category in **Palette**, and click on it.

9. Click on the top part of the box in the center. We will see that the top part shrinks according to the size of the label. Let it be like that.

10. Find the **button** widget in the **Control and Display** category in **Palette**, and click on it.

11. Click on the bottom part of the box, which is now the only place that is vacant.

12. We now have all widgets in place!

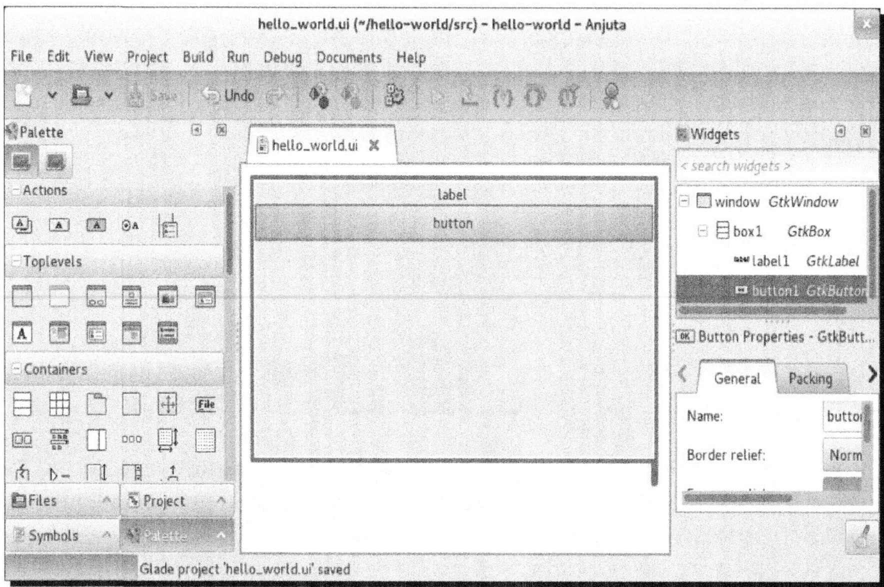

What just happened?

We have successfully added widgets into our window. Unfortunately, we can't just add a button and label into our window directly because of how GTK+ works. A window can only contain one widget. Therefore, we need a container that is capable of hosting more than one widget. That is why we need to add it before adding the button and label.

Understanding the hierarchy is very important when developing GTK+ applications. Let's look at the top part of the **Widgets** dock on the right-hand side; we can see how the widgets appear in the hierarchy. The topmost is the **window** object. The **window** object has a child that is **box1**. And **box1** has two children, namely **label1** and **button1**. The widgets are not placed in any specific place in the coordinate system, but rather packed one after another following the hierarchy.

Now go ahead and run this program to see what it looks like. Make sure you can click on the button.

Time for action – changing widget properties

As we can see, the result from our last activity is not satisfying. It does not look like what we expected in our mockup design. Now let's do something to fix this.

1. Click on the **label** widget on the top part of the box. Note that the label has been highlighted.

2. In the **Label Properties** section in the **Widgets** dock, click on the **Packing** tab.

3. Find the **Expand** option and choose **Yes**.

4. Finally, it now looks like our mockup!

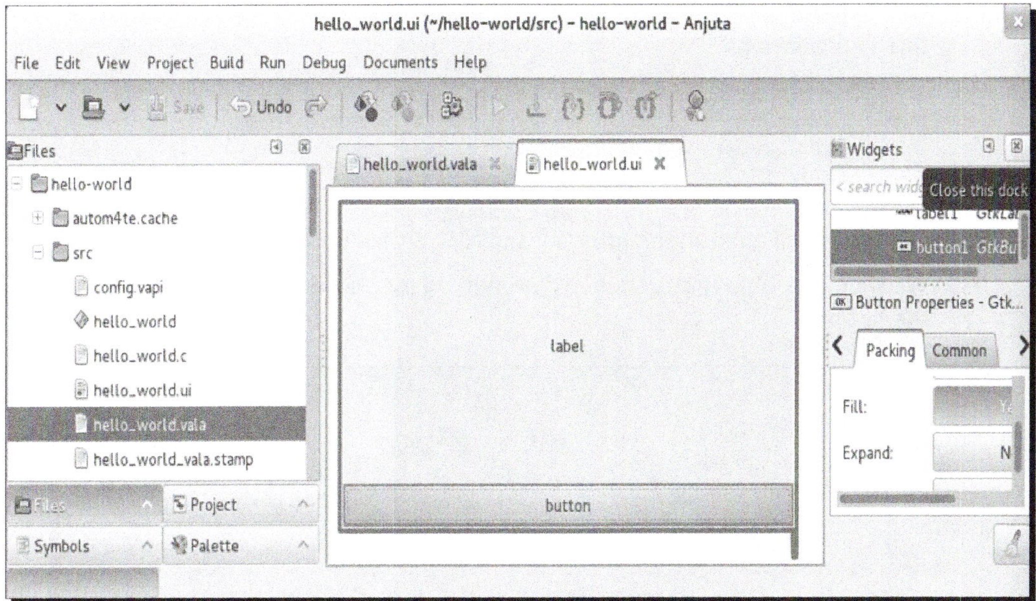

A responsive button

At this point we have the program that does nothing except show itself. Let's change it so the button responds to the click event. For example, suppose we want to print something when the button is clicked.

Time for action – making the button responsive

Now let's add some code to make this happen:

1. Click on the **button** object, which we created earlier, to get it highlighted.

2. Check **Button Properties** and find the **Signals** tab in it. If you can't see it, click on the > button on the right side of the tabs. Keep clicking on it until you find **Signals**. Click on **Signals**.

3. Our **button** is essentially a Gtk button, so expand the **GtkButton** entry on the list. There are few columns and rows. Find the **clicked** signal on the list.

4. On the **handler** column, click on the **clicked** signal so that a text entry is activated. Type `main_on_button1_clicked` in it.

5. Go back to the source code of `hello_world.vala`, and look within the body of the `Main` class. Add this code anywhere inside the class scope, or, to make it easier for you, find the `public void on_destroy` method inside the `Main` class and put this code above it:

```
[CCode (instance_pos = -1)]
public void on_button1_clicked(Button button) {
        stdout.printf("OK\n");
}
```

6. Now go ahead and run the program and click on the button.

7. We should be able to see **OK** being printed on the **Terminal** dock when we click the button.

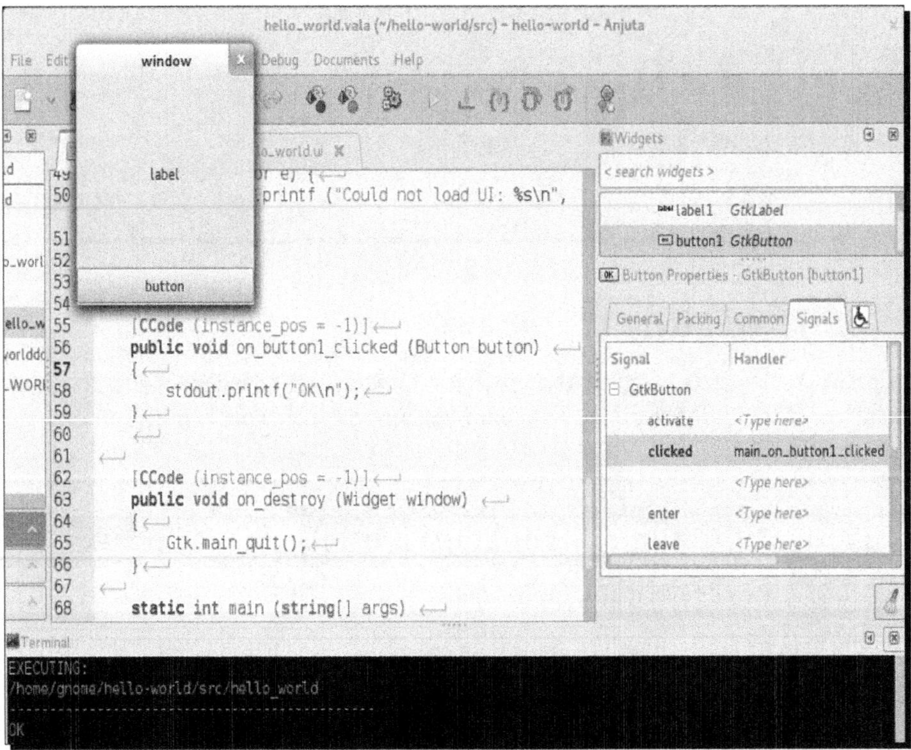

What just happened?

We have just connected a signal handler written in the source code with the named signal in the **button1** widget created in Glade. The signal name we connected is `clicked`, so whenever the button is clicked, the signal handler specified in the **Handler** column is called. We specify `main_on_button1_clicked`, which correlates with the function we wrote in `hello_world.vala` earlier, in the **Handler** column.

We named our handler function as `on_button1_clicked` and put it inside a class called `Main`. This is why we use `main_on_button1_clicked` in the signal handler name. One convention shown here is the use of the class name, which is written in lowercase, concatenated with the function name, separated by an underscore. The function name itself should give the impression that an event has occurred.

Ok, let's back up to our previous inspection of the `hello_world.vala` file. We have this piece of code:

```
var builder = new Builder ();
builder.add_from_file (UI_FILE);
builder.connect_signals (this);
```

The last line now makes sense here. The `connect_signals` method in the `builder` object is responsible for the signal's connection. Without this line, even with the previous instructions and writing of the handler function, the whole program will not work. This line basically ties all signals emitted by the user interface widgets into the `this` object, which is the `Main` object. So that is why we put our handler function inside `Main`.

Pop quiz – naming a signal

Good programming practices can make our life easier. One of them is to stick to a convention. One of the advantages is that when debugging, our mind can immediately trace the code. The convention can vary between organizations and even between projects. The developer must stick to one convention, especially in a project, and they can switch to another convention in another project, if necessary.

Imagine that we have a `Server` class and a function that handle the event when a connection is started.

Q1. Based on the convention we discussed earlier, what do you think is the best name we can give to the function?

1. `server_on_connection_started`.

2. `server_connection`.

3. `start_connecting`.

Tracking symbols

Symbols, be it a variable, a method, a constant, or something similar, can easily be tracked in Anjuta. Remember the `UI_FILE` constant we discussed before? Imagine that we are deep inside a source code file and stumble upon the following piece of code:

```
builder.add_from_file (UI_FILE);
```

We may be wondering what the value of `UI_FILE` is, who defined it, and so on.

Time for action – finding a symbol

Let's practice finding it out:

1. Activate the **Symbols** dock by clicking on it; if it is not available on the screen, go to the **View** menu and activate it from there.

2. We should immediately see `UI_FILE` listed there. However, imagine that our project is so big that the constant is buried inside. Let's go to the **Search** tab in the dock.

3. Type `UI_FILE` there. Note that it has a nice code completion to avoid mistyping.

4. `UI_FILE` is shown on the list along with the place where it is defined.

5. Double-click on the search result. The editor will show us the exact place where it is defined. Neat, eh?

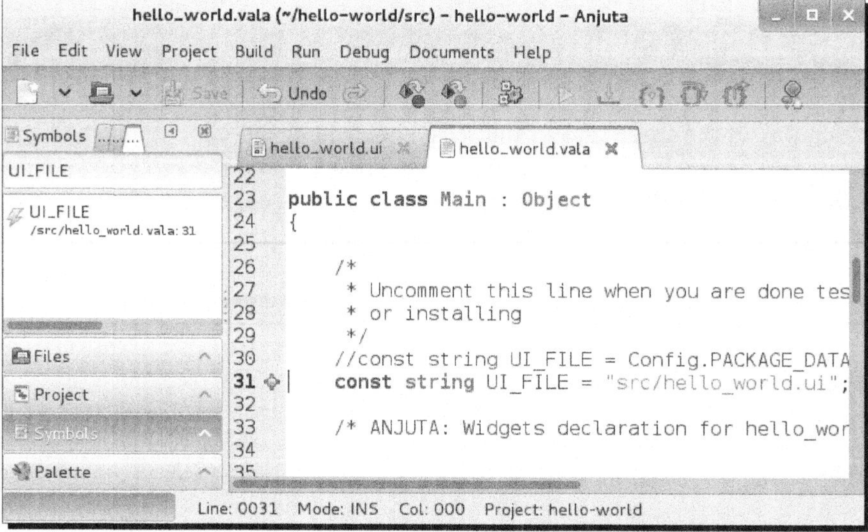

Getting help

When developing a software, we need a good reference tool to get some help. Devhelp is the tool that we are going to talk about. It is an offline **Application Programming Interface** (**API**) reference tool, which is used here because it is simple and fast. It opens a collection of manuals (called "books") that we can read and search from.

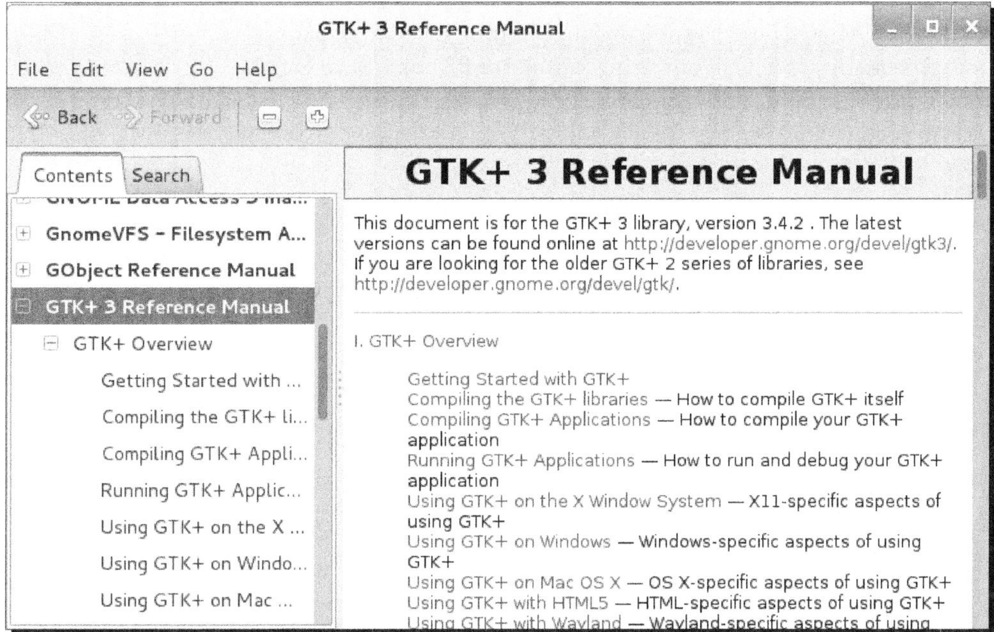

The usage is quite straightforward. The books are displayed on the left-hand side. To read a book, we can either follow the internal links shown on the body of the page on the right-hand side or we can expand it and see the chapters for quick navigation.

Summary

We have introduced ourselves to Vala programming by easily creating a Vala project in Anjuta with a wizard. We found that the IDE layout is quite simple to use; we can hide and show elements that we do not want to see. We also know the steps for building an application and how to find more information when the building has failed. When something is wrong with the build, we can filter out messages in order to avoid confusion.

Source code navigation is easy to do in Anjuta. Manipulating code is also easy as Anjuta provides some shortcuts for it (for example, when commenting and uncommenting blocks of code).

We managed to implement a UI based on a mockup design with Glade. We also know that Glade is deeply integrated into Anjuta, and we know that we can run Glade as a separate application. We saw how the UI is crafted in Glade and then read and used by our program, including how it works by connecting the signals of the UI objects into handler code.

When we need help during development, we know that Devhelp will be there for us by providing access to API reference documentation.

At this point, we should be ready to start learning GNOME application development. The basic skill needed is now in our hands. After our first exposure with Vala, let's take another step in GNOME application development by learning it in depth along with JavaScript in the next chapter.

Programming Languages

Long before GNOME 3, C was the first programming language for creating GNOME applications, and after it came C++, C#, Python, and the others. When GNOME was evolving close to Version 3, Vala and JavaScript became more and more popular and even became an important part of it. JavaScript has been around for a long time and people are familiar with it. Vala is quite new, but because the program written with it is fast and has a familiar syntax adopted from Java and C#, it is gaining popularity among GNOME application developers.

This chapter talks about these two programming languages. We will quickly look at the essentials of JavaScript and Vala, making sure that we have enough knowledge to make our applications with these languages.

In this chapter we shall learn about:

- Playing with data types in JavaScript
- Controlling iteration in JavaScript
- Basic object-oriented programming in JavaScript
- Constructing JavaScript objects
- Using JavaScript prototypes
- Modularizing a JavaScript program
- A Vala member access specifier
- Basic data types in Vala
- Gee collection library

Let's start first with implementing JavaScript with Seed.

Programming GNOME with JavaScript

There are actually two competing JavaScript implementations in GNOME, with differences in the engines used. The first one is Gjs, which is based on Spidermonkey, a JavaScript engine created by Mozilla. The second one, which we will use, is Seed. It is based on WebKit's JavaScript core engine. We chose Seed because it is used officially in GNOME 3.

Time for action – saying hello to Seed

Now it is time to see how Seed works.

1. Run the terminal from the **Terminal** menu in **Activities** in GNOME Shell or from **Applications | Accessories | Terminal**.

2. Run Seed by typing `seed` within the terminal console.

   ```
   $ seed
   ```

3. We are entering the Seed prompt:

   ```
   >
   ```

4. Type the following code, followed by the return key:

   ```
   print("Hello, world")
   ```

5. The text is printed out.

   ```
   Hello, world
   ```

What just happened?

Seed is an interpreter. When running Seed like this, we are entering the Seed interactive mode, which means that it interactively gives the result of the code that we typed. In this mode, we can type any valid JavaScript code in this shell. However, for those of you who are used to JavaScript programming, you can't type code like we do when coding for web applications. For example, you can't type the following code:

```
console.log("Hello, world")
```

This is because Seed does not provide objects such as `document` or `console`. So, only basic JavaScript is acceptable unless we can import the required objects.

Have a go hero – trying more JavaScript code here

While we are at it, let's try entering some JavaScript code, such as additions, subtractions, and variable assignment, in the shell. For example:

```
var a=1
var b=2
b+a
a-b
```

The list goes on. This is just to grasp the basic idea of the shell. If you have experience with using JavaScript but your skills are a bit rusty, you can use this as a warmup. We can also think of using this as a calculator, a smart one.

Say we give an unfinished line, for example:

```
var c=
```

We will see the prompt change into this:

```
..
```

This means that we need to finish it or else Seed will spew a syntax error message.

If done with this, feel free to quit by pressing the *Ctrl + C* key combination, and it will bring us back to the system's terminal console.

Time for action – running our program with Seed

Interactive mode is not the approach that we would use in our real applications. What we are going to do now is to put our code in a file and then run it. Are you ready?

1. Fire up Anjuta.
2. Create a new file by via **File | New**.
3. Fill the editor with this piece of code:

```
#!/usr/bin/env seed

print("Hello, world")
```

4. Save this file as `hello-world.js`. It is better to create a new directory for this (say, `hello-worldjs`) and put this file inside it.

You can click on the **Create folder** button, type `hello-worldjs`, and click on the newly created folder.

5. Click on the **Run** menu and choose **Execute**. A small dialog will appear; fill the
Program field with `/usr/bin/seed` and the **Arguments** field with `hello-world.`
`js`. Make sure that the **Run in terminal** option is checked.

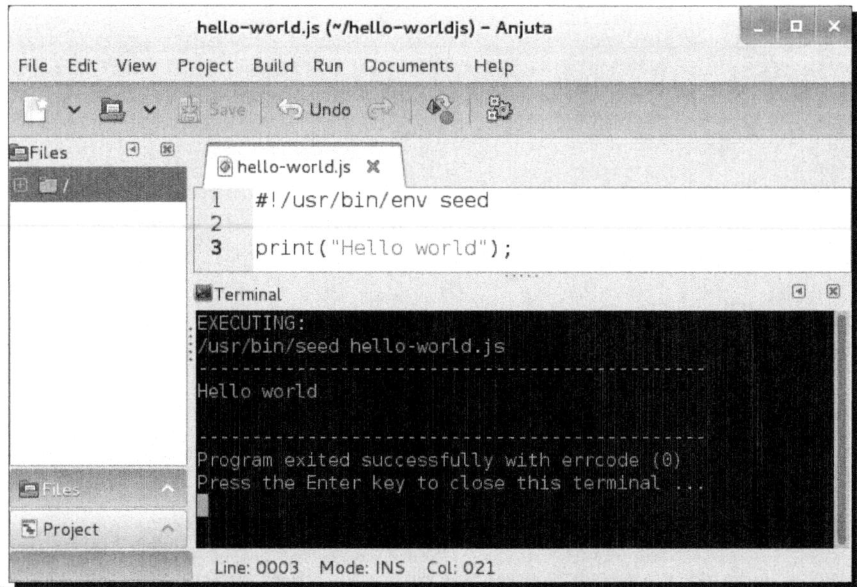

What just happened?

We call this method of program invocation as scripting. With this approach, the file itself is
loaded and run by Seed directly. It uses a similar method with other scripts such as Bash,
Perl, and Python. We can see from the first line that we use the hash bang (`#!`) sign to
indicate the program that is used as the interpreter of the script. We used `/usr/bin/`
`env` followed by `seed` instead of directly putting `/usr/bin/seed` there. We do it this way
because we don't want to strictly tighten the location of `seed`. With `env`, the system will
honor the system path setting to find the exact location of Seed. For example, if we have
`seed` in `/usr/local/bin` instead of in `/usr/bin`, the program will still work.

You might wonder why we still need to put `/usr/bin/seed` in the Run dialog rather than
entering `hello-world.js` directly. This is because we have not yet set the executable
property of the script. Let's bring out our Linux administration skill and go to the directory
where we placed `hello-world.js` and invoke this command in the terminal:

```
chmod +x hello-world.js
```

After this, we can put `hello-world.js` immediately in the **Program** field of the **Run** dialog. You may notice that we can no longer see this dialog when accessing the **Run** menu and **Execute** menu. This is because Anjuta now thinks that we already set the program arguments and are ready to execute. If we want to change this again, we can go to the **Run** menu and choose the **Program Parameters...** menu. Alternatively, we can run the script directly from the system console like this:

```
./hello-world.js
```

Loosely typed language

JavaScript is known as a loosely (weakly) typed programming language. It means that we can use a variable without declaring its type whether it is a number, string, or array. We simply use the `var` directive (or not) to declare a variable. We will soon find out how this works.

Time for action – playing with data types

Now, let's discuss the basic data types in JavaScript and see how we can interact with them. After this, we should be able to choose which type we should use depending on our needs.

1. Create a new file called `hello-world-data-types.js` and fill it with this:

    ```
    #!/usr/bin/env seed

    print("Hello world")

    var number = 1;
    print(number);
    number = number + 0.5;
    print(number);
    print(number.length);
    number = number + " is a number? no, it is now a string";
    print(number.length);
    print(number);
    number = (number.length == 0)
    print(number);
    number = undefined
    print(number);
    ```

2. Run it.

3. The `number` variable is printed, thus:

```
Hello world
1
1.5
[undefined]
1.5 is a number? no, it is now a string
39
0
[undefined]
```

What just happened?

We can now see two interesting things. First, that JavaScript can juggle between data types. We can change the type of one variable into another by just assigning a new value. The second, which we have talked about is that we do not need to declare the type of the variable. In this code, we have the `number` variable that we initially set with the value of `1`.

```
var number = 1;
print(number);
```

Now the `number` variable is just a plain integer.

```
number = number + 0.5;
print(number);
```

Then we add `0.5` into it, making it a floating point data type. JavaScript accepts this without any problem and we have 1.5 as the value now.

```
print(number.length);
```

Then we try to access the `.length` property of the number. Because the type of the `number` variable at this moment is a number, and because it does not have any length, the value of `number.length` is `[undefined]`.

We see now that JavaScript has the unknown value concept, which is described as `[undefined]`. If a variable is undefined, we can't access anything inside it and it will cause JavaScript to think that this is an error.

```
number = number + " is a number? no, it is now a string";
print(number);
```

Now we concatenated `number` with a string, effectively making it a string as a whole. Now `number.length` is defined by the interpreter and has a value of `39`, showing that it has 39 characters in it.

```
number = (number.length == 0)
print(number);
```

Here we assign number with a Boolean value coming from the (number.length == 0) expression. Because number.length is not 0, the expression returns false, and it is printed as 0. If it was true , it would be printed as 1.

```
number = undefined
print(number);
```

Now we set number to undefined; it is a reserved word, so we can just set it as shown previously.

It is fun, isn't it?

Pop quiz – what is the value now?

Q1. After the assignment of all data types that was performed earlier, at the very end of our code, what is the value of number.length now? Choose from the following (remember that just after we assigned it as a string, it had a value of 39):

1. 0, because we set number to undefined.

2. undefined, because we set number to undefined.

3. JavaScript will think this is an error because we try to access .length from an undefined value.

Controlling iteration

In programming, we almost always need to repeat certain parts of the code to be run. We do this by having an iteration control (also known as loop or repetition control) inside our code. In JavaScript it is quite easy.

Time for action – controlling Iteration

We can follow these steps to control iteration:

1. Create a new file called hello-world-iteration.js and put this code in it:

```
#!/usr/bin/env seed

print("Hello, world")
for (i = 0; i < 10; i ++) {
    print("Iteration number #" + i);
}
```

2. Run it.

_3._ We can see that the text is printed 10 times.

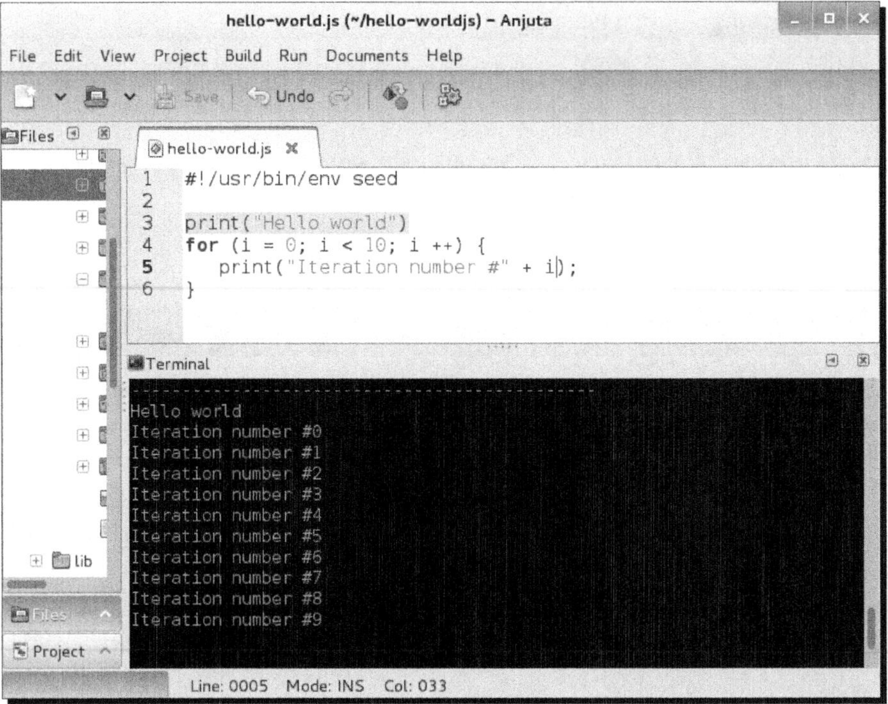

What just happened?

In the code, we tell JavaScript to do `10` iterations using the `for` loop. We can see that JavaScript starts the index from `0`, and not from 1, as we initially set the value of `i` (`i = 0` in the code). In each iteration we add `1` to `i` (see the `i++` expression in the `for` loop, which means "increase the value of `i` by 1"). The loop stops immediately when the `i` value breaks the constraint, which is 10. At the end of the loop, the value of `i` is 10. But because 10 is not lesser than 10 (in the code we put `i < 10`), it breaks the loop. Hence the text displays 0 to 9 instead of up to 10.

Have a go hero – counting down

We have done the counting up. Now how about counting down?

Time for action – manipulating an array

We can imagine an array as a collection of boxes that can hold a number of items with the same type. Let's try to fill those boxes.

1. Create a new script called `hello-world-array.js` and fill it to look like this:

```
#!/usr/bin/env seed

print("Hello world")
var boxes = []
for (i = 0; i < 10; i ++) {
    boxes[i] = i * 2;
}

for (i = 0; i < boxes.length; i ++) {
    print("Box content #" + i + " is " + boxes[i])
}
```

2. Run it.

3. We will see the text specifying the box number and its content.

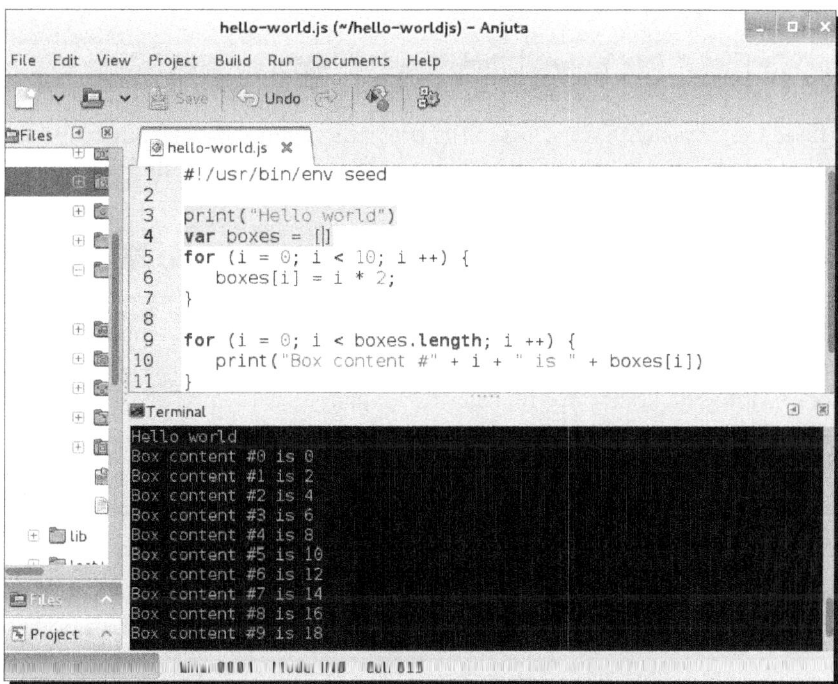

What just happened?

The first thing we do is to declare `boxes` as an array:

```
var boxes = []
```

Note that we did not set the size of the array; we just say that it is an array and let JavaScript do the magic. This is because the array can shrink or grow at any time whenever we modify its content. Then we fill in the boxes:

```
for (i = 0; i < 10; i ++) {
    boxes[i] = i * 2;
}
```

Then, on each box, we set the value to be *the index of the array times two*. We just set the content on the index `i` directly, without allocating anything, like in the C programming language. It's super easy. Then we print out the content of the array:

```
for (i = 0; i < boxes.length; i ++) {
    print("Box content #" + i + " is " + boxes[i])
}
```

The length of the array can be obtained from the `length` variable within an object. In this case, we can get the length from `boxes.length`. So whenever we fill an array, the length is adjusted automatically.

Have a go hero – fill with anything you want

We have filled the boxes with numbers in the previous section; how about other data types? Try to fill boxes with string or even mixed string and integer. Are you surprised?

Object-oriented programming (OOP) with JavaScript

If you are already familiar with object-oriented programming, be prepared that OOP in JavaScript is somewhat limited and does not follow the usual OOP practice. This is because the language itself is not a full OOP language. What we are trying to do here is to adapt the OOP concept within the limitations that JavaScript has.

Time for action – using the JavaScript object

Now it is time to eat the meat, the JavaScript object. We will use objects extensively in this book. Let's do that by first introducing to ourselves a simple one.

1. Create a new script called `hello-world-object.js` and fill with this code:

    ```
    #!/usr/bin/env seed

    print("Hello world")
    ```

```
var book = {};
print(book);
print(book.isbn);

book.isbn = "xxxx-1234-1234";
book.title = "A somewhat interesting book"
print(book);
print(book.isbn);
print(book.title);
```

2. Run it.

3. See the values printed:

```
Hello world
[object Object]
[undefined]
[object Object]
xxxx-1234-1234
A somewhat interesting book
```

What just happened?

Like any other data type, we can assign a variable with an object easily.

```
var book = {};
```

In this line, we define `book` as an empty object. Here, the object is initialized with curly brackets. This is the simplest form of an object.

```
print(book);
```

This prints `[object Object]` saying that this is an object of type `Object`.

```
print(book.isbn);
```

We try to access the `.isbn` property of the object here, but as it is empty, it is initially `[undefined]`.

```
book.isbn = "xxxx-1234-1234";
book.title = "A somewhat interesting book"
```

Here, we try to assign the property of the object with some values. At this point, we are free to put anything inside the object, and we don't have to initialize or declare it before using it.

```
print(book);
```

Here, we print the `book` variable again; it still says that it is an object of type `Object`.

```
print(book.isbn);
print(book.title);
```

But here the situation changes as the values are assigned and can be printed.

With great power comes great responsibility

As you may have noticed, in JavaScript, we are practically free to do anything with the data types. However, with this power, we have to thoroughly check our code for correctness. Sloppy programming with JavaScript will end up in disaster, because as the code grows, it becomes harder to track where the error is.

Because JavaScript is case sensitive, it will become even harder to track errors. Imagine if we have set this line somewhere in our code:

```
book.authorFirstName = "Random Joe"
```

Then, in other parts of the code, we try to modify the variable with this line:

```
book.authorFirstname = "Another Joe"
```

JavaScript will not complain about this because we are free to set anything inside our object. We must take responsibility for this error by double, no, triple checking our code so that we do not make typos like the previous one. Wait a second; have you spotted the bug that we are talking about?

Have a go hero – another way to fill the object

Try to modify a part of the previous code to look like this and see what happens:

```
var book = {
  isbn:"xxxx-1234-1234",
  title:"A somewhat interesting book"
}
```

We are now defining the ISBN and the title inside the object in a different way. Here we use a colon instead of the equals sign, and we put a comma in between the definitions. This notation is called **JSON (JavaScript Object Notation)**.

Constructing objects

After using the simplest form of a JavaScript object, let's now have a more sophisticated object. This marks our adventure with object-oriented programming with JavaScript.

Time for action – playing with constructors

When we talk about constructing an object, it means that we call a special function called a **constructor**. Let's see how to do it.

1. Create a new file called `hello-world-constructor.js` and fill it with this code:

```
#!/usr/bin/env seed

print("Hello world")

var Book = function(isbn, title) {
    this.isbn = isbn;
    this.title = title;
}

book = new Book("1234", "A good title");
print(book.isbn);
print(book.title);
```

2. Run it.

3. See the values printed:

```
Hello world

1234

A good title
```

What just happened?

This is actually similar to our previous code, with the difference that now we define it as a class, and then later instantiate it as an object.

```
var Book = function(isbn, title) {
    this.isbn = isbn;
    this.title = title;
}
```

This is our constructor of the `Book` class. Within it, we assign the `.isbn` property with the `isbn` variable passed as an argument in the constructor function. The same thing happens with the `.title` property.

```
book = new Book("1234", "A good title");
```

Here we create a new variable called book (note the lowercase!) by instantiating a Book class with the supplied arguments.

```
print(book.isbn);
print(book.title);
```

Now we can see the value of .isbn and .title as printed.

Class and object

The **class** is only a definition such as var Book = function(..) {...} in the previous code; it is not an object until we really instantiate it later with the new operator. When it becomes an object, we also call it an **instance of a class**. Previously, we did the instantiation differently by just using the curly brackets without any class definition.

By convention, we usually name our classes with CamelCase, which has a mix of uppercase and lowercase characters, where the first character in the first word is started with uppercase (for example, Book). In contrast, for object instances or variables, we used lowercase for the first character in the first word (for example, book).

Pop quiz – can you see the difference now?

Let's take a look at this code:

```
var Circle = function(radiusInPixel) {
    this.radius = radiusInPixel
}

var circle = new Circle(100);
```

Q1. What is circle and what is Circle? Which one of the following statements is correct?

1. Circle is a class because it has the definition, and circle is an object, instantiated from the Circle class.

2. circle is an object because it has the definition, and Circle is an instance of the circle object.

Using prototypes

In OOP, we can have methods or functions attached to an object. This means that the function is specific to a particular object in memory. If we call a function in one object, it does not interfere with another object of the same type that also has the same function. In JavaScript we use prototypes to achieve this feature.

Time for action – adding prototypes

Let's now add some methods to our class. Here we will use the `prototype` object to define them.

1. Create a new script called `hello-world-prototype.js` and fill it with this:

```
#!/usr/bin/env seed

print("Hello world")

var Book = function(isbn, title) {
    this.isbn = isbn;
    this.title = title;
}

Book.prototype = {
    printTitle: function(){
        print("Title is " + this.title);
    },

    printISBN: function() {
        print("ISBN is " + this.isbn);
    }
}

var book = new Book("1234", "A good title");
book.printTitle();
book.printISBN();
```

2. Run it.

3. See the values printed:

```
Hello world

Title is A good title

ISBN is 1234
```

What just happened?

In a JavaScript object, `prototype` is a special object that holds all the properties and methods inside a class or an object. So what we do here is to fill in the prototype with our own methods.

```
var Book = function(isbn, title) {
    this.isbn = isbn;
    this.title = title;
}
```

In this code, we have our constructor like before:

```
Book.prototype = {
```

Then, we start the declaration of the prototype, ready to fill it in with our own method definitions:

```
printTitle: function(){
    print("Title is " + this.title);
},
```

Here, we put our first method as described with a function body:

```
printISBN: function() {
    print("ISBN is " + this.isbn);
}
```

We use a colon instead of an equals sign to define the method, and we put a comma at the end of our method, meaning that there will come another method or member declaration after this line. Remember our experience from the previous code when defining the book object in a different way?

Then, our next method comes along. Here we end the definition without putting a comma.

```
var book = new Book("1234", "A good title");
```

After that, we declare a book variable by constructing the Book object with specified arguments.

```
book.printTitle();
book.printISBN();
```

Finally, we use our method by just calling it (note the brackets after the name of the method).

Have a go hero – adding more methods

Why don't we add more methods? Let's say we need these methods:

- `getISBN()`, which returns the isbn
- `getTitle()`, which returns the title of the book

Don't forget about the colon and the comma!

Time for action – modifying the prototype of an object

As mentioned previously, we can also put something inside the prototype of an object directly and not in the class. This is not something that we will do on an everyday basis, but we will learn it here just for our knowledge; it may come in handy later. Imagine that we want to replace a function defined in our prototype with another function at runtime!

1. Create a new script called `hello-world-proto.js` and fill with this:

```
#!/usr/bin/env seed

print("Hello world")

var Book = function(isbn, title) {
   this.isbn = isbn;
   this.title = title;
}

Book.prototype = {
   printTitle: function(){
      print("Title is " + this.title);
   },

   printISBN: function() {
      print("ISBN is " + this.isbn);
   }
}

var book = new Book("1234", "A good title");

book.printTitle();
book.printISBN();

book.__proto__ = {
   author: "Joe Random",
   printAuthor: function() {
      print("Author is " + this.author);
   }
}

book.printAuthor();

var anotherBook = new Book("4567", "A more better title");

anotherBook.printTitle();
anotherBook.printISBN();
anotherBook.printAuthor(); // this is invalid
```

2. Run it.

3. Note that it prints the author of the first book, but it fails to do so for the second one.

```
Hello world

Title is A good title

ISBN is 1234

Author is Joe Random

Title is A more better title

ISBN is 4567

** (seed:4911): CRITICAL **: Line 39 in hello-world.js:
TypeError 'undefined' is not a function (evaluating 'anotherBook.
printAuthor()')
```

What just happened?

To modify the prototype at runtime, we need to know a little secret. It's no longer accessible with the `prototype` property but rather with `__proto__`. In this line, we instantiate the `book` object:

```
var book = new Book("1234", "A good title");
```

And here, we add two properties inside the prototype which we access with `__proto__`:

```
book.__proto__ = {
    author: "Joe Random",
    printAuthor: function() {
        print("Author is " + this.author);
    }
}
```

Then, we try to use it immediately:

```
book.printAuthor();
```

However, we were not able to do this in another instance. Do you know why? Yes, because we only modify the `book` object, and this does not affect the `anotherBook` object.

```
var anotherBook = new Book("4567", "A more better title");

anotherBook.printAuthor(); // this is invalid
```

Pop quiz – how to make it global then?

Q1. What is the best way to add the `printAuthor` method in all objects created from the `Book` class?

1. Add `printAuthor` to `__proto__` in every object created, and then we will have the function available in all objects.

2. Just add `printAuthor` in the `Book` class prototype, and then all objects created from `Book` will have the function.

Have a go hero – changing the implementation details

Imagine that we want the `anotherBook` object to be used only for declaring special books. Because it is so special, we want to print *<book-title> is a really good title* in the `printTitle` function, with *<book-title>* being the actual title of the book.

Just redefine the function within `__proto__` in the `anotherBook` object.

Modularization

Imagine that we implemented a big project and we put it inside a single script. That would be a nightmare as it would be very difficult to debug. Hence, we should discuss this now, before our code gets bigger.

Time for action – modularizing our program

Now we are going to modularize our software.

1. Let's create a new file called `hello-world-module.js` and fill it with this:

```
#!/usr/bin/env seed

print("Hello world")

var BookModule = imports.book

var book = new BookModule.Book("1234", "A good title");
book.printTitle();
book.printISBN();
```

2. Create another new script called `book.js` and fill it with this:

```
var Book = function(isbn, title) {
  this.isbn = isbn;
  this.title = title;
}

Book.prototype = {
  printTitle: function(){
    print("Title is " + this.title);
  },

  printISBN: function() {
    print("ISBN is " + this.isbn);
  }
}
```

3. Then run `hello-world-module.js` (not `book.js`).

4. See the printouts.

What just happened?

From the output, we can see that it is exactly the same as the previous code. But here we split the code into two files.

```
var BookModule = imports.book

var book = new BookModule.Book("1234", "A good title");
```

Here, we ask Seed to attach the `BookModule` variable with the evaluation of `book` with the `imports` command. Here it is expected that we have `book.js` inside our current directory. With this, all objects in `book.js` are accessible from the `BookModule` variable. Hence, we construct the `book` object with the previous line.

Also note that, in `book.js`, we no longer have the hashbang line. This is not required because we don't use `book.js` as our entry point, but rather we use `hello-world-module.js`.

With this approach, we can lay out our objects in files and import them whenever necessary. This not only makes the memory usage efficient but also keeps the code structure clean.

This concludes our quick introduction to JavaScript as a GNOME application development programming language. Now let's move on to Vala.

Getting to know Vala

When compared to JavaScript, Vala is fairly new and is the only language being used in GNOME development since its conception. It has quite an interesting concept: the programmers are exposed to C# and Java-like syntax, but underneath, the code will be translated into pure C and then compiled to binary.

This approach will make GNOME programming more accessible, because developing a GNOME application with C is quite hard to understand for beginners. It involves many boilerplate code snippets that you must copy and paste into your source code tree and then modify according to the guidelines. This step is totally hidden by Vala.

Similar to our adventure with JavaScript, we will now learn the basics of the Vala language without implementing any graphical elements. As Vala is a full-blown object-oriented programming language, we will immediately use the OOP concept in our journey with Vala.

Let's now prepare a project that will be used as our experiment. Remember the steps from *Chapter 2, Preparing Our Weapons*? Good! Let's do it again with some changes. We will use `hello-vala` as the project name.

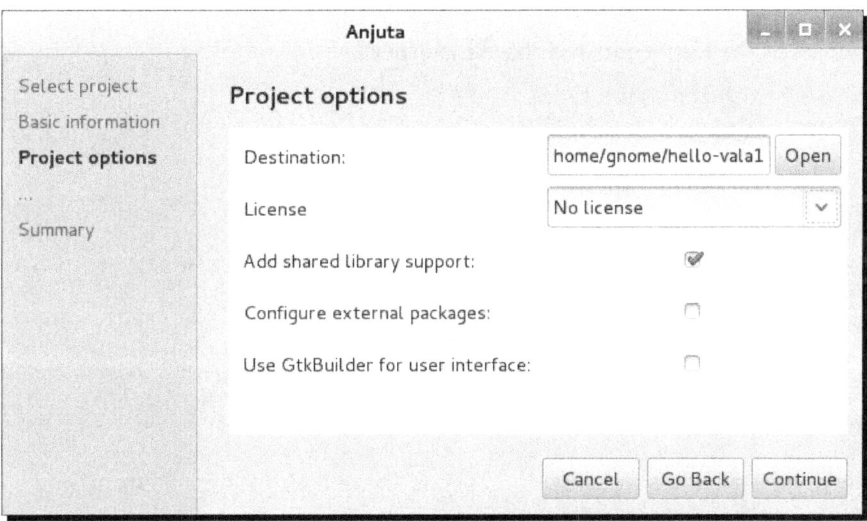

In the preceding screenshot, we can see in **Project options** that we choose **No license** to minimize modifications that we are going to do next. We also uncheck the **Use GtkBuilder for user interface** option because we want to do a simple text-based application to grasp the essentials of Vala.

Time for action – entry point to our program

We are now going to replace all the generated code with our own so that we understand
what makes an application from the ground up.

1. Edit the generated `hello_vala.vala` file and fill it with this:

```
using GLib;

public class Main : Object
{
  public Main ()
  {
  }

  static int main (string[] args)
  {
    stdout.printf ("Hello, world\n");
    return 0;
  }
}
```

2. Click on the **Run** menu and choose **Execute**.

3. See the text that is printed:

```
Hello, world
```

What just happened?

Here we start by looking at the `Book` class.

```
using GLib;
```

This line says that we are using the `GLib` namespace.

```
public class Main : Object
```

This is the definition of the `Main` class. It is stated here that it is derived from the
`GLib.Object` class. We don't put the full name `GLib.Object` but only `Object`
because we already stated in the first line that we are using the `GLib` namespace.

```
public Main ()
{
}
```

The preceding structure is the constructor of the class. Here we have an empty one.

```
static int main (string[] args)
{
    stdout.printf ("Hello, world\n");
    return 0;
}
}
```

This is our entry point to the program. If declared as static, the `main` function will be considered as the first function that will be run in the application. Without this function, we can't run the application.

And one more thing; there must be one and only one static `main` function, otherwise your program will not compile.

Have a go hero – look at the generated C code

Now we should have the generated C code available in the `src/` directory. Navigate the filesystem using the **Files** dock and find `hello_vala.c`. Let's open it and see how Vala transforms the Vala code into C code.

We can modify the C code, but your changes will be overwritten whenever you change the Vala code, and the C code will get regenerated.

Member access specifier

Vala defines a set of member access specifiers, which we can use to define which member of the class can be accessed by another class or by its inheriting classes. This idiom provides us a way to make a clean set of application programming interfaces (API), which is easy to use.

Time for action – defining member access

Let's take a look at how to specify the access to our class member.

1. Create a new file and save it as `book.vala` inside the `src/` directory. Fill it with this:

    ```
    using GLib;

    public class Book : Object {
        private string title;
        private string isbn;

        public Book(string isbn, string title) {
            this.isbn = isbn;
    ```

```vala
        this.title = title;
    }

    public void printISBN() {
    stdout.printf("%s\n", isbn);
    }

    public void printTitle() {
        stdout.printf("%s\n", title);
    }
}
```

2. We need to add this to the project. Click on the **Project** menu and choose **Add Source File...**.

3. In the next dialog, click on the **Target** option, find `hello_vala` inside `src/`, and then, in the file selection box below it, choose `book.vala`.

4. Modify the `main` function of `hello_vala.vala` to look like this:

```vala
using GLib;

public class Main : Object
{
  public Main ()
  {
     var book = new Book("1234", "A new book");
     book.printISBN ();
  }

  static int main (string[] args)
  {
     stdout.printf ("Hello, world\n");
     var main = new Main();
     return 0;
  }
}
```

5. Run it.

6. Note that the program cannot be built.

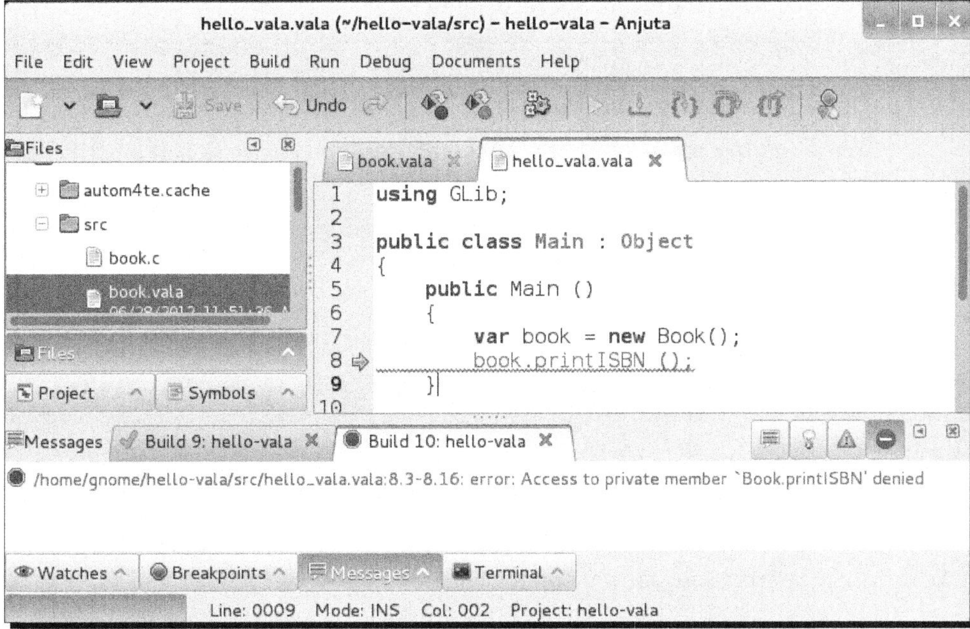

What just happened?

From the error message, we see that it rejects our access to call `Book.printISBN` (we read this dot notation as the `printISBN` member from the `Book` class).

```
var book = new Book("1234", "A new book");
book.printISBN ();
```

This is what we have in the `Main` class constructor. There we instantiate `Book` into the `book` variable, and call `printISBN` there.

```
void printISBN() {
stdout.printf(isbn);
}
```

However, this is what we have in the `Book` class. It looks innocent, but it turns out that we missed something crucial that makes this function inaccessible from outside the class.

The access specifiers

Here is a list of access specifiers that are recognized by Vala:

- `private`: The access is limited within the class or struct.
- `public`: The access is unlimited
- `protected`: The access is limited within the class and any class that inherits from the class
- `internal`: The access is limited within the classes inside the package

When we don't specify anything, the access is set to `private` by default. That is why our program cannot be built.

Pop quiz – how to fix this?

As mentioned previously, we don't put any specifiers in front of the `printISBN` function, so it is considered `private`. We can fix this by putting the correct access specifier in the `printISBN` function.

Q1. Which specifier from the following options do you think is correct?

1. `public`, because we want to access it from `Main` class which is outside the `Book` class.
2. None; we just need to fix how we call `printISBN` in the `Main` constructor.

Basic data types

Let's now move on, learning the basic data types available in Vala, meaning that we will take a look at how to interact with strings, numbers, and Boolean.

Time for action – experiment with data types

We will now create an imaginary BookStore program to explore the data types in Vala.

1. Create a new file called `bookstore.vala` and put it in `src/`. Fill it with these lines:

```
using GLib;

public class BookStore {
   private Book book;
   private double price = 0.0;
   private int stock = 0;
```

```vala
    public BookStore (Book book, double price, int stock) {
      this.book = book;
      this.price = price;
      this.stock = stock;
    }

    public int getStock() {
      return stock;
    }

    public void removeStock(int amount) {
      stock = stock - amount;
    }

    public void addStock(int amount) {
      stock = stock + amount;
    }

    public double getPrice() {
      return price;
    }

    public void setPrice(double price) {
      this.price = price;
    }

    public bool isAvailable() {
      return (stock > 0);
    }
  }
```

2. Add this file to our project.

3. Modify our `Main` class to look like this:

```vala
using GLib;

public class Main : Object
{
  public Main ()
  {
    var book = new Book ("1234", "A new book");
    book.printISBN ();

    var store = new BookStore (book, 4.2, 10);
    stdout.printf ("Initial stock is %d\n", store.getStock ());
    stdout.printf ("Initial price is $ %f\n", store.getPrice ());
    store.removeStock (4);
    store.setPrice (5.0);
```

```
            stdout.printf ("Stock is %d\n", store.getStock());
            stdout.printf ("and price is now $ %f\n", store.getPrice());
            var status = "still available";
            if (store.isAvailable() == false) {
              status = "not available";
            }
            stdout.printf ("And the book is %s\n", status);
        }

        static int main (string[] args)
        {
            stdout.printf ("Hello, world\n");
            var main = new Main();
            return 0;
        }
    }
```

4. Run it.

5. See how the data is manipulated and printed:

```
Hello, world

1234

Initial stock is 10

Initial price is $ 4.200000

Stock is 6

and price is now $ 5.000000

And the book is still available
```

What just happened?

Let's start analyzing from the calling code, the `Main` constructor.

```
    var store = new BookStore(book, 4.2, 10);
```

Here, we instantiate a new `store` object from the `BookStore` class. We initialize it with a `book` object, a floating point number, and an integer.

```
    public BookStore (Book book, double price, int stock) {
```

In the `BookStore` constructor, we have to specify the data types in the argument list as previously done. Then we say that we want to accept a `Book` object, a number in `double` precision, and an integer.

```
    this.book = book;
    this.price = price;
    this.stock = stock;
```

And then, we assign our private members of `book`, `price`, and `stock` with the arguments. Here we use `this.` to denote that we want to assign the `book` member from the private member with the `book` member from the argument. If we name our argument variable with a different name, for example, `bookObject`, we can omit `this` because it is no longer ambiguous; we know that `bookObject` must be coming from the argument list and not from our member. The same happens with `price` and `stock`.

```
stdout.printf ("Initial stock is %d\n", store.getStock());
```

This is how we print an integer with `printf`. We use `%d` as a placeholder for an integer.

```
stdout.printf ("Initial price is $ %f\n", store.getPrice());
```

And this is how we print a real number with `printf`. We use `%f` as a placeholder for it.

```
store.removeStock(4);
```

Then, we remove `4` books from the stock. Internally, this is defined in `BookStore.removeStock`, as follows:

```
stock = stock - amount;
```

There we just subtract using a mathematical expression because it is simply an integer.

```
var status = "still available";
if (store.isAvailable() == false) {
  status = "not available";
}
```

Next, we have a Boolean expression evaluation. If the value is `false`, we change the value of `status`. The type for `status` is `string`, and we can just assign the value.

```
stdout.printf ("And the book is %s\n", status);
```

Finally, we use `%s` as a placeholder in `printf` to put our string value there.

Gee, what is it?

Gee is a collection library written in Vala. The basic types of the collection are list, set, and maps. These are similar to array but with more powerful features.

Time for action – adding the Gee library

Let's take a look at Gee more closely. But first, let's try adding it to our project:

1. Click on the **Project** menu and choose **Add Library...**.
2. In **Select the target for the library**, find `hello_vala` under `src/`.

3. Then click on the **New library...** button.

4. Find **gee** from the list and check it in the **Module** option at the bottom of the dialog, and then find **HELLO_VALA**. This means that we add Gee into the C compilation step. Under the hood, this step modifies the `configure.ac` file to add Gee into the build system.

5. Then, from the **Files** dock, find `Makefile.am` in the `src/` directory and open it. Find the `hello_vala_VALAFLAGS` stanza and modify it to look like this:

```
hello_vala_VALAFLAGS =  \
    --pkg gtk+-3.0 \
    --pkg gee-1.0
```

6. Then, save and close the `Makefile.am` file. This step means that we add Gee into the Vala compilation step.

7. Then click on **Build** and choose **Clean Project**. This would clean the project from all the generated code and scripts prepared by the build system to make sure we pick up changes that we made in `Makefile.am` and `configure.ac`.

8. Try running our previous code again. There should be no error anymore.

What just happened?

We just added Gee into the project. Anjuta support for Vala is not yet perfect as we need to perform two actions (as we just did) to add a library into a project, one for C compilation and another for Vala compilation. Without these two steps, our program cannot be built because either Vala would not recognize the Gee namespace or the C compiler would not find the Gee header files and library.

Time for action – Gee in action

After installing Gee in our project, let's quickly check what capabilities Gee has to offer. Let's start from the simple ones, the array list.

1. Modify our `book.vala` file to look like this:

```vala
using GLib;
using Gee;

public class Book : Object {
    private string title;
    private string isbn;
    private ArrayList<string> authors;

    public Book(string isbn, string title) {
        this.isbn = isbn;
        this.title = title;
```

```
      authors = new ArrayList<string>();
   }

   public void addAuthor(string author) {
     authors.add(author);
   }

     public void printISBN() {
     stdout.printf("%s\n", isbn);
     }

   public void printTitle() {
     stdout.printf("%s\n", title);
   }

   public void printAuthors() {
     foreach (var author in authors) {
       stdout.printf("Author name: %s\n", author);
     }
   }
 }
```

2. Modify the `Main` class constructor to include these lines:

```
var book = new Book("1234", "A new book");
book.printISBN ();
book.addAuthor("Joe Random");
book.addAuthor("Joe Random Jr.");
book.printAuthors();
```

3. Run it.

4. See that it prints all of the authors of the book.

```
Hello, world
1234
Author name: Joe Random
Author name: Joe Random Jr.
Initial stock is 10
Initial price is $ 4.200000
Stock is 6
and price is now $ 5.000000
And the book is still available
```

What just happened?

Here we try to utilize the array list, which is one of many collection data structures provided by Gee.

```
using Gee;
```

In order to use Gee, first we declare that we are using the Gee namespace.

> We can actually omit this, but we need to always put the
> `Gee.` prefix in front of all Gee classes.

Now look at the member declaration in the `Book` class:

```
public class Book : Object {
    private string title;
    private string isbn;
    private ArrayList<string> authors;
```

The construct with angle brackets is called **generics programming**. This means that the data contained in the data structure (which is `ArrayList` in this context) is generic. If we have an array of type integer, we will put it as `ArrayList<int>`, and so on. Hence, in this particular line, we have `ArrayList`, which has content with type `string`, and we call the list with the name `authors`. In the constructor, we have to initialize the array list with this syntax:

```
public Book(string isbn, string title) {
    this.isbn = isbn;
    this.title = title;
    authors = new ArrayList<string>();
}
```

It means that we need to allocate an `ArrayList` object, which has content of type `string`. Note that only a declaration is not enough. If we forget this part, the program will crash.

```
public void addAuthor(string author) {
    authors.add(author);
}
```

Here, we use an `add` function, which is provided by the `ArrayList` class. As the name suggests, it will add the data into the array list; note that it can only accept `string` because we declare and initialize it with string content.

```
public void printAuthors() {
    foreach (var author in authors) {
        stdout.printf("Author name: %s\n", author);
    }
}
}
```

Here we iterate the content of the array list. We use the `foreach` command to iterate while assigning the value obtained on each iteration to the `author` variable. Note that we use the `var author in authors` expression. We don't specify the `author` variable to be `string`, but instead we use an automatic variable construction with the `var` keyword. In this line, `var` will get assigned a type depending on the content of the `authors` variable. Because the `authors` content type is `string`, the `author` variable bound to the `var` keyword will be also `string`. This kind of construction is really useful if we generalize a class to be able to handle any kind of data types depending on the data type stored in the collection or data structure.

Initializing members when declaring

In our previous code, we initialize the array list in the constructor. Another alternative is to initialize it while declaring in the declaration area, without initializing it in the constructor. We can do it like this:

```
private ArrayList<string> authors = new ArrayList<string>();
```

When your code grows and you have more than one constructor, this alternative is better than initializing in the constructor because you must copy all of the initialization code to all constructors.

Time for action – watching for signals

Vala has a construct for emitting and watching signals, which is a mechanism of subscribing to information when something happens in the code. We can subscribe to a signal by connecting the function that will perform some action into the signal. Let's see how it works.

1. Modify our `bookstore.vala` file ad add two new declarations:

```
public class BookStore {
  ...
  public signal void stockAlert();
  public signal void priceAlert();
```

2. Modify our `removeStock` and `setPrice` functions in `bookstore.vala` to be like this:

```
public void removeStock(int amount) {
  stock = stock - amount;
  if (stock < 5) {
    stockAlert();
  }
}
public void setPrice(double price) {
  this.price = price;
```

```
    if (price < 1) {
      priceAlert();
    }
  }
```

3. Modify our `Main` constructor to be like this:

```
public Main ()
  {
      var book = new Book("1234", "A new book");
      book.printISBN ();
      book.addAuthor("Joe Random");
      book.addAuthor("Joe Random Jr.");
      book.printAuthors();

      var store = new BookStore(book, 4.2, 10);

      store.stockAlert.connect(() => {
        stdout.printf ("Uh oh, we are going to run out stock
soon!\n");
        });

      store.priceAlert.connect(() => {
        stdout.printf ("Uh oh, price is too low\n");
      });
      stdout.printf ("Initial stock is %d\n", store.getStock());
      stdout.printf ("Initial price is $ %f\n", store.getPrice());
      store.removeStock(4);

      store.setPrice(5.0);
      stdout.printf ("Stock is %d\n", store.getStock());
      stdout.printf ("and price is now $ %f\n", store.getPrice());

      store.removeStock(4);

      var status = "still available";
      if (store.isAvailable() == false) {
        status = "not available";
      }
      stdout.printf ("And the book is %s\n", status);
      store.setPrice(0.2);
```

4. Run it.

5. See the printed message:

```
Hello, world

1234

Author name: Joe Random
```

```
Author name: Joe Random Jr.
Initial stock is 10
Initial price is $ 4.200000
Stock is 6
and price is now $ 5.000000
Uh oh, we are going to run out stock soon!
And the book is still available
Uh oh, price is too low
```

What just happened?

The warning message printed that the stock is running out and the price is too low is not printed by `BookStore` class but rather by the `Main` class. This assumes a scenario where the `Main` class subscribes to the signals and will do something about it when `Main` receives the information from the signals.

```
public signal void stockAlert();
public signal void priceAlert();
```

First, we have to define the signal in the class that we want to publish the signal from. In `BookStore`, we declare these two signals. Note that we only declare the method signature with the `signal` keyword. We don't declare the body of the function. It is essential of the signal that the object that subscribes to these signals provides functions to handle the emitted signals.

```
if (stock < 5) {
   stockAlert();
}
...
if (price < 1) {
   priceAlert();
}
```

These two snippets show how we emit the signal. When `stock` is less than 5, we emit the `stockAlert` signal, and if `price` is less than 1, we emit the `priceAlert` signal. The `BookStore` class doesn't care about what happens next; it only announces the signals, and that's it.

```
store.stockAlert.connect(() => {
   stdout.printf ("Uh oh, we are going to run out stock soon!\n");
});

store.priceAlert.connect(() => {
   stdout.printf ("Uh oh, price is too low\n");
});
```

While here, the `Main` class constructor connects itself with these two signals. We can see the construct for providing a function body by using the `=>` operator. This construct is called **closure** or **anonymous function**. The parameter of this function is defined before `=>`, which in this context is indicating that no parameters were supplied. This is shown by empty parentheses.

Inside the function body, we declare what should happen when the signal is emitted by the `store` object. Here, we just print some alert text. In reality, we could do anything from disconnecting network and displaying images to any other actions we want.

```
store.removeStock(4);
...
store.setPrice(0.2);
```

Here the actual signals are emitted and the text is printed.

Have a go hero – putting parameters in signals

We can put parameters in our signal, too. We can just put the parameters we want in the signal declaration. Then, when connecting to a signal, put the parameters before the `=>` operator. Now how about modifying the `priceAlert` signal to have one parameter, which is the price of the book?

Summary

It is fairly easy and quick to create an application and get it up and running with both Seed and Vala. So why do we want to learn both and use them in this book?

JavaScript is an interpreted language; we can see the guts of the program and modify it directly without recompilation. Vala, on the other hand, is a compiled language. We need to have access to the source code to modify it. If we want to make a commercial software on top of the GNOME platform, Vala makes a pretty good choice.

Making a program with JavaScript in Seed is pretty straightforward and does not require project management in Anjuta, while in Vala, we need to take care of the dependencies manually. Let's hope this can be fixed in the future version of Anjuta.

Now we know the basic construct of the JavaScript and Vala code, from manipulating basic data types to using the object-oriented programming concept.

We see that JavaScript programming is pretty relaxed, while Vala is strict. A better code structure using modularization would help simplify development and make debugging easier.

After knowing all of this, now we are ready to go to the next chapter, which uses the GNOME platform libraries, which is the foundation of creating a GNOME application.

4

Using GNOME Core Libraries

GNOME core libraries are a collection of foundation utility classes and functions. It covers many things from simple date-conversion functions to virtual filesystem access management. GNOME would not be as powerful as it is now without its core libraries. There are a lot of UI libraries out there that are not successful because of the lack of this kind of power. No wonder there are many libraries outside GNOME that also use GNOME core libraries to support their functionalities.

GNOME core libraries are composed from GLib and GIO, which are non-UI libraries for supporting our UI applications. These libraries connect our programs with files, networks, timers, and other important aspects in the operating system. Without this knowledge, we can probably make a beautiful program, but we would be incapable of interacting with the rest of the system.

In this chapter we shall learn about:

- The GLib main loop and basic functions
- The GObject signaling system and properties
- The GIO files, stream and networking
- The GSettings configuration system

Ok, let's get started.

Before we start

There are a few exercises in this chapter that need access to the Internet or the local network. Make sure you have a good connection before running the program. Another exercise requires access to removable hardware and mountable filesystems.

In this chapter, we will do something different regarding the Vala exercises. Because the nature of the discussions are independent of each other, each Vala exercise is done in its own project instead of continuously modifying a file in a single project. So, in each Vala exercise we will create a new project and work inside that project. The name of the project will be noted so you can easily compare your project with the source code that accompanies this book. Similar to the previous chapter, the project we create here is a Vala GTK+ (simple) project. In the project properties, we should not tick on the **GtkBuilder support for user interface** option and should pick **No license** in the **License** option.

In each exercise, the JavaScript code follows the Vala code and it is kept inside one file per exercise. The functionalities of the JavaScript code would be exactly the same. So you can opt to choose whether you want to use either the Vala or the JavaScript code, or both.

The GLib main loop

GLib provides a main event loop, which takes care of the events coming from various sources. With this event loop, we can catch these events and do the necessary processing.

Time for action – playing with the GLib main loop

Here, we will introduce ourselves to the GLib main loop.

1. Create a new Vala project called `core-mainloop` and use this code in the `Main` class:

```vala
using GLib;

public class Main : Object
{
  int counter = 0;

  bool printCounter() {
    stdout.printf("%d\n", counter++);
    return true;
  }

  public Main ()
  {
```

```vala
      Timeout.add(1000, printCounter);
    }

    static int main (string[] args)
    {
      Main main = new Main();
      var loop = new MainLoop();
      loop.run ();
      return 0;
    }
  }
```

2. And this is the JavaScript code's counterpart; you can name the script as
    `core-mainloop.js`:

```javascript
#!/usr/bin/env seed

GLib = imports.gi.GLib;
GObject = imports.gi.GObject;

Main = new GType({
  parent: GObject.Object.type,
  name: "Main",
  init: function() {
    var counter = 0;
    this.printCounter = function() {
      Seed.printf("%d", counter++);
      return true;
    };
    GLib.timeout_add(0, 1000, this.printCounter);
  }
});
var main = new Main();
var context = GLib.main_context_default();
var loop = new GLib.MainLoop.c_new(context);
loop.run();
```

3. Run it. Do you notice that the program prints the counter and stays running?
    You can do nothing except press the *Ctrl + C* key combination to kill it.

What just happened?

We have set up a GLib main loop with a single source of events, a timeout.

Initially, we set the `counter` variable to `0`.

```vala
    int counter = 0;
```

We prepare a function called `printCounter` to print the `counter` variable's value, and increase its value by one immediately after printing. Then we return `true` to indicate that we want the counter to continue.

```
bool printCounter() {
    stdout.printf("%d\n", counter++);
    return true;
}
```

In the constructor, we create a `Timeout` object with a `1000` ms interval pointing to our `printCounter` function. This means that `printCounter` will be called at every 1-second interval, and it will be repeatedly called as long as `printCounter` returns `true`.

```
public Main ()
{
    Timeout.add(1000, printCounter);
}
```

In the `main` function, we instantiate the `Main` class, create a `MainLoop` object, and call `run`. This will cause the program to stay running until we manually terminate it. When the loop is running, it can accept events submitted to it. The `Timeout` object that we created earlier produces such an event. Whenever the timer interval expires, it notifies the main loop, which in turn calls the `printCounter` function.

```
static int main (string[] args)
{
    Main main = new Main();
    var loop = new MainLoop();
    loop.run ();
    return 0;
}
```

Now, let's take a look at the JavaScript code. If you notice, the class structure is a bit different from what we learned in the previous chapter. Here we use Seed Runtime's construction of class.

```
GLib = imports.gi.GLib;
GObject = imports.gi.GObject;
```

Here, we import `GLib` and `GObject`. Then we construct a class called `Main`, which is based on `GObject`.

Here is how we do it. The following code says that we subclass `GType` into a new class called `Main` and pass the object structure into the argument.

```
Main = new GType({
    parent: GObject.Object.type,
    name: "Main",
```

The first member of the object is `parent`, which is the parent of our class. We assign it with `GObject.Object.type` to denote that our class is derived from `Object` in the `GObject` module that we imported previously. Then we name our class as `Main`. After that, we put the functions inside the `init` function, which is also the constructor of the class.

The content of the class member is similar to what we've seen in the Vala code and it is quite straightforward.

```
init: function() {
  var counter = 0;
  this.printCounter = function() {
    Seed.printf("%d", counter++);
    return true;
  };
  GLib.timeout_add(0, 1000, this.printCounter);
}
});
```

Then we have the code that is analogous to what we have in Vala's static `main` function. Here we create our `Main` object and create the GLib's main loop.

```
var main = new Main();
var context = GLib.main_context_default();
var loop = new GLib.MainLoop.c_new(context);
loop.run();
```

Have a go hero – stopping the timeout

Our program counts forever. Can you make it stop after the counter reaches 10?

You can just play with the `printCounter` return value.

Or even better, can you make it stop totally, meaning that the program would exit after the counter reaches 10?

You can ignore the return value and rearrange the code, and somehow pass the `loop` object into the `Main` class. In the `printCounter` function, you can call `loop.quit()` whenever it reaches 10 to make the program break the main loop programmatically.

GObject signals

GObject provides a signaling mechanism that we can hook into. In the previous chapter, we have discussed the Vala signaling system. Internally, it is actually using the GObject signaling system, but it is so transparent that it is seamlessly integrated into the language itself.

Time for action – handling GObject signals

Let us see how to do it in JavaScript:

1. Create a new script called `core-signals.js` and fill it with the following code:

```
#!/usr/bin/env seed

GLib = imports.gi.GLib;
GObject = imports.gi.GObject;

Main = new GType({
  parent: GObject.Object.type,
  name: "Main",
  signals: [
      {
        name: "alert",
        parameters: [GObject.TYPE_INT]
      }
    ],
  init: function(self) {
    var counter = 0;

    this.printCounter = function() {
      Seed.printf("%d", counter++);
      if (counter > 9) {
        self.signal.alert.emit(counter);
      }
      return true;
    };

    GLib.timeout_add(0, 1000, this.printCounter);
  }
});

var main = new Main();

var context = GLib.main_context_default();
var loop = new GLib.MainLoop.c_new(context);
```

```
main.signal.connect('alert', function(object, counter) {
  Seed.printf("Counter is %d, let's stop here", counter);
  loop.quit();
});
loop.run();
```

2. Run it and notice the messages printed:

```
0

1

2

3

4

5

6

7

8

9

Counter is 10, let's stop here
```

What just happened?

With the GObject signaling system, we can subscribe for notifications that are emitted by an object. We just need to provide a handler that will perform some action upon receiving the signal.

Here, we declare our signal in an array by putting an object with names and parameters as the content of the object. The parameter type is the type that is known by the GLib system. If our signal does not have any parameters, we can omit it.

```
signals: [
  {
    name: "alert",
    parameters: [GObject.TYPE_INT]
  }
],

main.signal.connect('alert', function(object, counter) {
  Seed.printf("Counter is %d, let's stop here", counter);
  loop.quit();
});
```

Then we subscribe to the signal and provide a closure that just prints the `counter` value and breaks the main loop. Note that the parameter is defined in the second parameter of the closure. The first parameter is reserved for the object itself.

Finally, we emit the signal by calling the signal by its name. `self` is the `Main` class we pass in the `init` function.

```
if (counter > 9) {
   self.signal.alert.emit(counter);
}
```

As soon as we call this, the signal will be processed in the main loop and will be delivered to the objects that subscribe to it.

Have a go hero – writing it in Vala

Compared with the previous code, signal declaration, emission, and subscription are easier in Vala, as we've seen it the last time. How about trying to write the previous code in Vala?

GLib properties

Properties are key-value pairs in a storage system that are available in all instances of GObject, which is the base class for all objects in the GNOME system. One useful feature of properties is that we can subscribe for changes when the value is changed.

Time for action – accessing properties

We are going to learn how to set and get a value to and from a property as well as monitor the changes.

1. Create a new script called `core-properties.js` and fill it with this code:

```
#!/usr/bin/env seed

GLib = imports.gi.GLib;
GObject = imports.gi.GObject;

Main = new GType({
  parent: GObject.Object.type,
  name: "Main",
  properties: [
    {
      name: 'counter',
      type: GObject.TYPE_INT,
```

```
          default_value: 0,
          minimum_value: 0,
          maximum_value: 1024,
          flags: (GObject.ParamFlags.CONSTRUCT
              | GObject.ParamFlags.READABLE
              | GObject.ParamFlags.WRITABLE),
      }
    ],
    init: function(self) {
      this.print_counter = function() {
        Seed.printf("%d", self.counter++);
        return true;
      }

      this.monitor_counter = function(obj, gobject, data) {
        Seed.print("Counter value has changed to " + obj.counter);
      }

      GLib.timeout_add(0, 1000, this.print_counter);
      self.signal.connect("notify::counter", this.monitor_counter);
    }
});

var main = new Main();
var context = GLib.main_context_default();
var loop = new GLib.MainLoop.c_new(context);
loop.run();
```

2. And this is the Vala counterpart (you can create a new project called `core-properties` and fill `core_properties.vala` with this code):

```
using GLib;

public class Main : Object
{
  public int counter {
    set construct;
    get;
    default = 0;
  }

  public bool print_counter() {
    stdout.printf("%d\n", counter ++);
    return true;
  }
```

```vala
    public void monitor_counter() {
      stdout.printf ("Counter value has changed to %d\n", counter);
    }

    public Main ()
    {
    }

    construct {
      Timeout.add(1000, print_counter);
      notify["counter"].connect ((obj)=> {
        monitor_counter ();
      });
    }

    static int main (string[] args)
    {
      Gtk.init (ref args);
      var app = new Main ();

      Gtk.main ();
      return 0;
    }
}
```

3. Run it and notice the messages printed. Note that you can press the *Ctrl + C* combination keys to stop the program.

```
Counter value has changed to 0

Counter value has changed to 1

0

Counter value has changed to 2

1

Counter value has changed to 3

2

Counter value has changed to 4

3

Counter value has changed to 5

4

Counter value has changed to 6

5..
```

What just happened?

In the JavaScript code, we need to declare the properties inside the `properties` array, and fill it with the property's object.

Here we describe that our property has the name `counter` and is of type integer. It needs to declare the default, minimum, and maximum values. It also needs the flags. From the flags, we can see `GObject.ParamFlags.CONSTRUCT`, which means that the property is initialized in the construction phase. It means that the default value is set when the object is created. We also see that it is readable and writable.

```
properties: [
    {
        name: 'counter',
        type: GObject.TYPE_INT,
        default_value: 0,
        minimum_value: 0,
        maximum_value: 1024,
        flags: (GObject.ParamFlags.CONSTRUCT
              | GObject.ParamFlags.READABLE
              | GObject.ParamFlags.WRITABLE),
    }
]
```

In the following code, we subscribe for changes. We use the signaling system and the name of the signal is constructed with the `notify::` keyword followed by the property's name. After this, every change that happens to the property will trigger the signal handler.

```
self.signal.connect("notify::counter", this.monitor_counter);
```

Here we set the value of the property by increasing its value. Note that here we modify the value; hence the value monitor will be triggered first, and then the actual value is printed by `printf`.

```
this.print_counter = function() {
    Seed.printf("%d", self.counter++);
    return true;
}
```

And the following code shows how to read the value:

```
this.monitor_counter = function(obj, gobject, data) {
    Seed.print("Counter value has changed to " + obj.counter);
}
```

In contrast with the JavaScript code, the properties declaration in Vala is very simple. The declaration is similar to the normal variable declaration with some additions.

In the following code, the `set construct` expression means that it is writable and the default value is initialized in the construction phase. `get` means that it is readable, and `default` defines the default value.

```
public int counter {
    set construct;
    get;
    default = 0;
}
```

However, there is no mechanism to set the minimum and maximum value.

Then we see how reading and writing the property are done like reading and writing a normal variable. From outside the class, we can use the normal way to refer a member variable, which is by using an object name followed by a dot and the property name.

```
public bool print_counter() {
    stdout.printf("%d\n", counter ++);
    return true;
}
```

```
public void monitor_counter() {
    stdout.printf ("Counter value has changed to %d\n", counter);
}
```

Subscribing for changes also uses the usual signaling mechanism, with the exception that we insert the property name in square brackets following the signal name, `notify`.

```
notify["counter"].connect ((obj)=> {
    monitor_counter ();
}
```

There is something new in the code; something we have not seen before. It is the `construct` keyword. It is basically an alternative way to construct an object similar to the normal constructors. This style of construction is close to how GObject construction is being carried out in the actual generated C code.

Despite the differences between these JavaScript and Vala codes, both allow the use of a property just like a plain member of the class. So, in both languages, you can access the `counter` property as `main.counter` (assuming that the object's name is `main`).

Pop quiz – why the value of zero is printed out

From the output, we saw this:

```
Counter value has changed to 0
```

Q1. We did not set the counter to 0 explicitly, did we? So, why did it happen?

1. Because the property has the `set construct` keyword defined.

2. Because 0 is the default value.

Have a go hero – making a property read-only

When a property is read-only, we can no longer set its value. Now, let's try to make the `counter` property read-only. Hint: Play with the property flag.

Configuration files

In many cases we need to somehow read from a configuration file in order to customize how our program should behave. Here, we will learn how to use the simplest configuration mechanism in GLib using a configuration file. Imagine that we have a configuration file and it contains the name and version of our application so that we can print it somewhere inside our program.

Time for action – reading configuration files

Here's how to do it:

1. Create a configuration file; let's call it `core-keyfile.ini`. Its content is as follows:

   ```
   [General]
   name = "This is name"
   version = 1
   ```

2. Create a new Vala project and name it `core-keyfile`. Put the `core-keyfile.ini` file inside the project directory (but not in `src`).

3. Edit `core_keyfile.vala` to look like this:

   ```vala
   using GLib;

   public class Main : Object
   {
     KeyFile keyFile = null;
     public Main ()
   ```

```
    {
      keyFile = new KeyFile();
      keyFile.load_from_file("core-keyfile.ini", 0);
    }

    public int get_version()
    {
      return keyFile.get_integer("General", "version");
    }

    public string get_name()
    {
      return keyFile.get_string("General", "name");
    }

    static int main (string[] args)
    {
      var app = new Main ();
      stdout.printf("%s %d\n", app.get_name(), app.get_version());

      return 0;
    }
}
```

4. The JavaScript code (let's call it `core-keyfile.js`) looks like this (remember to put the `.ini` file in the same directory as the script):

```
#!/usr/bin/env seed

GLib = imports.gi.GLib;
GObject = imports.gi.GObject;

Main = new GType({
  parent: GObject.Object.type,
  name: "Main",
  init: function(self) {

    this.get_name = function() {
      return this.keyFile.get_string("General", "name");
    }

    this.get_version = function() {
      return this.keyFile.get_integer("General", "version");
    }
```

```
        this.keyFile = new GLib.KeyFile.c_new();
        this.keyFile.load_from_file("core-keyfile.ini");
    }
});

var main = new Main();
Seed.printf("%s %d", main.get_name(), main.get_version());
```

5. Run the program and look at the output:

```
"This is name" 1
```

What just happened?

The configuration file we are using has a key-value pairs structure conforming to the Desktop Entry Specification document of freedesktop.org. In the GNOME platform, this structure is commonly used, mainly in the .desktop files, which are used by the launcher. People using Windows might find this similar to the .ini format, which is also used for configuration.

GLib provides the KeyFile class to access this type of configuration file. In our constructor, we have this snippet:

```
keyFile = new KeyFile();
keyFile.load_from_file("core-keyfile.ini", 0);
```

It initializes an object of KeyFile, and loads the core-keyfile.ini file into the object.

If we jump a bit in our core-keyfile.ini file, we have a section, as shown, written inside a pair of square brackets.

```
[General]
```

And then all the entries following it can be accessed by specifying the section name. Here we provide two methods, get_version() and get_name(), as shortcuts to get the value of the name and version entries in the configuration file.

```
public int get_version()
{
    return keyFile.get_integer("General", "version");
}

public string get_name()
{
    return keyFile.get_string("General", "name");
}
```

Inside the methods, we just get the integer value from the `version` entry and get the string value from the `name` entry. We also see that we obtain the entries under the `General` section. And in these methods we just return the value immediately.

As shown in the following code, we consume the values from the methods and print them:

```
stdout.printf("%s %d\n", app.get_name(), app.get_version());
```

Quite easy, isn't it? The JavaScript code is also easy and straightforward; so it does not need to be explained further.

Have a go hero – multi-section configuration

Let's try adding more sections inside the configuration file and accessing the values. Imagine that we have a specific section called `License` that has `license_file` and `customer_id` as the entries. Imagine that we will use this information later to check whether the customer has the right to use the software.

GIO, the input/output library

In real life, our program must be able to access files wherever they are stored, locally or remotely. Imagine that we have a set of files that we need to read. The files are spread both locally and remotely. GIO will make it easy for us to manipulate these files as it provides an API to interact with our files in an abstract way.

Time for action – accessing files

Let's see how it works:

1. Let's create a new script called `core-files.js`, and fill it with these lines:

```
#!/usr/bin/env seed

GLib = imports.gi.GLib;
Gio = imports.gi.Gio;
GObject = imports.gi.GObject;

Main = new GType({
  parent: GObject.Object.type,
  name: "Main",
  init: function(self) {
    this.start = function() {
      var file = null;
      var files = ["http://en.wikipedia.org/wiki/Text_file",
"core-files.js"];
```

```
      for (var i = 0; i < files.length; i++) {
        if (files[i].match(/^http:/)) {
          file = Gio.file_new_for_uri(files[i]);
        } else {
          file = Gio.file_new_for_path(files[i]);
        }

        var stream = file.read();
        var data_stream = new Gio.DataInputStream.c_new(stream);
          var data = data_stream.read_until("", 0);

          Seed.print(data)
      }
    }
  }
});

var main = new Main();
main.start();
```

2. Alternatively, you can create a Vala project called `core-files`. Fill `src/core_files.vala` with this code:

```
using GLib;

public class Main : Object
{
  public Main ()
  {
  }

  public void start ()
  {
    File file = null;
    string[] files = {"http://en.wikipedia.org/wiki/Text_file",
"src/core_files.vala"};

    for (var i = 0; i < files.length; i++) {
      if (files[i].has_prefix("http:")) {
        file = File.new_for_uri(files[i]);
      } else {
        file = File.new_for_path(files[i]);
      }

      var stream = file.read();
      var data_stream = new DataInputStream(stream);
```

```vala
        size_t data_read;
        var data = data_stream.read_until("", out data_read);
        stdout.printf(data);
    }
  }

  static int main (string[] args)
  {
    var app = new Main ();
    app.start();
    return 0;
  }
}
```

3. Run the program, and notice that it fetches the Wikipedia page from the Internet as well as the source code of the program from the local directory.

```
Terminal                                                          _  □  X
 File  Edit  View  Search  Terminal  Help
l, true);
}</script>
<script src="/w/index.php?title=Special:BannerController&amp;cache=/cn.js&amp;30
3-4" type="text/javascript"></script>
<script src="//bits.wikimedia.org/en.wikipedia.org/load.php?debug=false&amp;lang
=en&amp;modules=site&amp;only=scripts&amp;skin=vector&amp;*" type="text/javascri
pt"></script>
<script src="//geoiplookup.wikimedia.org/" type="text/javascript"></script><!--
Served by srv261 in 0.098 secs. -->
        </body>
</html>
using GLib;

public class Main : Object
{
        public Main ()
        {
        }

        public void start ()
        {
                File file = null;
                string[] files = {"http://en.wikipedia.org/wiki/Text_file", "src
/core_files.vala"};
```

What just happened?

GIO aims to provide a set of powerful virtual filesystem APIs. It provides a set of interfaces that serve as a foundation to be extended by the specific implementation. For example, here we use the GFile interface that defines the functions for a file. The GFile API does not tell us where the file is located, how the file is read, or other such details. It just provides the functions and that's it. The specific implementation that is transparent to the application developers will do all the hard work. Let's see what this means.

In the following code, we get the file location from the array `files`. Then we check if the location has an HTTP protocol identifier or not; if yes, we create the `GFile` object using `file_new_for_uri`, otherwise we use `file_new_for_path`. We can, of course, use `file_new_for_uri` even for the local file, but we need to prepend the `file://` protocol identifier to the filename.

```
if (files[i].match(/^http:/)) {
  file = Gio.file_new_for_uri(files[i]);
} else {
  file = Gio.file_new_for_path(files[i]);
}
```

This is the only difference between handling the remote file and the local file. And after that we can access files either from the local drive or from a web server by using the same function with GIO.

```
var stream = file.read();
var data_stream = new Gio.DataInputStream.c_new(stream);
var data = data_stream.read_until("", 0);
```

Here we use the `read` function to get the `GFileInputStream` object. Notice here that the API provides the same function wherever the file is.

The resulting object is a stream. A **stream** is a sequence of data that flows from one end to the other. The stream can be passed to an object and can transform it to become another stream or just consume it.

In our case, we get the stream initially from the `file.read` function. We transfer this stream into `GDataInputStream` in order to easily read the data. With the new stream, we ask GIO to read the data until we find nothing, which means it has reached the end of the file. And then we spit the data out onto the screen.

Network access with GIO

GIO provides adequate functions to access the network. Here we will learn how to create socket client and server programs. Imagine that we are building a simple chat program that can send data from one end to another.

Time for action – accessing a network

For brevity, we will do it only in JavaScript now; you can look at the Vala program in
core-server and core-client projects code that accompany this book. Ok, so let's see
what are the steps needed to access the network.

1. Create a new script called `core-server.js` and fill it with these lines:

```javascript
#!/usr/bin/env seed

GLib = imports.gi.GLib;
Gio = imports.gi.Gio;
GObject = imports.gi.GObject;

Main = new GType({
  parent: GObject.Object.type,
  name: "Main",
  init: function(self) {
    this.process = function(connection) {
      var input = new Gio.DataInputStream.c_new (connection.get_
input_stream());
      var data = input.read_upto("\n", 1);
      Seed.print("data from client: " + data);
      var output = new Gio.DataOutputStream.c_new (connection.get_
output_stream());
      output.put_string(data.toUpperCase());
      output.put_string("\n");
      connection.get_output_stream().flush();
    }

    this.start = function() {
      var service = new Gio.SocketService();
      service.add_inet_port(9000, null);
      service.start();
      while (1) {
        var connection = service.accept(null);
        this.process(connection);
      }
    }
  }
});

var main = new Main();
main.start();
```

2. Run this script. The program will stay running until we press *Ctrl + C*.

3. Then create another script called `core-client.js`; here is the code:

```
#!/usr/bin/env seed

GLib = imports.gi.GLib;
Gio = imports.gi.Gio;
GObject = imports.gi.GObject;

Main = new GType({
  parent: GObject.Object.type,
  name: "Main",
  init: function(self) {

    this.start = function() {
      var address = new Gio.InetAddress.from_string("127.0.0.1");
      var socket = new Gio.InetSocketAddress({address: address,
port: 9000});
      var client = new Gio.SocketClient ();
          var conn = client.connect (socket);

          Seed.printf("Connected to server");

      var output = conn.get_output_stream();
      var output_stream = new Gio.DataOutputStream.c_new(output);

          var message = "Hello\n";
      output_stream.put_string(message);
      output.flush();

      var input = conn.get_input_stream();
      var input_stream = new Gio.DataInputStream.c_new(input);
      var data = input_stream.read_upto("\n", 1);
      Seed.printf("Data from server: " + data);
    }
  }
});

var main = new Main();
main.start();
```

4. Run this program and notice the output of both the server and the client programs. They can talk to each other!

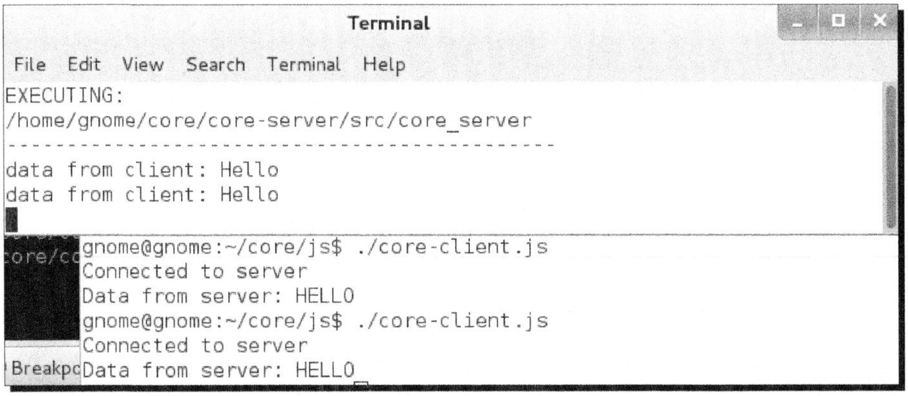

What just happened?

GIO provides high-level as well as low-level networking APIs that are really easy to use. Let's take a look at the server first.

Here we open a service in port number `9000`. It is an arbitrary number; you can use your own number if you want, with some restrictions:

```
var service = new Gio.SocketService();
service.add_inet_port(9000, null);
service.start();
```

You can't run the service if there is already another service running with a port number that is the same as yours. Also, you have to run your program as root if you want to use a port number below 1024.

And then we enter an infinite loop that is called when the service is accepting an incoming connection. Here, we just call our process function to handle the connection. That's it.

```
while (1) {
   var connection = service.accept(null);
   this.process(connection);
}
```

The server's basic activity is defined as easily as that. The details of the processing is another story.

Then, we create a `GDataInputStream` object based on the input stream coming from the connection. And then we read the data in until we find the end of line character which is \n. It is one character, so we put 1 there as well. And then we print the incoming data.

```
    var input = new Gio.DataInputStream.c_new            (connection.get_
input_stream());
    var data = input.read_upto("\n", 1);
    Seed.print("data from client: " + data);
```

To make things interesting, we want to return something to the client. Here we create an object of the `GDataOutputStream` class that is coming from the connection object. We change the data coming from the client to uppercase, and we send it back through the stream. In the end, we make sure everything is sent by flushing down the pipe. That's all on the server side.

```
    var output = new Gio.DataOutputStream.c_new (connection.get_output_
stream());
    output.put_string(data.toUpperCase());
    output.put_string("\n");
    connection.get_output_stream().flush();
```

On the client side, initially, we make an object of `GInetAddress`. The object is then fed into `GInetSocketAddress` so we can define the port of the address that we want to connect to.

```
    var address = new Gio.InetAddress.from_string("127.0.0.1");
    var socket = new Gio.InetSocketAddress({address: address, port:
    9000});
```

Then we connect the `socket` object with `SocketClient` into `GSocketClient`. After this, if everything is OK, the connection to the server is established.

```
    var client = new Gio.SocketClient ();
    var conn = client.connect (socket);
```

On the client side, in principle, the process occurs in the opposite way as it would occur on the server side. Here we create `GDataOutputStream` first, based on the stream coming from the connection object. Then we just send the message into it. We also want to flush it so all the remaining data in the pipeline is flushed out.

```
    var output = conn.get_output_stream();
    var output_stream = new Gio.DataOutputStream.c_new(output);

    var message = "Hello\n";
    output_stream.put_string(message);
    output.flush();
```

Then, we expect to get something from the server; so we create an input stream object. We read from it until we find a newline, and we print the data.

```
var input = conn.get_input_stream();
var input_stream = new Gio.DataInputStream.c_new(input);
var data = input_stream.read_upto("\n", 1);
Seed.printf("Data from server: " + data);
```

Have a go hero – making an echo server

Echo server is a service that returns everything that is sent to it as it is, without any modifications. For example, if we send "Hello", the server will also send back "Hello". Sometimes it is used for checking whether the connection between two hosts is working. How about modifying the server program to be an echo server?

We can put it in an infinite loop, but if we type "quit", the server disconnects.

Understanding GSettings

Previously, we have used the GLib configuration parser to read our application configuration. Now we will try to use a more advanced settings system with GSettings. With this, we can access configurations throughout the GNOME platform, including all the applications that use the system.

Time for action – learning GSettings

Let's see what the GSettings configuration system looks like as visualized by the `dconf-editor` tool:

1. Launch a terminal.
2. Run `dconf-editor` from the terminal.

3. Navigate through the `org` tree on the left-hand side of the application, and go through **gnome**, **desktop**, and then **background**.

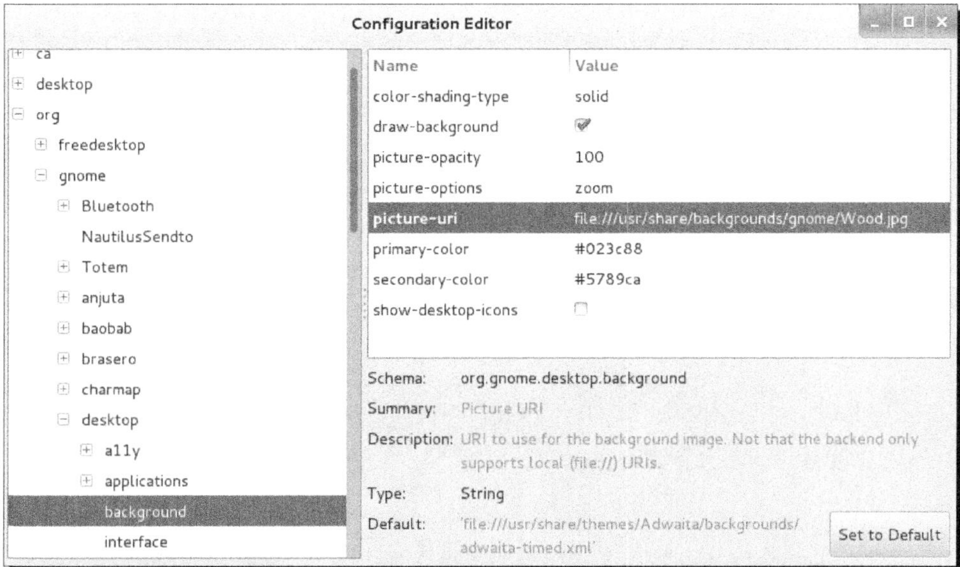

What just happened?

GSettings is a new introduction in GNOME 3. Before, the configuration was handled with GConf. In GNOME 3, every shipped GNOME application has been migrated to use GSettings. The concept of storing the settings in GConf and GSettings remains the same, that is, by using key-value pairs. However, GSettings contains improvements in many aspects, including more restrictive usage by enforcing schema as metadata. With GConf, we can freely store and read any values from the system.

GSettings is actually only a top-level layer. Underneath, there is a low-level system called dconf, which handles the actual storing and reading of the values. The tool we discuss here shows the keys and values in a hierarchy so we can browse, read, and even write a new value (if the schema says it's writable, of course).

In the screenshot we can see that `org.gnome.desktop.background` has many entries; one of them is `picture-uri`, which contains the URI of the desktop's background image.

GSettings API

In this book, the API is more interesting than the administrative tools. After we see GSettings visually, it is time to access GSettings through API.

Time for action – accessing GSettings programmatically

Imagine that we create a tool to set the background image of our GNOME desktop. Here is
how to do it:

1. Create a new Vala project called `core-settings`, and modify `core_settings.vala` with the following:

```vala
using GLib;

public class Main : Object
{
  Settings settings = null;
  public Main ()
  {
    settings = new Settings ("org.gnome.desktop.background");
  }

  public string get_bg()
  {
    if (settings == null) {
      return null;
    }

    return settings.get_string ("picture-uri");
  }

  public void set_bg(string new_file)
  {
    if (settings == null) {
      return;
    }
    if (settings.set_string ("picture-uri", new_file)) {
      Settings.sync ();
    }
  }

  static int main (string[] args)
  {
    var app = new Main ();
    stdout.printf ("%s\n", app.get_bg());
    app.set_bg ("file:///usr/share/backgrounds/gnome/Wood.jpg");
    return 0;
  }
}
```

2. The JavaScript code is quite straightforward; here we have a snippet of it just to see the adaptation needed from the Vala code:

```
init: function(self) {
  this.settings = null;

  this.get_bg = function() {
    if (this.settings == null)
      return null;

    return this.settings.get_string("picture-uri");
  }

  this.set_bg = function(new_file) {
    if (this.settings == null)
      return;

    if (this.settings.set_string("picture-uri", new_file)) {
      Gio.Settings.sync();
    }
  }

  this.settings = new Gio.Settings({schema: 'org.gnome.desktop.background'});
}
```

3. Run it and see the change in your current desktop background image. Your current desktop background will change to the file specified in the code.

What just happened?

In this exercise, we use the already installed schema owned by the desktop, which is `org.gnome.desktop.background`, so we can just use the API to access the settings. Let's take a look at the details.

First, we initiate the connection to GSettings by specifying the schema name, which is `org.gnome.desktop.background`, and it returns a GSettings object.

```
settings = new Settings("org.gnome.desktop.background");
```

Then we put a simple safety net just in case the initialization fails. In the real world, we can perform reinitialization rather than just a simple return.

```
if (settings == null) {
  return null;
}
```

After that, we obtain a value of type `string` under the key `picture-uri`, and we can consume it in any way we want.

```
return settings.get_string("picture-uri");
```

Finally, we set the value using the same key. If it is successful, we ask GSettings to save it to the disk by calling the `sync` function. Easy, right?

```
if (settings.set_string ("picture-uri", new_file)) {
  Settings.sync ();
}
```

Summary

In this chapter, we learned a lot about the GNOME core libraries. Even though we did not touch everything in the libraries, we managed to tackle all the basics and essentials needed to build our GNOME application.

We know now that GLib provides a main loop that handles all the events from various sources. We discussed the GObject property and the signaling system. We also tried to look into the events processed by the main loop by posting with the timeouts, and signals when a value of a property has changed. Regarding the programming languages, we found out that Vala is more integrated with GNOME, and JavaScript requires more code to use GObject properties or signals.

We had an exercise of accessing files both locally and remotely, and we found out that the API provided by GIO is very easy to use because it abstracts the way we access those files wherever they are.

With GIO, we also did an experiment of building a simple client and server chat program and we found out that to create such an interesting program requires quite a minimal amount of code, both in JavaScript and Vala.

Finally, we had a discussion about GSettings and tried to read and write the GNOME desktop's background image with it.

After we master the foundation of the GNOME application, the next step is to learn the basics of a graphical program in the next chapter.

5

Building Graphical User Interface Applications

GTK+ has been the de facto graphical user interface (GUI) toolkit for GNOME since the project's inception. Lately, Clutter joined as the alternative, providing a fluid animating user interface powered by OpenGL. These two make a good set of base toolkits to choose from when developing a GUI application for GNOME.

In this chapter, we will learn how to create applications with GTK+ and Clutter. Specifically, we will take a look at:

- Creating a basic GTK+ application
- Programming with plain GTK+
- GUI programming with Clutter

Before we start

Developing an application with Clutter requires that you have a working OpenGL-enabled environment as mentioned in *Chapter 1, Installing GNOME 3 and SDK*. If your environment is not supported, the program will not start at all. However, GTK+ application development does not require any hardware support.

Creating a basic GTK+ application

Let's start by using the basic widgets of GTK+: label and button. We saw a mockup once in *Chapter 2, Preparing Our Weapons*, and here again, we will use a mockup as our blueprint to create an application. But now, we will add a feature to the mockup to make our plan more concrete. Imagine that we want to create an application, which is shown by the following mockup:

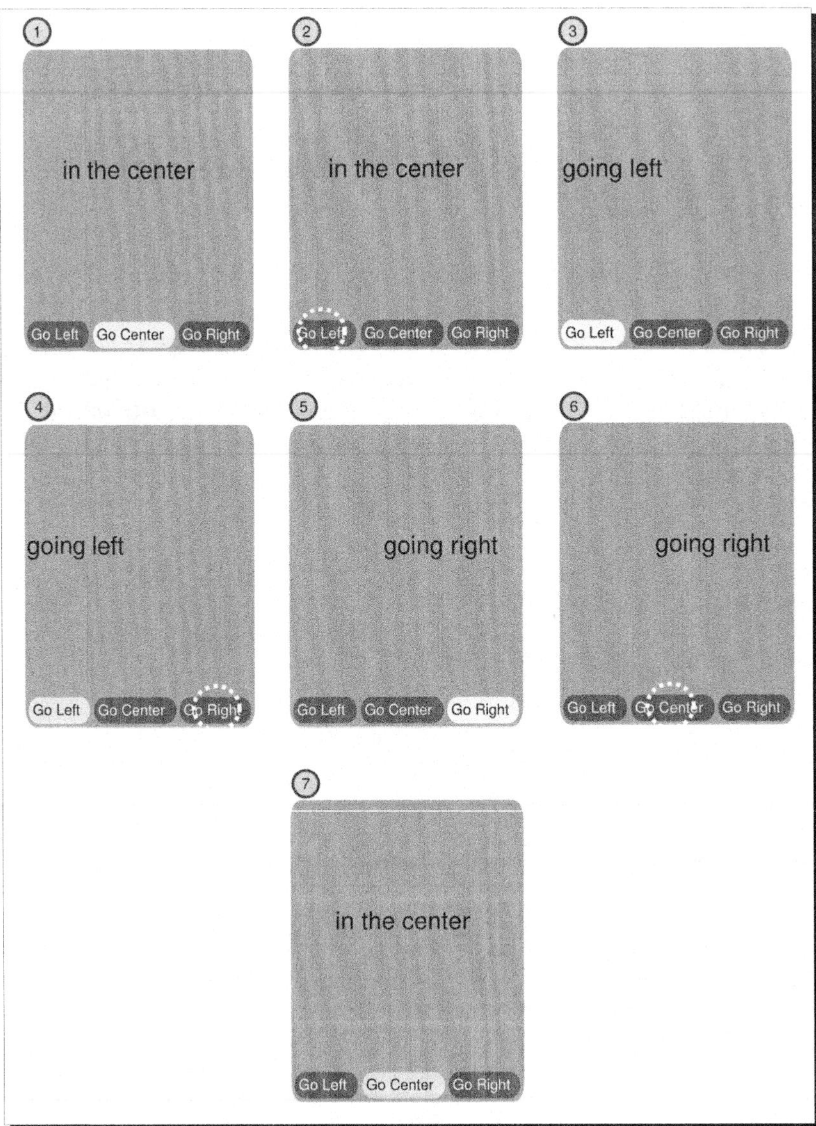

Each image on the mockup shows a particular state of the application. By following the state from one image to the next, it makes the whole sequence flow, which is called the **interaction flow**. Concretely, this shows us the interaction by the user immediately followed by the response of the application. The user interaction is represented by a graphical icon, which is drawn on top of the item on the application screen that the user is interacting with. In this mockup we only have click interaction, which is represented by a dotted circle to indicate that a mouse click is performed on the item.

Let's see the mockup closely. The first application state is shown by image number 1. It shows a label that is aligned to the center, and three buttons with the middle one in the pressed state. The image number 2 shows that the user clicks on the first button. The image number 3 shows the application's response. We see that the image is moved to the left and the button state is changed to the pressed state. Also shown there is the middle button's state, which is set to the normal state. If we follow the next image until the end, we have the complete possible interaction in our application.

From here we can try to plan what widgets need to be used. For the window, we could use a simple GtkWindow. We can use a GtkLabel for the label in the center of the application. If we use a normal GtkButton for the buttons, we need to reset all the buttons when one of the buttons is pressed. So here we can use a special button called GtkRadioButton to get the feature of setting all the buttons to the inactive state except the button that we press. When we know what widgets to use, then we can start doing the implementation.

Time for action – implementing the mockup

We briefly did a GUI application with Vala in *Chapter 2, Preparing Our Weapons*, so now we will create an application in JavaScript to experiment with labels and buttons according to the mockup.

1. Run Glade as a standalone program and create a new file called `gtk-basic-widgets.ui` and put it into a dedicated directory called `gtk-basic-widgets`.

2. On the **Palette** dock, find a **Box** object inside the **Containers** section. Click on it and click on the blank window on the right. When asked, the **Number of items** value is 2. You can use the − and **+** buttons or just enter the number 2 inside it.

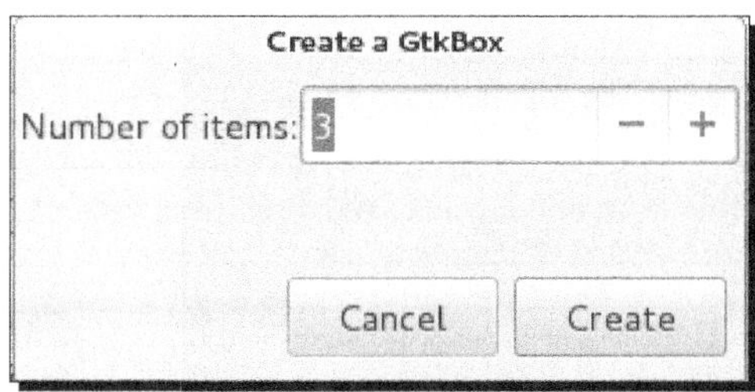

3. Now we can see that the box on the window is divided into two boxes; let's call them top and bottom box.

4. Again, click on the **Box** object inside the **Containers** section and click on the bottom box. Our bottom box will be divided into three boxes.

5. Our second group of boxes here is named automatically as **box2**. Check the **Orientation** value in the **General** tab of **box2**. Change this to **Horizontal**.

6. In the **General** tab, set the **Homogeneous** value to **Yes**.

7. Now we have our bottom box divided horizontally into three boxes. Let's remember these new boxes as left, center, and right boxes.

8. Find the label on the **Control and Display** section in the **Palette** dock. Click on it, and then click on the top box. Now we have the label put into the top box.

9. Find **label1** on the **Widgets** dock, and click on the **Packing** tab. Change the value of **Expand** to **Yes**, by just clicking on its value.

10. Now our label expands the area on the top box.

11. Find **Toggle Button** on the **Control and Display** section in the **Palette** dock. Click on it and click on the left box. Continue to click on **Toggle Button** and then click on the middle box, and then the right box.

12. For the middle and right buttons, we need to specify the button group so that they can be selected. In the **General** tab of these buttons, find the **Group** option. Click on the ellipsis button (shown with three dots) and select **radiobutton1**.

13. Now we have all buttons filling the bottom boxes.

14. Click on the middle button, set the **Active** value (it can be found in the **General** tab) as **Yes**.

15. Click on the label, open the **General** tab, and set the value of **Label** to **in the center**.

16. Click on the left button, click on the **Label on optional image** option, and fill **Label** with **Go Left**. Repeat the same actions with the middle and right button, and set the labels to **Go Center** and **Go Right** respectively.

17. For all the buttons, we go to the **General** tab on each button and set the value of **Draw indicator** to **No**, and **Horizontal alignment for child** to **0.5**.

18. Create a new script called `gtk-basic-widgets.js` with code that looks like this:

```
#!/usr/bin/env seed

Gtk= imports.gi.Gtk;
GObject = imports.gi.GObject;
Main = new GType({
        parent: GObject.Object.type,
        name: "Main",
        init: function(self) {
```

```
        this.go_left = function(object) {
    if (object.active) {
                self.label.set_label("going left");
                self.label.set_alignment(0, 0.5);
    }
        }

        this.go_center = function(object) {
    if (object.active) {
                self.label.set_label("in the center");
                self.label.set_alignment(0.5, 0.5);
    }
        }

        this.go_right = function(object) {
            if (object.active) {
      self.label.set_label("going right");
                self.label.set_alignment(1, 0.5);
    }
        }

        var ui = new Gtk.Builder()
        this.ui = ui;
        ui.add_from_file("gtk-basic-widgets.ui");
        var window = ui.get_object("window1");
        window.resize(300, 400);
        window.show_all();
      window.signal.destroy.connect(Gtk.main_quit);

        this.label = ui.get_object("label1");
          ui.get_object("radiobutton1").signal.toggled.
connect(this.go_left);
            ui.get_object("radiobutton2").signal.toggled.
connect(this.go_center);
        ui.get_object("radiobutton2").set_active(true);
        ui.get_object("radiobutton3").signal.toggled.
connect(this.go_right);
        }
});

Gtk.init(Seed.argv);
var main = new Main();
Gtk.main();
```

19. Run the application. Try to press the buttons and see whether we fulfill the mockup.

What just happened?

As we saw in *Chapter 2*, *Preparing Our Weapons*, we can't just add the widgets (buttons and a label) directly into a window because the window can only take one widget. Hence, we need a container widget that can hold more than one widget. Because of the desired appearance, we first divide the window into two parts: top and bottom. Then we put another container inside the bottom part. With these containers set, we can then put our widgets inside.

In this example, we use GtkBox (shown as **Box** in Glade) as the container and set the orientation to indicate how we want to divide the parts. GtkBox does not have a visible part. It lets the widgets that are placed inside to cover the whole area that is allocated to it. When we pack a widget inside Box, the widget gives a hint to Box about its preferred height, then Box will calculate and allocate an area according to the height and let the widget draw itself into the area. Box automatically arranges the widgets that are added into it according to the orientation that we have specified. So, we don't put the widgets with certain coordinates but rely on how Box arranges them.

Our first box is a vertical box and we want the bottom part to be of a rather constant size and the top part to adjust its size according to the size of the window. To do that, we specifically make the label1 widget, which is placed inside the top box, expand by setting the **Expand** packing option to **Yes** when it is packed, so the label will give extra space that it can get when the parent's size grows. Together with the **Fill** option, which is already set to **Yes** by default, Box will give maximal height instead of giving the actual height of the label.

What happened here is that `Box` will calculate the preferred size for all widgets inside the top and bottom parts and find out the remaining size available according to the size of the window. After that, it maximizes the size of the `label1` widget, which is inside the top part, by adding the remaining size to the original size of the label.

We can't split the bottom part directly because a `Box` object can only have one orientation. In order to do that, we add a new horizontal `Box` widget inside the bottom part. Now, the situation is a bit different. Here, our `Box` orientation is horizontal and what we want is to split it into three parts equally, so we need to enable the **Homogeneous** option.

In our toggle buttons, we use `radiobutton1` as our group leader. With this, when one of the buttons is pressed then all other buttons are made inactive. We also make the appearance to look like normal buttons by disabling the **Draw indicator** option and making the labels inside the buttons be aligned to the center.

In this example, we have put many widgets in the hierarchy, meaning that some widgets have parents and children. For example, the window contains the children of all widgets attached to it and its children. The vertical `Box` widget has children of label and the horizontal `Box` widget and its children. The horizontal `Box` widget has all buttons as its children, and so on. Understanding the hierarchy is very important so we can know the structure of the application. The hierarchy is visible in Glade in the **Inspector** dock.

```
Gtk.init(Seed.argv);
    var main = new Main();
    Gtk.main();
```

Here we have the initialization code of GTK+. `Gtk.init` prepares the graphical environment so that our application is run as a GUI application. `Seed.argv` provides a list of arguments that are passed into our application. In this example it is an empty list. Then we initialize our `Main` class. After that, we enter the GTK+ main loop by calling `Gtk.main`.

In this part of the code, we load the `gtk-basic-widgets.ui` file with a `Gtk.Builder` object:

```
this.ui = new Gtk.Builder()
    this.ui.add_from_file("gtk-basic-widgets.ui");
```

Make sure that the path is correct.

Then we get the reference of our window by just finding its name, which is `window1`.

```
    var window = this.ui.get_object("window1");
```

If you change the name to something else, then you need to change it in this code too.

We can use the `get_object` function to find any widgets that we use in Glade as long as the name is correct.

Then we resize the window and show everything in it on the screen.

```
window.resize(300, 400);
    window.show_all();
```

This part will terminate the application whenever the window is closed.

```
window.signal.destroy.connect(Gtk.main_quit);
```

If we don't have this code, the application will still be running even if the window is closed. One way to check whether your application is still running is to run the `ps` command in a terminal.

In the following code, we connect the toggled signal of all the buttons to their respective handler. A toggled signal is emitted by a button whenever the state is changed, either from the active to inactive state or vice versa.

```
this.label = ui.get_object("label1");
                ui.get_object("radiobutton1").signal.toggled.
connect(this.go_left);
                ui.get_object("radiobutton2").signal.toggled.
connect(this.go_center);
ui.get_object("radiobutton2").set_active(true);

    ui.get_object("radiobutton3").signal.toggled.connect(this.go_
right);
```

When the `radiobutton1` button is toggled, the signal handler `go_left` function is called. For `radiobutton2`, it is `go_center`, and for `radiobutton3`, it is `go_right`. For `radiobutton2`, we initialize it to be active so that it matches with the mockup's initial state.

In the `go_left` function, we set the label to **going left**, and we make the label to be left aligned by setting the first variable of the `set_alignment` function to 0. The second variable is for the vertical alignment.

```
this.go_left = function(object) {
  if (object.active) {
      self.label.set_label("going left");
        self.label.set_alignment(0, 0.5);
  }
}
```

It is always set to `0.5`. The alignment value range is from `0` (left) to `1` (right). The vertical alignment value is also from `0` (top) to `1` (bottom). Remember also that when we set **Horizontal alignment for child** for all buttons to `0.5` in Glade, it means that the label inside the button is set to be center aligned.

What we really want is to set these settings only when the button is active, and not otherwise. Hence, we guard the function with `if (object.active)` in order to avoid the label and alignment setting to be called twice. In this example, the guard does not make any difference if we don't have it. But in a real live application, the guard is sometimes necessary in order to avoid duplicate calls, which can lead to confusion and even make the performance slower if there are some heavy calculations inside the handler.

A similar thing happens to the `go_center` and `go_right` functions. But there, we set the alignment to be centered with an argument of `0.5` and right alignment with an argument of `1`.

Pop quiz

Q1. If we have the value of horizontal alignment as `0.3`, where is the place of a widget visually?

1. Center
2. Slightly to the right
3. Slightly to the left

Q2. If we have the value of vertical alignment as `0.3`, where is the place of a widget visually?

1. Center
2. Slightly to the right
3. Slightly to the left

Have a go hero – creating a Vala version

Now you can try to port this simple code to a Vala version by using the example we've used in *Chapter 2, Preparing Our Weapons*. The port should be straightforward and pretty easy.

Time for action – adding icons to the buttons

Now imagine that we want to add icons to our buttons. Icons are usually added into buttons to explain more about the intended functionality represented by the button. This will become more important if the label on the button is short or ambiguous. Let's go through the following steps to add icons to the buttons:

1. While still on `gtk-basic-widgets.ui`, click on the left button.
2. Navigate to the **General** tab and find the **image widget** option just under the **Label with optional image** option.

3. Click on the ellipsis button and it will bring up a dialog.

4. Click on the **New** button and it will create an image widget.

5. Now find this widget on the widget list. It should be initially named `image1`.

6. Click on the image, navigate to the **General** tab, and find **Stock ID** under **Edit image**. Click on it and find the **Left** icon. The icon name is `gtk-justify-left`.

7. Repeat the process, but now use the **Center (gtk-justify-center)** and **Right (gtk-justify-right)** icons for the middle and right buttons.

8. In the code, add these lines in the constructor:

```
var s = Gtk.Settings.get_default();
s.gtk_button_images = true;
```

9. Run it.

What just happened?

The images were created outside the widget hierarchy in the application. It means that it neither has parent widgets nor children. It is just created "somewhere" in the code. We use these images by tying them to the buttons. By default, these images will not be displayed.

```
var s = Gtk.Settings.get_default();
s.gtk_button_images = true;
```

With this code, the images are then displayed by GTK+.

Have a go hero – adjusting the icon placement

Go on, explore the available properties visible in the **General** tab in the **Widgets** dock. There is the **Image position** property that can be used to adjust the placement of the icon. With that property, we can set the right alignment icon to be placed on the right and the center alignment icon to be placed at the center of the button. What you need to do is just activate that switch and that's it!

Porting the code without GtkBuilder

We've always been using Glade to design our UI, and GtkBuilder to load the design at runtime. We will use Glade in the rest of our book, but now let's try to do GTK+ programming at a lower level to grasp the essentials of GTK+, which is not obvious when using Glade. This knowledge becomes more important when our project becomes larger and larger, and at some point will stumble upon performance problems, layout problems, and so on.

Time for action – programming with raw GTK+

Now we will execute a JavaScript code that uses raw GTK+ programming to implement the mockup and the interaction flow.

1. Create a JavaScript file named `gtk-basic-widgets-sans-glade.js` inside a directory with a similar name without the `.js` extension.

2. Use this code for the script:

```
#!/usr/bin/env seed

Gtk = imports.gi.Gtk;
GObject = imports.gi.GObject;

Main = new GType({
  parent: GObject.Object.type,
  name: "Main",
  init: function(self) {
    this.go_left = function(object) {
      if (object.active) {
                        self.label.set_label("going left");
                        self.label.set_alignment(0, 0.5);
      }
            }

                this.go_center = function(object) {
        if (object.active) {
```

```
                                        self.label.set_label("in the center");
                                        self.label.set_alignment(0.5, 0.5);
        }
            }

                this.go_right = function(object) {
                        if (object.active) {
        self.label.set_label("going right");
                                self.label.set_alignment(1, 0.5);
        }
            }

    var window = new Gtk.Window();
    window.signal.destroy.connect(Gtk.main_quit);

    var topBottomBox = new Gtk.Box();
    topBottomBox.orientation = Gtk.Orientation.VERTICAL;
    topBottomBox.set_homogeneous(false);

    window.add(topBottomBox);

    var label = new Gtk.Label();
    this.label = label;
    label.set_text("in the center");
    topBottomBox.pack_start(label, true, true, 0);

    var buttonBox = new Gtk.Box();
    buttonBox.set_homogeneous(true);

    topBottomBox.pack_start(buttonBox, false, false, 0);

    var leftButton = new Gtk.RadioButton.with_label(null, "Go
left");
    var centerButton = new Gtk.RadioButton.with_label_from_
widget(leftButton, "Go center");
    var rightButton = new Gtk.RadioButton.with_label_from_
widget(leftButton, "Go right");

    leftButton.signal.clicked.connect(this.go_left);
    centerButton.signal.clicked.connect(this.go_center);
    rightButton.signal.clicked.connect(this.go_right);

    leftButton.draw_indicator = centerButton.draw_indicator =
rightButton.draw_indicator = false;

    centerButton.active = true;

    leftButton.xalign = 0.5;
    centerButton.xalign = 0.5;
    rightButton.xalign = 0.5;
```

```
        buttonBox.pack_start(leftButton, false, true, 0);
        buttonBox.pack_start(centerButton, false, true, 0);
        buttonBox.pack_start(rightButton, false, true, 0);

        window.show_all();
        window.resize(300, 400);
    }
});

Gtk.init(Seed.argv);
var main = new Main();

Gtk.main();
```

3. Run it; it should have the exact same visual as the version that uses Glade and GtkBuilder.

What just happened?

We won't discuss the part of the code that is similar to our previous experiment, but rather look at the manual widgets' declarations more closely.

First we create a GtkWindow and connect the `destroy` signal so that the application will terminate gracefully whenever the window is closed.

```
var window = new Gtk.Window();
    window.signal.destroy.connect(Gtk.main_quit);
```

In this part, we prepare a box that splits the window into top and bottom parts. In here, we explicitly say that our box is a vertical and non-homogeneous box. Then we add it into the window, which is a single-child container widget.

```
var topBottomBox = new Gtk.Box();
topBottomBox.orientation = Gtk.Orientation.VERTICAL;
topBottomBox.set_homogeneous(false);
    window.add(topBottomBox);
```

Next, we prepare a label and pack it into the top box. In Glade, we explicitly specify the number of items to be placed into the box, while in manual GTK+ programming, we just pack it into the box, one by one without any possibilities to declare in advance the number of items. Glade requires the number just to prepare the placeholders where we can put our items.

```
var label = new Gtk.Label();
this.label = label;
label.set_text("in the center");
topBottomBox.pack_start(label, true, true, 0);
```

In this code, we pack the `label` variable with the Fill and Expand properties' values set to `true`. `0` there means that we should not add any padding during packing.

After that, we prepare the box for the buttons. We only set the `homogeneous` property without touching the orientation as it is already horizontal by default. And here, we just pack it without the Fill and Expand values set:

```
var buttonBox = new Gtk.Box();
buttonBox.set_homogeneous(true);
    topBottomBox.pack_start(buttonBox, false, false, 0);
```

In this part, we create the first button:

```
        var leftButton = new Gtk.RadioButton.with_label(null, "Go left");
```

And next, two buttons are added with `leftButton` as the group leader:

```
var centerButton = new Gtk.RadioButton.with_label_from_
widget(leftButton, "Go center");
    var rightButton = new Gtk.RadioButton.with_label_from_
widget(leftButton, "Go right");
```

This part just connects the clicked signals of these buttons:

```
leftButton.signal.clicked.connect(this.go_left);
centerButton.signal.clicked.connect(this.go_center);
rightButton.signal.clicked.connect(this.go_right);
```

In here, we set the `draw_indicator` property to `false` so that our radio button will look like a plain button:

```
    leftButton.draw_indicator = centerButton.draw_indicator =
rightButton.draw_indicator = false;
```

This part is for activating the middle button as shown in the first state of the mockup:

```
    centerButton.active = true;
```

These parts are to set the alignment of the labels inside the buttons. The value of `0.5` means that all of them are aligned to the center:

```
leftButton.xalign = 0.5;
centerButton.xalign = 0.5;
    rightButton.xalign = 0.5;
```

After that, we pack the buttons with only the Fill property to be set to `true`.

The rest of the code looks similar to the GtkBuilder-enabled code. What we can see from this is that manual GTK+ programming will give you more knowledge on GTK+ API.

```
buttonBox.pack_start(leftButton, false, true, 0);
buttonBox.pack_start(centerButton, false, true, 0);
    buttonBox.pack_start(rightButton, false, true, 0);
```

If your `.ui` file in your project becomes larger and larger, loading the file during startup may take a while. In this case, you can consider doing the packing manually, especially if your `.ui` file is stable enough, in that it has not changed a lot during the development. On the other hand, if your `.ui` file keeps changing, using Glade and GtkBuilder may be worth a consideration because manual GTK+ can sometimes make your head dizzy. This is because, unfortunately, the API itself is not really intuitive and can be easily misused.

However, it is a very good idea to keep your user interface clean and well structured, so you can go ahead in either way. Planning in advance about what widgets to use by using the mockup is one good practice.

GUI programming with Clutter

Clutter is usually used for creating more compelling GUI applications as it provides rich animation and effective features, and is also used for rendering with OpenGL. Yet, it hides all OpenGL-specific programming from the developers. Different from GTK+, Clutter is a scene graph based canvas, which we can put anything into in any place we want. Every object on the stage is a 2D surface, while the stage itself is a 3D space.

Time for action – implementing the mockup with Clutter

Let's introduce ourselves to Clutter by implementing the mockup and its interaction flow with Clutter.

1. Create a new JavaScript file called `clutter-basic.js` in a directory called `clutter-basic-vala`.

2. Fill the script with this code:

```
#!/usr/bin/env seed

Clutter = imports.gi.Clutter;
Pango = imports.gi.Pango;
GObject = imports.gi.GObject;

Main = new GType({
    parent: GObject.Object.type,
    name: "Main",
```

```
init: function(self) {
  var stageColor = new Clutter.Color();
  stageColor.from_string("#b0b0b0");

  var labelColor = new Clutter.Color();
  labelColor.from_string("#000000");

  var buttonColor = new Clutter.Color();
  buttonColor.from_string("#505050");

  var buttonPressedColor = new Clutter.Color();
  buttonPressedColor.from_string("#a0a0a0");

  var buttonTextColor = new Clutter.Color();
  buttonTextColor.from_string("#000000");

  var buttonLeft = new Clutter.Rectangle();
  buttonLeft.width = 100;
  buttonLeft.height = 40;
  buttonLeft.x = 0;
  buttonLeft.y = 360;
  buttonLeft.color = buttonColor;
  buttonLeft.set_border_color(stageColor);
  buttonLeft.set_border_width(1);

  var buttonCenter = new Clutter.Rectangle();
  buttonCenter.width = 100;
  buttonCenter.height = 40;
  buttonCenter.x = 100;
  buttonCenter.y = 360;
  buttonCenter.color = buttonColor;
  buttonCenter.set_border_color(stageColor);
  buttonCenter.set_border_width(1);

  var buttonRight = new Clutter.Rectangle();
  buttonRight.width = 100;
  buttonRight.height = 40;
  buttonRight.x = 200;
  buttonRight.y = 360;
  buttonRight.color = buttonColor;
  buttonRight.set_border_color(stageColor);
  buttonRight.set_border_width(1);

  var s = Clutter.Stage.get_default();
  s.color = stageColor;
  this.s = s;
  s.width = 300;
  s.height = 400;
```

```
    var fd = Pango.FontDescription.from_string("Sans 16");
    var label = new Clutter.Text();
    label.set_font_description(fd);
    label.set_text("in the center");
    label.color = labelColor;
    label.x = (s.width - label.width)/2;
    label.y = 100;

    var buttonFd = Pango.FontDescription.from_string("Sans 12");

    var buttonLeftText = new Clutter.Text();
    buttonLeftText.set_font_description(buttonFd);
    buttonLeftText.set_text("Go Left");
    buttonLeftText.color = buttonTextColor;
    buttonLeftText.x = (buttonLeft.width - buttonLeftText.width)
/2;
    buttonLeftText.y = (buttonLeft.height - buttonLeftText.height)
/2 + buttonLeft.y;

    var buttonCenterText = new Clutter.Text();
    buttonCenterText.set_font_description(buttonFd);
    buttonCenterText.set_text("Go Center");
    buttonCenterText.color = buttonTextColor;
    buttonCenterText.x = (buttonCenter.width - buttonCenterText.
width) /2 + buttonLeft.width;
    buttonCenterText.y = (buttonCenter.height - buttonCenterText.
height) /2 + buttonCenter.y;

    var buttonRightText = new Clutter.Text();
    buttonRightText.set_font_description(buttonFd);
    buttonRightText.set_text("Go Right");
    buttonRightText.color = buttonTextColor;
    buttonRightText.x = (buttonRight.width - buttonRightText.
width) /2 + buttonLeft.width + buttonCenter.width;
    buttonRightText.y = (buttonRight.height - buttonRightText.
height) /2 + buttonRight.y;

    buttonLeft.set_reactive(true);
    buttonLeft.signal.button_press_event.connect(function(self) {
      buttonLeft.color = buttonPressedColor;
      buttonRight.color = buttonCenter.color = buttonColor;
      label.save_easing_state();
      label.set_text("going left");
      label.set_x(0);
      label.restore_easing_state();
```

```
        return true;
    });

    buttonCenter.set_reactive(true);
    buttonCenter.signal.button_press_event.connect(function(self)
    {
        buttonCenter.color = buttonPressedColor;
        buttonRight.color = buttonLeft.color = buttonColor;
        label.save_easing_state();
        label.set_text("in the center");
        label.set_x((s.width - label.width)/2);
        label.restore_easing_state();

        return true;
    });

    buttonRight.set_reactive(true);
    buttonRight.signal.button_press_event.connect(function(self) {
        buttonRight.color = buttonPressedColor;
        buttonLeft.color = buttonCenter.color = buttonColor;
        label.save_easing_state();
        label.set_text("going right");
        label.set_x(s.width - label.width);
        label.restore_easing_state();

        return true;
    });

    buttonCenter.color = buttonPressedColor;

    s.add_actor(buttonLeft);
    s.add_actor(buttonRight);
    s.add_actor(buttonCenter);
    s.add_actor(buttonLeftText);
    s.add_actor(buttonRightText);
    s.add_actor(buttonCenterText);

    s.add_actor(label);
    s.show_all();
    }
});

Clutter.init(Seed.argv);
var main = new Main();

Clutter.main();
```

3. If you want Vala instead of JavaScript code, let's create a new Vala project using a similar setting with non-GUI application settings when creating a project in Anjuta. Let's create a new project called `clutter-basic-vala`.

4. Edit the `src/Makefile.am` file and find this part:

```
clutter_basic_vala_VALAFLAGS = \
   --pkg gtk+-3.0
```

Replace the two lines and edit it to look exactly like this:

```
clutter_basic_vala_VALAFLAGS = \
   --pkg clutter-1.0
```

5. Edit the `configure.ac` file and find this line:

```
PKG_CHECK_MODULES(CLUTTER_BASIC_VALA, [gtk+-3.0])
```

Replace the whole line with this line:

```
PKG_CHECK_MODULES(CLUTTER_BASIC_VALA, [clutter-1.0])
```

6. To avoid repeating codes in our book, let's try to port the JavaScript code to Vala; it is pretty straightforward and based on our previous exposure to both programming languages, this would be an easy task.

7. Run the program and it will look like the following screenshot:

What just happened?

We can immediately see that the code size is huge. This is because Clutter is more low-level than GTK+. It only has very basic widgets and we need to create our own widgets from scratch. We can also see that the interaction is more fluid and pleasing because of the implicit animations provided by Clutter.

In the technical aspect, we can see that the objects can be placed anywhere on the stage. We call the objects in Clutter **actors**. We can apply a role of animation or effects to them and move them around the stage.

Compared to JavaScript, coding Clutter with Vala requires a bit of setting up in the beginning. We need to adjust the build system by modifying the `configure.ac` and `Makefile.am` files.

The adjustment enables the build system to pick up the Clutter library both during compilation in the Vala and during the building of the generated C-code files. What we did was we removed the GTK+ library by removing the `gtk+-3.0` settings both in `Makefile.am` and `configure.ac` and we replaced it instead with `clutter-1.0`. This is because we don't need GTK+ at all in this example. With JavaScript, it is far more easier as we don't need to do anything and it will work automatically.

Let's see the code more in depth to get a better understanding of how Clutter works.

The main code is pretty simple and similar to the GTK+ counterpart. We have `init` and the main loop function.

```
Clutter.init(Seed.argv);
var main = new Main();
Clutter.main();
```

First, we define a few colors that are used in the application. We can see that it parses the hexadecimal RGB color format and then we store that into a variable:

```
var stageColor = new Clutter.Color();
stageColor.from_string("#b0b0b0");
```

Imagine this as our button widget. We hardcode the size and location to simplify the code, and then set the color to one of the colors we defined earlier.

In real applications, the size and location should be coming from either a calculation or pre-defined settings.

```
var buttonLeft = new Clutter.Rectangle();
buttonLeft.width = 100;
buttonLeft.height = 40;
buttonLeft.x = 0;
```

```
buttonLeft.y = 360;
buttonLeft.color = buttonColor;
buttonLeft.set_border_color(stageColor);
buttonLeft.set_border_width(1);
```

This part defines a stage to place all the widgets. The stage is comparable to the GtkWindow widget that we had earlier.

```
var s = Clutter.Stage.get_default();
s.color = stageColor;
this.s = s;
s.width = 300;
s.height = 400;
```

This part of the code defines a font description. It takes the description from a string and returns a logical representation of a font, which is then used by the labels:

```
var fd = Pango.FontDescription.from_string("Sans 16");
```

After that, we define the label's text, font, color, and location:

```
var label = new Clutter.Text();
label.set_font_description(fd);
label.set_text("in the center");
label.color = labelColor;
label.x = (s.width - label.width)/2;
label.y = 100;
```

And here we define the text of a button. A quite good improvement can be seen here, that is, we no longer hardcode the position of the text:

```
var buttonFd = Pango.FontDescription.from_string("Sans 12");
var buttonLeftText = new Clutter.Text();
buttonLeftText.set_font_description(buttonFd);
buttonLeftText.set_text("Go Left");
buttonLeftText.color = buttonTextColor;
buttonLeftText.x = (buttonLeft.width - buttonLeftText.width) /2;
buttonLeftText.y = (buttonLeft.height - buttonLeftText.height) /2 +
buttonLeft.y;
```

Then, we set the button to be reactive. Without this code, the button would not be able to react to an event coming into it.

```
buttonLeft.set_reactive(true);
```

This defines the handler of the `button-press-event` event. In the handler, we set the pressed button and reset the color of other buttons to achieve a pressed feeling. Then, we ask for an implicit animation by saving the easing state before changing the label's property and restoring it afterwards. Implicit animations mean that we don't specifically ask for a certain type of animation in our code. Instead, we rely on Clutter to do animation whenever we change a property in an actor.

```
buttonLeft.signal.button_press_event.connect(function(self) {
    buttonLeft.color = buttonPressedColor;
    buttonRight.color = buttonCenter.color = buttonColor;
    label.save_easing_state();
    label.set_text("going left");
    label.set_x(0);
    label.restore_easing_state();

    return true;
});
```

As soon as we change the value, Clutter will treat that value as the target value, and it will set up a timer and on each frame of the timer, it increases (or decreases) the current value of the property towards the target. All of this happens in the background and happens automatically.

Here in our `actor` label, we make two changes that may be transformed with animations by Clutter, which are changing the text and changing the position of the text. Please note here that we set the text first before changing the position because the position requires the new width of the text, which is available until we set the text value. If we put this in a reverse sequence, then the label position will not be correct.

One more thing to observe is that our function must return `true` whenever we have done something when reacting to the signal. If, somehow, we skip or refuse to do something about the signal, we have to return `false` so another event handler in the queue will take care of the signal.

```
s.add_actor(buttonLeft);
s.add_actor(buttonRight);
s.add_actor(buttonCenter);
s.add_actor(buttonLeftText);
s.add_actor(buttonRightText);
s.add_actor(buttonCenterText);
s.add_actor(label);
```

In here, we add all the actors into the stage so it can be shown as follows:

```
s.show_all();
```

Ultimately, we show all actors and the stage together.

Have a go hero – playing with the animations

There are numerous transformations that we can apply to the buttons or the label. For example, when the button is pressed we can scale up the button so it will be bigger, and when we release the button we scale it back down to the original size. And all of this will be animated. We can add more closures to handle the `button-release-event` event to restore the original values of the actors that we want to animate.

Summary

In this chapter, we have learnt about creating GUI applications using both GTK+ and Clutter. We know that the system requirements for each toolkit are different and we also learnt about the kind of applications that can be created using these toolkits.

With GTK+, we have learnt that GTK+ provides ready-to-use widgets. We have also learnt to use some of them, such as Button, Box, Window, and Label. We know how to set the alignment of the widgets and manage them by setting their properties. We know how to connect an event to a handler that will react to the event and do something useful.

With Clutter we learnt that it can create an application with pleasing visual animations. But we also know the limitations. One of them being it only provides a very basic foundation before we can easily use them to make an application.

We also learnt that the development of a GUI application can be made a lot easier by using mockup and interaction flow. We know that we can plan in advance by selecting what widgets to use in our application.

In the next chapter, we will learn to extend GTK+ by creating our own widgets.

6
Creating Widgets

As we have seen from our experience in the previous chapter, GTK+ provides standard widgets. In some cases, we can survive using GTK+ standard widgets in our applications. But when our application design and requirements become more and more complex, implementing our own widgets is inevitable. Especially so when we do several projects which share similar design and requirements. Otherwise, we will end up with copying code and this will become a maintenance nightmare.

Implementing our own widget can also mean customizing widgets, which is adding or removing functionalities that are not available in the original widgets. In this chapter, we will learn how to create GTK+ widgets from scratch and also extend them. We will also talk about how to paint or draw the widget internally using the Cairo canvas API.

Specifically, we will discuss the following topics:

- Overriding widgets
- Adding new functionalities to a widget
- Implementing a custom widget
- Maintaining widgets in a compiled library

So let's get started.

Before we take off

We are going to use the raw GTK+ programming instead of using Glade in this chapter.
Hence, our Vala projects will use the same settings that we used in *Chapter 3, Programming
Languages* and *Chapter 4, Using GNOME Core Libraries*. The project we create here is a Vala
GTK+ (simple) project; disable **GtkBuilder support for the user interface** and enable the **No
license** option.

Overriding the widget's standard functions

Usually, we customize how a widget behaves and change how it looks by simply putting
different default values in one of its properties. This is not a problem if we just want to
customize the widget once or twice. We can just instantiate it as an object and customize
the properties. But if we want to reuse the widget, we need to subclass the widget and
customize the subclass further. Subclassing means that we create a new widget class based
on a particular existing widget class.

Time for action – overriding the set_title function

Now let's subclass `GtkWindow` and imagine that we want to change the behavior of
the `set_title` function of `GtkWindow`. The function is used to set the window's title
with the specified string passed in the argument. The new behavior that we want to
introduce here is to always add a special word into the window's title whenever we
set the `set_title` function.

1. Create a new Vala project called `custom-overriding`.

2. In the `src/custom_overriding.vala` file, use the following code:

```vala
using GLib;
using Gtk;

public class CustomWindow : Window
{
  public CustomWindow ()
  {
  }

  public new void set_title (string newTitle)
  {
    title = "Custom: " + newTitle;
  }
```

```
    static int main (string[] args)
    {
      Gtk.init (ref args);
      var window = new CustomWindow ();
      window.set_title ("My window");
      window.show_all ();
      window.destroy.connect(Gtk.main_quit);

      Gtk.main ();

      return 0;
    }
}
```

3. Our JavaScript equivalent code looks like the following. Put it inside a script file called `custom-overriding.js`:

```
#!/usr/bin/env seed

Gtk = imports.gi.Gtk;
GObject = imports.gi.GObject;

CustomWindow = new GType({
  parent: Gtk.Window.type,
  name: "CustomWindow",
  class_init: function(klass, prototype) {
    prototype.set_title = function(newTitle) {
      this.title = "Custom: " + newTitle;
    }
  },
});

Gtk.init(Seed.argv);
var window = new CustomWindow();
window.set_title("My window");
window.signal.destroy.connect(Gtk.main_quit);
window.show_all();
Gtk.main();
```

4. Run it and see that the title is automatically prepended with **Custom: word** as shown in the following screenshot:

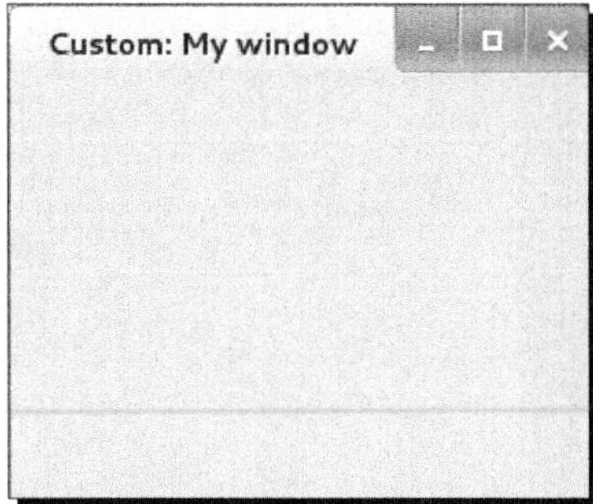

What just happened?

Let's take a look at the Vala code first.

In the following declaration, we tell Vala that we have a new class called `CustomWindow` and it is a derivative of `Window`:

```
public class CustomWindow : Window
```

There is no need to explicitly say `GtkWindow` here because we are using the `Gtk` and `GLib` namespaces with these lines:

```
using GLib;
using Gtk;
```

With the previous code, we have the possibility of the full name of `Window` being either `Gtk.Window` or `GLib.Window`. But because there is no such thing as `GLib.Window`, we are now pretty sure that we are subclassing this new `CustomWindow` class from `Gtk.Window`.

We then have an empty constructor here; because it is empty, we can omit this if we want:

```
public CustomWindow ()
{
}
```

In the following part, we declare a function called `set_title`. Here, we override the `set_title` function with our own function:

```
public void set_title(string newTitle)
{
   title = "Custom: " + newTitle;
}
```

In order to do this, the function arguments (also called method signatures) must be exactly the same, otherwise Vala will issue a warning message when we call the function with the following line of code:

```
window.set_title ("My window");
```

This function is called instead of the original `Gtk.Window` class' `set_title` function. Inside the body of our `set_title` function, we set the value of the `title` property with the `Custom:` string and concatenate it with `newTitle`, which is being provided as the argument of the function.

The next time we want to reuse this in our applications, we need to instantiate our `CustomWindow` class instead of the normal `Window` class by just issuing the following code:

```
var window = new CustomWindow ();
```

Then our newly defined window object will have all the functionalities coming from `Gtk.Window` as well as the new behavior set in the `set_title` function.

With Seed, we define the new behavior in `set_title` by using the following JavaScript code:

```
class_init: function(klass, prototype) {
  prototype.set_title = function(newTitle) {
    this.title = "Custom: " + newTitle;
  }
}
```

This is a bit different from what we have learned in *Chapter 4, Using GNOME Core Libraries*, where we put a new function directly inside the `init` function. In the previous code, we put the function inside `prototype`, a bit similar to what we have seen in *Chapter 3, Programming Languages*, even though it is conceptually different.

Actually, we can directly use it inside the `init` function. However, to make it more readable and clearly identify that it is an overridden function, we put this declaration inside the `prototype` parameter of `class_init`. This mimics how GObject works in a C-language code that we connect to the virtual functions (in short, the functions that can be overridden in the derived class) in the `class_init` function.

This is how we do it in JavaScript because the language itself, as we discussed in *Chapter 4, Using GNOME Core Libraries*, is not a real OOP language. Actually, we can define the function in both the places at the same time, but only the function defined inside the `init` function will be used. This is because all the functions created in `class_init` are created when the class is created; and the functions created in `init` are created when the object is instantiated. Therefore, the functions that we declare in `class_init` are overridden in `init` when the object is created later on as both have the same name.

Adding new functionalities

Let's now imagine that we want to add new functionalities in our widget, not only new behaviors of some old functionality. Imagine that we want to implement a window which has an internal text entry to perform live searches. This widget would display a text entry immediately after we press any key on the keyboard. The text inside the text entry would then be used by another entity in our application to perform a live search.

Time for action – making a composite widget

We knew earlier that a window can't add more than one child into it, so how are we going to add a text entry and the actual content of the window? Let's discuss it:

1. Create a script called `custom-composite.js` and fill it with the following code:

```
#!/usr/bin/env seed

Gtk = imports.gi.Gtk;
GObject = imports.gi.GObject;

CustomWindow = new GType({
  parent: Gtk.Window.type,
  name: "CustomWindow",
  signals: [
      {
        name: "search-updated",
        parameters: [GObject.TYPE_STRING]
      }
    ],

  class_init: function(klass, prototype) {
    prototype.show_search_box = function() {
      this.entry.show();
      this.entry.has_focus = true;
    }
    prototype.hide_search_box = function() {
      this.entry.hide();
    }
    prototype.super_add = prototype.add;
    prototype.add = function(widget) {
      if (widget != this.box) {
        this.box.pack_start(widget, true, true);
      } else {
        this.super_add(widget);
```

```
        }
      }
    },
    init: function(self) {
      this.box = new Gtk.Box();
      this.box.orientation = Gtk.Orientation.VERTICAL;
      this.entry = new Gtk.Entry();
      this.add(this.box);
      this.box.pack_start(this.entry, false, true);
      this.box.show();

      this.entry.signal.key_release_event.connect(function(obj,
event) {
        self.signal.search_updated.emit(self.entry.text);
        return false;
      });

      this.signal.key_press_event.connect(function(obj, event) {
        if (!self.entry.get_visible()) {
          self.show_search_box();
        }
        return false;
      });
    }
});

Gtk.init(Seed.argv);
var window = new CustomWindow();
var label = new Gtk.Label({label:'This is a text'});
window.add(label);
window.resize(400, 400);

window.signal.connect('search-updated', function(object, value) {
  label.set_text('Searching for keyword: ' + value);
});

label.show();
window.show();

Gtk.main();
```

2. Alternatively, you can create a Vala project called `custom-composite` and fill `src/custom_composite.vala` with the following code snippet:

```vala
using GLib;
using Gtk;

public class CustomWindow : Window
{
  Entry entry;
  Box box;
  public signal void search_updated(string value);

  void show_search_box() {
    entry.show();
    entry.has_focus = true;
  }

  void hide_search_box() {
    entry.hide();
  }

  public override void add(Widget widget) {
    if (widget != box) {
      box.pack_start(widget, true, true);
    } else {
      base.add(widget);
    }
  }

  public CustomWindow ()
  {
    box = new Box(Orientation.VERTICAL, 0);
    entry = new Entry();
    box.pack_start (entry, false, true);
    box.show();

    add(box);

    key_release_event.connect((event) => {
      search_updated(entry.text);
      return false;
    });

    key_press_event.connect((event) => {
      if (!entry.get_visible()) {
        show_search_box();
      }
```

```
        return false;
      });
    }

    static int main (string[] args)
    {
      Gtk.init (ref args);
      var window = new CustomWindow();
      var label = new Label("This is a text");

      window.add(label);
      window.resize(400,400);
      window.search_updated.connect((value) => {
        label.set_text("Searching for keyword " + value);
      });

      label.show();
      window.show();
      Gtk.main ();

      return 0;
    }
}
```

3. Run the program and start typing as shown in the following screenshot:

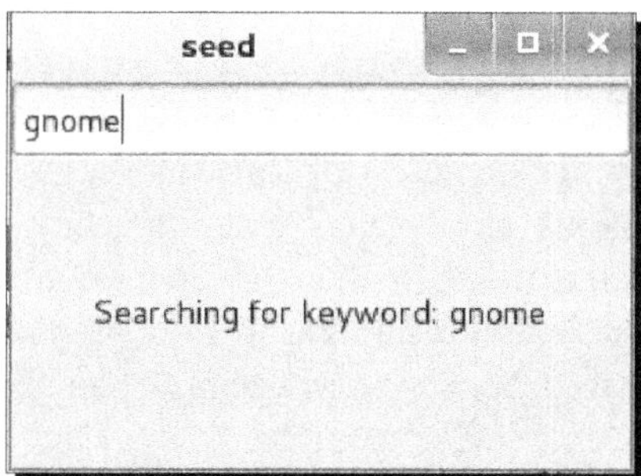

What just happened?

We have just created a composite widget, that is, a widget that is composed from a few widgets. Our new `CustomWindow` widget is built using `GtkWindow`, `GtkBox`, and `GtkEntry` and the only interface exposed to the application is the one that is coming from `GtkWindow`. This is because the widget that we want to extend is the `GtkWindow` class and not the `GtkEntry` class or the `GtkBox` class, so we pick `GtkWindow` to be our base class.

We also add a new signal that is triggered when the user types something into the text entry. The signal outputs the content of the text entry, making it useful to provide the data into something such as a search engine.

Let's see the JavaScript code first:

```
CustomWindow = new GType({
    parent: Gtk.Window.type,
    name: "CustomWindow",
```

The preceding class definition tells Seed that our new `CustomWindow` class is a subclass of `GtkWindow` and we name this as `CustomWindow`.

Next, we declare a new signal of type string called `search-updated`:

```
signals: [{
  name: "search-updated",
  parameters: [GObject.TYPE_STRING]
     }],
```

We use this signal to tell that our text entry contains a new data that can be used for further processing.

To make it easier to tell the whole story, let's start with the `init` function first:

```
init: function(self) {
   this.box = new Gtk.Box();
   this.box.orientation = Gtk.Orientation.VERTICAL;
   this.entry = new Gtk.Entry();
```

Here, we declare two supporting objects inside our window `GtkBox` and `GtkEntry` inside `init`. At this point, our `CustomWindow` object is about to be created. We must not put this inside `class_init` because the `class_init` function is called only once when the class is created. What we want is that these two supporting objects be created when the `CustomWindow` object is created, hence we put it inside the `init` function.

Back to the idea, what we want is to put `GtkEntry` inside `CustomWindow`. But because of the limitation of a window that it can't have more than a single child widget, we use `GtkBox` to take over the container's role in our `CustomWindow` class. We lay the widgets out vertically, with `GtkEntry` positioned on the top.

In the following line, we add the box directly into our window:

```
this.add(this.box);
```

But what happens if, in our application, we want to add another widget to our window? Isn't the `CustomWindow` content now already filled with the `box` object? That is correct. So we need to come up with something that would put the added widget inside the `box` object, instead of putting it into the `CustomWindow` class. We will do this in `class_init` by redefining the `add` function. We will see it shortly.

The next step is to pack the `GtkEntry` class and show the `box` object:

```
this.box.pack_start(this.entry, false, true);
this.box.show();
```

We add a `key-release-event` event handler in the following code snippet. So, whenever a key is released, we emit the signal stating that some data is available in the text entry:

```
this.entry.signal.key_release_event.connect(function(obj, event) {
    self.signal.search_updated.emit(self.entry.text);
    return false;
});
```

We trigger the signal by passing the text entry's content. We do this in the key release event instead of doing it in the key press event for performance reasons. We know that when we type something, the text is only ready when we finish typing, that is, after the key is released. If we trigger the signal in the key press event, consider a case when we do a long press to input multiple duplicate characters into the text entry, the signal will be continuously emitted and if we use a not-so-effective search engine, the process could make the application run slower.

Here, we use the `key-press-event` event to initially show the text entry whenever a key is pressed in our application:

```
this.signal.key_press_event.connect(function(obj, event) {
    if (!self.entry.get_visible()) {
        self.show_search_box();
    }
    return false;
});
```

Let's move to `class_init`, which contains our method declarations:

```
class_init: function(klass, prototype) {
    prototype.show_search_box - function() {
        this.entry.show();
        this.entry.has_focus = true;
    }
    prototype.hide_search_box = function() {
        this.entry.hide();
    }
```

We add new utility functions inside our `class_init` function, so that it will be already available when the object is created later on. The previous functions are about displaying (including grabbing a keyboard focus) and hiding the text entry. This part that follows is about modifying the `add` function of `GtkWindow`:

```
prototype.super_add = prototype.add;
prototype.add = function(widget) {
  if (widget != this.box) {
    this.box.pack_start(widget, true, true);
  } else {
    this.super_add(widget);
  }
}
```

As we've seen in the `init` function, we add a box into our `CustomWindow` class. In our previous function we have a special treatment that if the added widget is our own `box` object, we simply call the function in the base class, which is basically the original `add` function of `GtkWindow`. We do it by first saving the original function in the `super_add` variable. After saving the function, we redefine the `add` function by packing the added widget into our box.

Let's see how to utilize our new `CustomWindow` widget in an application. In the following code, we just declare a new object from our `CustomWindow` class:

```
Gtk.init(Seed.argv);
var window = new CustomWindow();
```

Then, we create a new label and add it into our window. Note that here the label is packed into our internal box object:

```
var label = new Gtk.Label({label:'This is a text'});
window.add(label);
```

Then we have the following line:

```
window.resize(400, 400);
```

You can see in the preceding code line that we did not declare the `resize` function, but we get this for free from our base class, which is the `GtkWindow` class. It also means that this is not necessarily declared inside `GtkWindow`, but it can be declared in the `GtkWindow` class' parent class, or even in the parent class of `GtkWindow` class' parent, and so on.

This part of the code shows how to use our new signal:

```
window.signal.connect('search-updated', function(object, value) {
  label.set_text('Searching for keyword: ' + value);
});
```

Whenever our signal is emitted, we display the content of the text entry inside the label. In real-world applications, we would provide the value to a search engine, which can either search the document for the word or search from some data in a database.

Next, let's dissect the Vala code. Here, we simply say that our `CustomWindow` class is subclassed from the `Window` class:

```
public class CustomWindow : Window
```

Now, we declare the `entry` and `box` widgets; note that we have not done anything with these:

```
Entry entry;
Box box;
```

Then, we declare the new signal. Remember that we use an underscore instead of a dash as a word separator for signals in Vala:

```
public signal void search_updated(string value);
```

We define the `add` function here and pack the widget if the widget is not our box:

```
public override void add(Widget widget) {
  if (widget != box) {
    box.pack_start(widget, true, true);
  } else {
    base.add(widget);
  }
}
```

And if it is, we use the original `GtkWindow` class' `add` function. Here, we simply use `base.add()` and are not doing any magic trick like we did with the JavaScript code.

> We use the `override` keyword to indicate that this function overrides the original add function from the parent class. Without this keyword, the function is considered as a totally new function and not related to the parent class' add function.

The rest of the code is quite straightforward and similar to what we have in the JavaScript code, which was covered earlier.

Maintaining compatibility

If we look closely at our `CustomWindow` class, we actually break a compatibility with `GtkWindow`. `GtkWindow` can only take a single child widget, but our `CustomWindow` class can take more than one widget because they will be packed into our internal box. If we want to maintain compatibility with `GtkWindow`, then we must handle this issue by rejecting the subsequent add requests whenever our `CustomWindow` class already has a child inside.

We also forgot to redefine the `remove` function, so whenever we want to remove the child widget, we will always fail because the child widget is stored inside our internal `box` object, and not inside the `CustomWindow` class. The `GtkWindow` class' `remove` function will reject this, because the parent of the child (which is our internal box) is not the same anymore (which is `CustomWindow`).

We can fix this. For the first problem, we can check the number of children in our internal `box` object. If it is more than two (the `GtkEntry` class and the child itself) after we add a new widget, reject the request. For the second problem, we can just redefine the `remove` function and remove the child widget from our internal `box` object.

We can use `this.box.get_children().length` to get the number of children inside the internal box object.

Have a go hero – hiding the entry after use

We have prepared the `hide_search_box` function but we have not used it anywhere. Here is an idea: how about hiding the search box when we press the *Esc* key?

We can check the *Esc* key by checking the value of `event.key.keyval` in the `key-press-event` handler.

Implementing a GTK+ custom widget

The next step is to implement a custom widget, which is not extending from a currently existing widget, but rather creates a widget from scratch. We will need to do this if we really can't find any similar widgets from GTK+ standard widgets, which can do what we require from the widget that we want to implement.

We can only do this with Vala; unfortunately, as the version of Seed used during the writing of this book can't handle the overriding of a function properly when called from within a class.

Our example does not really reflect the real life situation just discussed because you can easily search a widget which can be readily used, instead of implementing it from scratch. However, the example is provided to simply show the effort involved and how to do it.

Imagine that we need a widget which fulfills the following requirements:

- The widget should be be able to draw a decoration, such as a rectangle, inside its area
- When we click the widget with a mouse, the color changes, indicating that it is being pressed
- When we release the mouse, the color goes back to the normal state's color
- When we click the widget with a mouse, there would be a signal telling that the widget is activated, and when we release the mouse, another signal would be triggered telling that it is now deactivated

Time for action – implementing the custom widget

Ok, let's do an implementation according to our previous design:

1. Create a new Vala project called `custom-new`; edit `src/custom_new.vala` and fill it with the following code:

```vala
using GLib;
using Gtk;

public class CustomWidget : DrawingArea
{
  StateFlags state;
  const int MARGIN = 20;
  public signal void activated();
  public signal void deactivated();

  void update_state (int newState)
  {
    switch (newState) {
    case 1: state = StateFlags.SELECTED;
     break;
    case 0:
    default:
        state = StateFlags.NORMAL;
      break;
    }
```

```vala
    queue_draw ();
}

public override bool draw(Cairo.Context cr) {
  StyleContext style = get_style_context ();
    style.set_state (state);

  int w = get_allocated_width ();
  int h = get_allocated_height ();

    Gtk.render_background (style, cr, 0, 0, w, h);

  cr.rectangle (MARGIN, MARGIN,
              w - (MARGIN * 2),
              h - (MARGIN * 2));
  cr.stroke ();
  return true;
}

public CustomWidget()
{
  update_state (0);
  add_events (Gdk.EventMask.BUTTON_PRESS_MASK
          | Gdk.EventMask.BUTTON_RELEASE_MASK);

  button_press_event.connect ((e) => {
    update_state (1);
    activated();
    return true;
  });

  button_release_event.connect ((e) => {
    update_state (0);
    deactivated();
    return true;
  });
}

static int main (string[] args)
{
  Gtk.init (ref args);
  var window = new Window();
  var widget = new CustomWidget();

  window.add (widget);
  window.show_all ();
```

```
        Gtk.main ();

        return 0;
    }
}
```

2. Run the program and try testing it with the requirements that we set earlier.

What just happened?

From the code, we can see that it is quite simple to implement our own widget from scratch. Let's dig it up more.

```
    public class CustomWidget : DrawingArea
```

Our class declaration shows that we are using `GtkDrawingArea` as our base class. The `GtkDrawingArea` class is a blank widget, doing nothing and showing nothing. The feature of this widget is that we can draw something on top of it. In GTK+ terminology, we call this widget as drawable. We choose `GtkDrawingArea` because it fits with our requirements and it is the usual widget that developers use to implement a new widget from scratch.

```
    StateFlags state;
```

The following is a variable which will hold the state of the widget, whether it is pressed or not:

```
    const int MARGIN = 20;
```

This is a constant called `MARGIN` which holds a value of `20`. It will be used as the margin of the rectangle from the edge of the widget. Writing the name of a constant with all uppercase letters is the convention used in the whole GNOME project, so it's good to always follow this convention when we do GNOME application development.

These are the two signals that we provide in our widget:

```
public signal void activated();
   public signal void deactivated();
```

This is a utility function which saves the state of the widget and then calls `queue_draw`:

```
void update_state (int newState)
{
  switch (newState) {
  case 1: state = StateFlags.SELECTED;
    break;
  case 0:
  default:
    state = StateFlags.NORMAL;
    break;
  }
  queue_draw ();
}
```

The `state` variable basically holds our own interpretation of the state and maps it to the condition of the widget. From the requirements, we want the color to change when the widget is clicked upon or the mouse is released from it. Here, we map the color with the state. Whenever nothing is pressed (or when the mouse is released), we set the state to be in the NORMAL state. Conversely, when the mouse is pressed, we set the state to be in the SELECTED state. These two states are part of an enumeration of many possible states, such as NORMAL, SELECTED, ACTIVE, INSENSITIVE, and so on.

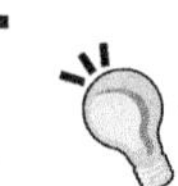

We can learn more about the different possible states by looking for `GtkStateFlags` in DevHelp.

We have the freedom to map these states, but we should apply common sense when doing this. It means that when the widget is pressed, we would think that the widget is now either active or selected or focused instead of being insensitive or disabled. Then we find the closest meaning of this hypothetical state with the previous flags. Hence, in our widget, for the pressed state, we map it with SELECTED and when it is not pressed, we map it with the NORMAL state.

At the end of the function, we call `queue_draw` to make the widget refresh the drawings of the widget. What it basically does is ask GTK+ to call our `draw` function as soon as possible.

The following is our `draw` function, which is responsible for the visual appearance of our widget:

```
public override bool draw(Cairo.Context cr) {
```

We can draw anything on the top of our widget in this function. What we get from the system passed in the argument is the `Cairo Context` object. Cairo is the vector-based canvas system used by GTK+ for drawing the widgets. `Context` is a handle object created by GTK+ with which we can control what to draw, where to draw, and so on. This is similar to the canvas in HTML5.

From the requirements, we must fill the widget with a color depending on the state. So what is the color that we should use? We don't need (and we must not do it!) to declare a color in our widget directly. Instead, we should rely on the GTK+ theming system.

The first thing we do in this function is to get a style context:

```
StyleContext style = get_style_context ();
style.set_state (state);
```

The context controls, among other things, the color or pattern that is used in certain states. This is the state that we set in the `update` function. Then we set the context with the state information. And after doing this, the style context would automatically switch to the specified state.

We call the `render_background` function, which will fill the color or pattern into our widget in the specified area:

```
int w = get_allocated_width ();
int h = get_allocated_height ();
Gtk.render_background (style, cr, 0, 0, w, h);
```

In this case, we fill the whole area with our color or pattern, starting from the `0,0` coordinates along with the full width and full height of the allocated size of the widget. So we expect that the color or pattern will fill the widget entirely. The actual color or pattern used is specified in the GTK+ theme. If the theme says that the color for the NORMAL state is blue, GTK+ will use blue color to fill the widget, and so on.

After drawing a background according to the requirements, we should draw a foreground with a rectangle. Here, we simply draw a rectangle with the size of the widget reduced almost to the value of MARGIN which is 20 pixels. Here, we expect that the rectangle is drawn within the widget area:

```
cr.rectangle (MARGIN, MARGIN,
              w - (MARGIN * 2),
              h - (MARGIN * 2));
```

In Cairo, we can give many commands, but nothing will be rendered before we really commit them. For drawing stroke commands such as the preceding `rectangle` command, we use the `stroke` function to commit the drawing to the canvas.

```
cr.stroke ();
```

After this, the rectangle is really drawn to the widget.

We return a `true` value from the function, indicating that there should be no more processing needed from other parts of the GTK+ system.

```
return true;
```

So, what would trigger the `draw` function to be called? Many of them, including `queue_draw` that we discussed earlier. Another possibility is when we resize the window which hosts the widget, or when some other window is obscuring part of the widget, and so on. Concretely, anything that makes GTK+ think that the widget must be redrawn, will trigger the `draw` function. Because the `draw` function may be called repeatedly all the time, we must carefully design the content of this function to be as minimal as possible. In order to get a pleasing visual appearance of the widget, we should avoid heavy computations or call functions, which process slowly, in the `draw` function. For example, if our widget shows an animation, in order to get a smooth and fluid animation, we must have a frame rate of 60 **frames per second (fps)**. This means that we would expect the `draw` function to be called 60 times a second. This also means that the `draw` function must be executed within 16.67 milliseconds. If we can't achieve this, the animation would stutter, and the whole user experience could be jeopardized.

Now let's see the constructor:

```
public CustomWidget ()
{
    update_state (0);
```

Here, we initialize the `state` variable to `0`, meaning that the widget is expected to be drawn with the `NORMAL` state because no mouse press would occur initially.

The following code is essential to be called inside the constructor. This asks the GTK+ system to pass the button press and release events to the widget whenever they occur:

```
add_events (Gdk.EventMask.BUTTON_PRESS_MASK
        | Gdk.EventMask.BUTTON_RELEASE_MASK);
```

If we don't do this, the widget will not know whether it is pressed or not, hence the following two event handlers would not be called at all:

```
button_press_event.connect((e) => {
  update_state (1);
  activated();
  return true;
});

button_release_event.connect((e) => {
  update_state (0);
  deactivated();
  return true;
});
```

In these event handlers, we return `true` to indicate that the processing is final and we don't want GTK+ to pass the event to other widgets that are possibly in the event pipeline.

We should now notice in our example that the major differences between creating a widget from scratch and subclassing an existing widget in our previous example is in the `draw` function and the event subscription in the constructor. Actually, we could also subclass an existing widget and also implement our own drawing functions. In some particular cases, we could even mix our own drawing with the original drawing function by calling `base.draw()` in our `draw` function.

Maintaining widgets in a library

When we have quite a few custom widgets that are used in many projects, it is important to make a library out of them so that we don't copy the source code around and then lose track of whether we have modified one of them or not. By collecting them into a library, we only have a single source code and a single library that we can use for those projects.

In *Chapter 3, Programming Languages*, we talked about modularization of the JavaScript code, which is conceptually the same as the preceding principle. With Vala, the process needs more efforts; but at the end of the day, we can reap the benefits of collecting our widgets in a library.

Time for action – creating a library

Let's concentrate on how we should do it in Vala. We will create two projects, one as the example library and the other as the user of that library, using the following steps:

1. First, let's create a Vala project called `custom-library`.

2. In `src/custom_library.vala`, we fill the code from the `custom_new.vala` file from the `custom-new` project. We can just copy and paste the code and make some slight adjustments as follows:

   1. Wrap the class declaration with a namespace declaration, so that our code will look like the following:

      ```
      namespace CustomWidget {
      public class CustomWidget : DrawingArea
      ```

   2. Don't forget to put the closing curly bracket at the end of the code.

   3. Remove the `static main` function from the class.

   4. Using the **Files** dock, replace the `src/Makefile.am` file's whole code with the following code:

      ```
      AM_CPPFLAGS = \
        -DPACKAGE_LOCALE_DIR=\""$(localedir)"\" \
        -DPACKAGE_SRC_DIR=\""$(srcdir)"\" \
        -DPACKAGE_DATA_DIR=\""$(pkgdatadir)"\" \
        $(CUSTOM_LIBRARY_CFLAGS)

      AM_CFLAGS =\
         -Wall\
         -g

      lib_LTLIBRARIES = libcustomwidget.la

      libcustomwidget_la_SOURCES = \
        custom_library.vala config.vapi

      libcustomwidget_la_VALAFLAGS =   \
        --pkg gtk+-3.0 --library=libcustomwidget -X -fPIC -X
      -shared -H custom_widget.h

      libcustomwidget_la_LDFLAGS - \
        -Wl,--export-dynamic
      ```

3. Build the project by pressing the *Shift + F7* key combination. Make sure there are no errors and you should find `custom_widget.h` and `libcustomwidget.vapi` in the `src` directory, and a set of library files in the `.libs` directory. This means that the library is now ready to be used.

4. Create another project called `custom-library-client` as an example on how to use the library we created previously. Fill the `src/custom_library_client.vala` file with the following code:

```vala
using GLib;
using Gtk;
using CustomWidget;

public class Main : Object
{
  public Main ()
  {
    Window window = new Window();
    var w = new CustomWidget.CustomWidget();
    window.set_title ("Hello custom widget");

    window.add(w);
    window.show_all();
    window.destroy.connect(on_destroy);
  }

  public void on_destroy (Widget window)
  {
    Gtk.main_quit();
  }

  static int main (string[] args)
  {
    Gtk.init (ref args);
    var app = new Main ();
    Gtk.main ();
    return 0;
  }
}
```

5. Create a `lib/` directory inside our project, and get these files from the `custom-library` project: `src/custom_widget.h`, `src/libcustomwidget.vapi`, and all files with a `.libs/libcustomwidget.so` prefix. Copy the files into the `lib/` directory which was just created.

6. Replace and fill `src/Makefile.am` with the following:

```
AM_CPPFLAGS = \
  -DPACKAGE_LOCALE_DIR=\""$(localedir)"\" \
  -DPACKAGE_SRC_DIR=\""$(srcdir)"\" \
  -DPACKAGE_DATA_DIR=\""$(pkgdatadir)"\" \
  $(CUSTOM_LIBRARY_CLIENT_CFLAGS)

AM_CFLAGS =\
   -Wall\
   -g -I../lib/

bin_PROGRAMS = custom_library_client

custom_library_client_SOURCES = \
  custom_library_client.vala config.vapi

custom_library_client_VALAFLAGS =  \
  --pkg gtk+-3.0 --pkg libcustomwidget --vapidir ../lib

custom_library_client_LDFLAGS = \
  -Wl,--export-dynamic -lcustomwidget -L../lib

custom_library_client_LDADD = $(CUSTOM_LIBRARY_CLIENT_LIBS)
```

7. Open the **Run** menu and choose **Program Parameters**. In the upcoming dialog, expand the **Environment Variables** box.

8. Create a new entry `LD_LIBRARY_PATH` and fill the value field with the full path of the `lib/` directory, which we have created. For example, in my computer, I have the `custom-library-client` project in `/home/gnome/src/ custom-library-client`, so I entered `/home/gnome/src/ custom-library-client/lib` in the value field.

9. After this, we can run the application. We should see a similar application as the previous example, but now with the window's title set as shown in the following screenshot:

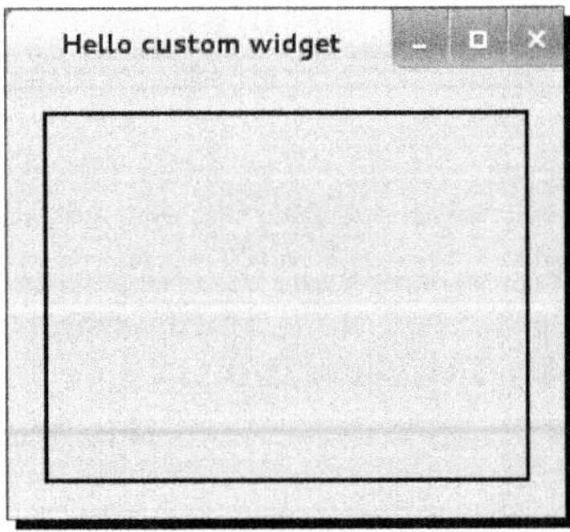

What just happened?

In the library project, we enclosed the class with the `CustomWidget` namespace. This enables us to put this line in the client application:

```
Using CustomWidget;
```

In the library, we remove the `static main` function. This is mandatory since a library should never have a `main` function. As we knew earlier that there must be exactly one `main` function as the entry point to our application, and in this case, the entry point is in the `custom-library-client` project.

Then we make modifications to `Makefile.am` to tell both Vala and C compilers that we want to create a library instead of making an application.

The following line tells that we want to create a library with the name of `libcustomwidget.la`:

```
lib_LTLIBRARIES = libcustomwidget.la
```

In practice, this will produce `libcustomwidget.la` and a set of `libcustomwidget.so` library files.

Then, the following line tells that our `libcustomwidget` library is built from the following files:

```
libcustomwidget_la_SOURCES = \
    custom_library.vala config.vapi
```

The following line of code tells us that when compiling the Vala code into a C-language source code and finally the Binary executable file, we want to make a library with the mentioned name, and pass `-fPIC -shared` into the C compiler (`-X` is the option to pass any flag stated after `-X` to the C compiler).

```
libcustomwidget_la_VALAFLAGS =  \
    --pkg gtk+-3.0 --library=libcustomwidget -X -fPIC -X -shared -H
custom_widget.h
```

The preceding two flags are the most important flags when creating a library, which enables the library to be shared and to be loaded into any location in the memory (**PIC** itself stands for **Position-independent Code**). At last, we tell the compiler that we have generated a C header file called `custom_widget.h`. This file is needed by the C compiler in the client project.

We then build the project instead of running it because we don't have the `main` function in this project. The resulting files must be copied either system-wide in `/usr/include` (for `custom_widget.h`), `/usr/lib` (for the `libcustomwidget.so.*` files), and `/usr/share/vala/vapi` (for the `libcustomwidget.vapi` file) or simply copy all of them into the `lib` directory in the client project.

Let's move to the client project.

The only interesting part in the client project is in the `src/Makefile.am` file.

We specify `--pkg libcustomwidget` as an additional library. We also specify that the `libcustomwidget.vapi` would be available in the `../lib` directory:

```
custom_library_client_VALAFLAGS =  \
    --pkg gtk+-3.0 --pkg libcustomwidget --vapidir ../lib
```

Without this, Vala would not know where to find the `.vapi` file, except if we install it system-wide.

This part of the file that follows is for the linker, that it should resolve the symbol using the `libcustomwidget` library found in `../lib/libcustomwidget.so*`:

```
custom_library_client_LDFLAGS = \
    -Wl,--export-dynamic -lcustomwidget -L../lib
```

While running the application, we set `LD_LIBRARY_PATH` to the full path which contains the `libcustomwidget.so.*` files. We don't need to do this when we have the libraries installed system-wide.

At the end of the day, we should ship the `.vapi` file, the `.h` file, and the library files and install them system-wide so the application can easily find and use them, as it is now very easy to use the GTK+ libraries. One big advantage of this library approach is that the library is not only usable by Vala programs, but also can be directly used with C programs or any other programming languages, provided that the header file and the library can be bound into the programming languages in question.

Summary

In this chapter we have learned how to extend an existing widget, combine existing widgets into a new widget, as well as create a new widget. We see that it is quite easy to add or remove functionalities of an existing widget. We also know that it is very important to make our widget backward compatible with the original interface when we extend a widget.

When we created the custom widget, we discussed a bit about painting with Cairo canvas. We touched on the GTK+ styling API so that we can rely on the theming system for the coloring and other paint styles, and avoid hardcoding in our program. We also talked about the importance of keeping the painting function optimal, so that we can keep the performance in a good shape.

Finally, creating widgets is essentially also creating a library. We talked about how to do this with Vala. With this experience so far, we now have more confidence to develop a GNOME application not only by picking already-made widgets, but also extending and creating new ones, and integrating them in our application.

In the next chapter, we will talk about multimedia programming with GStreamer. We will discuss how to utilize the GStreamer framework to play and manipulate media files.

7
Having Fun with Multimedia

Multimedia capabilities are one of the strong points of GNOME. It provides numerous APIs for developers to easily present multimedia content. This opens quite a broad spectrum of application ideas that can be implemented; for example, a simple audio/video conversion tool, a music or video stream player, CCTV monitoring, or a full-blown education application, to name a few.

In this chapter, we will take a look at the basic usage of GStreamer by presenting audio and video content with the GStreamer API. Specifically, we will discuss the following:

- The GStreamer concept
- Playing audio and video
- Applying filters to stream

Let's get into more detail now.

Packages required

This chapter uses software, namely the MPEG codecs, which are not freely available in the default Linux distribution repositories. Fedora users need to add a third-party repository in order to be able to use the software. Type the following command on the terminal to add this third-party library:

```
su -c 'yum localinstall --nogpgcheck http://download1.rpmfusion.org/
free/fedora/rpmfusion-free-release-stable.noarch.rpm http://download1.
rpmfusion.org/nonfree/fedora/rpmfusion-nonfree-release-stable.noarch.rpm'
```

The following packages need to be installed:

- **Fedora**: `gstreamer-plugins-bad`, `gstreamer-plugins-ugly`, `gstreamer-ffmpeg`, and `gstreamer-tools`

- **Ubuntu/Debian**: `gstreamer0.10-plugins-bad`, `gstreamer0.10-plugins-ugly`, `gstreamer0.10-plugins-ffmpeg`, `gstreamer0.10-tools`, and `libgstreamer-plugins-base0.10-dev`

Understanding the basic concept of GStreamer

GStreamer is a media-processing framework used by GNOME to support its multimedia feature. It has a plugin infrastructure which provides an abstraction layer for opening, encoding, decoding, and filtering media streams. It means that as long as there is a plugin for a certain multimedia format, we can open or write files or play media with that format. The following diagram shows the simplified architecture of the GStreamer API:

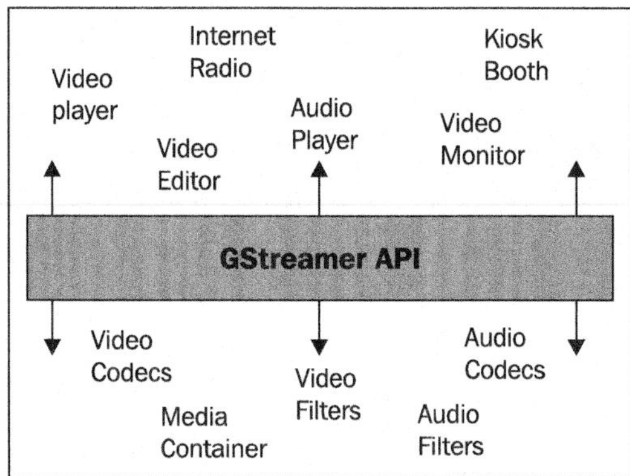

As we can see from the diagram, the application can just use the APIs provided by GStreamer and the implementation of a particular codec or filter can also use the API. The application does not need to know the details of a codec or a filter and vice versa. Unfortunately, in the real world, there are still audio and video player applications which implement everything shown in the diagram by themselves and they differ between each other.

GStreamer has the concept of **elements**. It is the basic part of the entities involved in a media stream. There is an element where the stream originates, there is another element where the stream ends, and also additional elements in between where the stream is manipulated while being passed through it.

We can imagine the data as water. Water flows into a system where the elements are connected with pipes. They are put into the system by an element such as a water gallon, a glass, a respiratory system, or even a reactor, which hypothetically produces water from oxygen and hydrogen molecules.

Inside the system, the water can be manipulated so that the color or smell can be changed by the filter elements. We can even combine these filters.

After that, the water exits the system through an element such as a bucket, a glass, a spray, or even a vaporizer.

Each element at least has a door, which is source, sink, or both. **Source** is where the data flows from and **sink** is where the data flows into. These doors are called **pads**. An element could have more than one pad, for example, for elements which can produce both audio and video streams. These pads can be both statically or dynamically created.

We can see the visualization of the elements as shown in the following diagram:

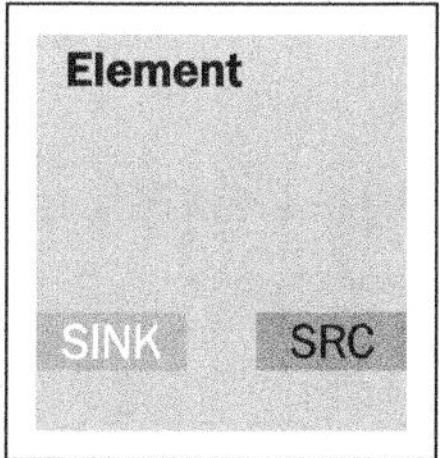

Each element has it own states, which is either of the following:

- **Null**: The default state of an element
- **Ready**: The state where the stream is ready and waiting to be flown
- **Paused**: The state where the stream is open but the flow is frozen
- **Playing**: The state where the stream is open and is flowing

The data is passed into the system by using buffers as the pipes pass the water into the system. The whole system is orchestrated by employing events which carry control information. The events are sent to the elements so they can react according to the events delivered.

The events—or in GStreamer terms, messages—are delivered through a bus. The bus is created by the pipeline. And by tapping into the bus, we can subscribe to the messages posted there.

Accessing the GStreamer pipeline with the command line

GStreamer provides a tool to help us test the pipeline just by using a command line. This is a very handy tool to quickly see whether the pipeline is correct or not. Let's imagine a concrete example. Suppose that we want to play a stereo MP3 file. The source element would be the MP3 file opener, which is `filesrc`, and we pass the stream to the next element to `mad`, which is the MP3 decoder. The decoded stream can be then passed to the `audioconvert` element, which converts the raw audio stream into, say, a mono channel.

This newly-modified stream, when passed to `audioresample`, for example, converts it into an audio stream of 8 KHz. Then the final stream is passed to `alsasink` to play the stream into the sound card.

Time for action – testing the pipeline

We can implement this pipeline by using the command line and by using the GStreamer tool, `gst-launch`. Let us see how we can achieve this:

1. Open a terminal and type this command in a single line:

```
$ gst-launch-0.10 filesrc location=bass.mp3 ! mad ! audioconvert
! audio/x-raw-int,channels=1 ! audioresample ! audio/x-raw-int,
rate=8000 ! alsasink
```

2. Listen to the audio being played and see the following output printed on the screen:

```
Setting pipeline to PAUSED ...

Pipeline is PREROLLING ...

Pipeline is PREROLLED ...

Setting pipeline to PLAYING ...

New clock: GstAudioSinkClock

Got EOS from element "pipeline0".

Execution ended after 9311663370 ns.

Setting pipeline to PAUSED ...

Setting pipeline to READY ...

Setting pipeline to NULL ...

Freeing pipeline ...
```

What just happened?

We can visualize the pipeline as shown in the following diagram:

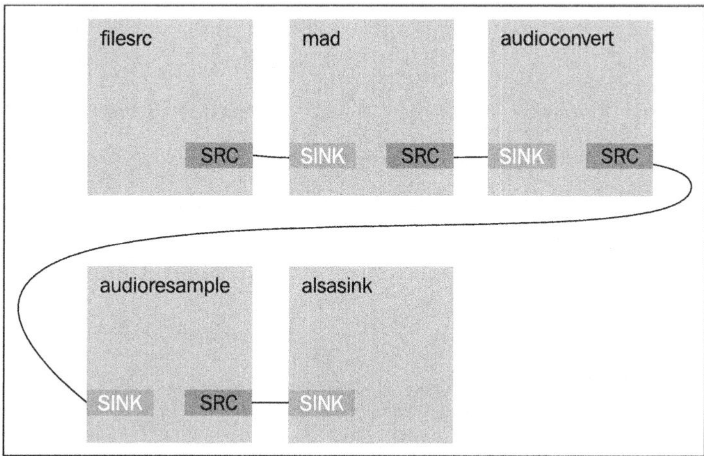

The `gst-launch` tool establishes the pipeline as specified in the command line. We connect the elements involved by using an exclamation mark in between them.

First, we start the pipeline with `filesrc` and specify the property of the location by typing the filename which we want to play, as shown here:

```
filesrc location=bass.mp3 !
```

Then we pass the stream to the `mad` element, which is a MP3 decoder, by using the mad library:

```
mad !
```

Then we pass it to the `audioconvert` element:

```
audioconvert ! audio/x-raw-int,channels=1 !
```

Here, we specify the source pad to transform the stream into an integer-format audio with only one channel. Then we pass it to `audioresample` element:

```
audioresample ! audio/x-raw-int, rate=8000 !
```

We specify the source pad to transform the stream into an 8-KHz audio stream.

Finally, we pass the stream to the `alsasink` element, which outputs the stream into the soundcard via the **Advanced Linux Sound Architecture (ALSA)**.

```
alsasink
```

Finally, we hear the audio being played!

Time for action – programmatically playing the audio

Knowing how to interact with GStreamer elements using the command-line tool is very useful to check whether your pipeline design would work or not. Now let's try to do this programmatically:

1. Create a new script called `audio.js` and fill it with the following code:

```
#!/usr/bin/env seed

GLib = imports.gi.GLib;
Gst = imports.gi.Gst;
GObject = imports.gi.GObject;

Main = new GType({
        parent: GObject.Object.type,
        name: "Main",
        init: function() {
                var pipeline = new Gst.Pipeline({ name: 'pipe' });
                var filesrc = Gst.ElementFactory.make ('filesrc',
'source');
                var mad = Gst.ElementFactory.make ('mad',
'decoder');
                var converter = Gst.ElementFactory.make
('audioconvert', 'converter');
                var resampler = Gst.ElementFactory.make
('audioresample', 'resampler');
                var alsasink = Gst.ElementFactory.make
('alsasink', 'sink');

                pipeline.add (filesrc);
                pipeline.add (mad);
                pipeline.add (converter);
                pipeline.add (resampler);
                pipeline.add (alsasink);

                filesrc.location = "bass.mp3";
                filesrc.link(mad);
                mad.link(converter);

                var caps = Gst.caps_from_string("audio/x-raw-
int,channels=1")
                converter.link_filtered(resampler, caps);

                caps = Gst.caps_from_string("audio/x-raw-
int,rate=8000")
                resampler.link_filtered(alsasink, caps);
```

```
                this.play = function() {
                        pipeline.set_state (Gst.State.PLAYING);
                };
        }
});

Gst.init(Seed.argv);
var main = new Main();
main.play();

var context = GLib.main_context_default();
var loop = new GLib.MainLoop.c_new(context);

loop.run();
```

2. Alternatively, you can also create a Vala project without UI and a license, called `audio.vala`. Fill the `src/audio.vala` file with the following code:

```
using Gst;
using GLib;

public class Main : GLib.Object
{
  Pipeline pipeline;

  public Main ()
  {
        pipeline = Gst.parse_launch ("filesrc location=bass.mp3 !
mad ! audioconvert ! audio/x-raw-int,channels=1 ! audioresample !
audio/x-raw-int, rate=4000 ! alsasink") as Gst.Pipeline;
  }

  public void play() {
    pipeline.set_state (State.PLAYING);
    }

  static int main (string[] args)
  {
    Gst.init (ref args);
    var app = new Main ();
    app.play();

    new MainLoop().run();

    return 0;
  }
}
```

3. Modify `configure.ac` from the following code:

```
PKG_CHECK_MODULES(AUDIO, [gtk+-3.0 ])
```

to this:

```
PKG_CHECK_MODULES(AUDIO, [gstreamer-0.10 ])
```

4. Modify `src/Makefile.am` from this:

```
audio_VALAFLAGS =  \
  --pkg gtk+-3.0
```

to this:

```
audio_VALAFLAGS =  \
  --pkg gstreamer-0.10
```

5. Don't forget to copy the `bass.mp3` file in the same directory where you run the program.

6. Run it, and you will hear the same audio being played from the previous experiment.

What just happened?

If we take a look at both versions of the code written in Vala and JavaScript, there is quite a significant difference between them. This is not because of the nature of the language but rather because both are using alternative ways to interact with GStreamer.

Let's start with the JavaScript code. In the following code, we define all the elements involved and the pipeline:

```
var pipeline = new Gst.Pipeline({ name: 'pipe' });
var filesrc = Gst.ElementFactory.make ('filesrc', 'source');
var mad = Gst.ElementFactory.make ('mad', 'decoder');
var converter = Gst.ElementFactory.make ('audioconvert', 'converter');
var resampler = Gst.ElementFactory.make ('audioresample',
'resampler');
var alsasink = Gst.ElementFactory.make ('alsasink', 'sink');
```

In each element we need to declare the name of the element we want and the name by which we want to refer to it. After that we keep it in a local variable for easy access.

We then add all the elements to the pipeline:

```
pipeline.add (filesrc);
pipeline.add (mad);
pipeline.add (converter);
pipeline.add (resampler);
pipeline.add (alsasink);
```

At this point, the elements are just added but not connected to each other. Then, we specify the `location` property of the `filesrc` element as shown here:

```
filesrc.location = "bass.mp3";
filesrc.link(mad);
mad.link(converter);
```

This is to tell the element that we want to open the `bass.mp3` file. After that we connect the `filesrc` element to the `mad` element. The next step is to continue the wiring by connecting the `mad` element to the `converter` element.

The following code sets the capabilities of the `converter` element, that is, to process the integer-format raw audio stream using just a single channel.

```
var caps = Gst.caps_from_string("audio/x-raw-int,channels=1")
converter.link_filtered(resampler, caps);
```

With the capabilities in hand, we connect the `converter` element to `resampler` with the `link_filtered` function instead of using the `link` function.

This code reuses the `caps` variable and resets it with the new value:

```
caps = Gst.caps_from_string("audio/x-raw-int,rate=8000")
resampler.link_filtered(alsasink, caps);
```

In the preceding code, we set the bit rate to `8000` Hertz. Then we connect the `resampler` element with the `caps` variable to the `alsasink` element. The `alsasink` element is used to command the sound card to play the audio. At this point, we do not need to do more connection, so that's it.

When we need to play the audio, what we need to do is to trigger the state of the pipeline with the `Gst.State.PLAYING` value.

```
pipeline.set_state (Gst.State.PLAYING);
```

When this is set, the flow starts and ends up in the sound card, so we can hear the audio.

In the Vala version, we slightly change the code to show that there is more than one way to achieve the result. But first let's review the build infrastructure.

We modified `configure.ac` to include the `gstreamer-0.10 pkgconfig` build flag into our build infrastructure so that the C compiler recognizes and knows where to pick up the header files and the required libraries. Here is the code:

```
PKG_CHECK_MODULES(AUDIO, [gstreamer-0.10 ])
```

Then, we modify the `Makefile.am` file to let the Vala compiler know that we want to use the `Gst` namespace, which comes from `gstreamer-0.10` package.

```
audio_VALAFLAGS =  \
   --pkg gstreamer-0.10
```

Notice that we only have a single line of code to construct the pipeline as shown here:

```
pipeline = Gst.parse_launch ("filesrc location=bass.mp3 ! mad !
audioconvert ! audio/x-raw-int,channels=1 ! audioresample ! audio/x-
raw-int, rate=4000 ! alsasink") as Gst.Pipeline;
```

In the preceding code, we just copy and paste the command-line code version into the `Gst.parse_launch` function. This function returns `Gst.Element`, but we need to convert that into `Gst.Pipeline` by just appending `as Gst.Pipeline` to specify the casting at the end of the line. After that, we start the flow by setting the state.

```
pipeline.set_state (State.PLAYING);
```

Notice that in both the versions, we use the `GLib` main loop so that the system knows about the events and does not quit immediately. The result is that we need to press *Ctrl + C* to exit the program because we don't handle the any event notifying the end of the stream.

Time for action – handling the events

Now let's continue learning about getting events from the stream so that we can react properly to each event. Imagine that we need to terminate the application after the stream ends. Unfortunately, we can only do this with Vala as the current version of the GObject introspection library used by Seed does not contain the necessary functions to establish our goal. Execute the following steps to handle these events:

1. We can use the audio project and modify the `audio.vala` file to be like the following snippet of code:

```
public class Main : GLib.Object
{
  Pipeline pipeline;
  public signal void eos ();

  bool bus_handler (Bus bus, Message message) {
    if (message.type == MessageType.EOS) {
      stdout.printf ("End of stream!\n");
      eos ();
    }
    return true;
  }

  public Main ()
  {
        pipeline = Gst.parse_launch ("filesrc location=bass.mp3 !
  mad ! audioconvert ! audio/x-raw-int,channels=1 ! audioresample !
  audio/x-raw-int, rate=4000 ! alsasink") as Gst.Pipeline;
      var bus = pipeline.get_bus ();
      bus.add_watch (bus_handler);
```

```vala
      }

    public void play() {
      pipeline.set_state (State.PLAYING);
      }

    static int main (string[] args)
    {
      Gst.init (ref args);
      var loop = new MainLoop();
      var app = new Main ();
      app.play();

      app.eos.connect (() => {
        loop.quit();
      });

      loop.run();

      return 0;
    }
  }
```

2. Build and run it. We will see that the program just terminates after printing the following output:

```
End of stream!
```

What just happened?

What we want is just to react whenever we know that the stream ends. So, we can think of calling a callback upon receiving the event and need to figure out how to trigger the event.

This part of the code gets a GStreamer bus from the pipeline:

```vala
    var bus = pipeline.get_bus ();
    bus.add_watch (bus_handler);
```

As we discussed earlier, the bus carries all the messages posted into it. So we just need to tap the bus by using the `add_watch` function.

After that, we set up the other parts; first, our own signal:

```vala
    public signal void eos();
```

And the second one is a signal handler:

```vala
    bool bus_handler (Bus bus, Message message) {
      if (message.type == MessageType.EOS) {
        stdout.printf ("End of stream!\n");
```

```
        eos();
    }
    return true;
}
```

In the preceding code, we set up our own signal to relay the GStreamer message as an event to the client of our class. We do it like this because our client may not know anything about the GStreamer messages, so we simplify the signal by wrapping the GStreamer event with our own event.

The message handler is quite simple, we check whether the message type is an **End Of Stream (EOS)** message or not. If it is, then we just print out a text and emit our own signal.

The following code shows how the client is connected to our signal:

```
app.eos.connect(() => {
    loop.quit();
});
```

Upon receiving the signal, it just exits the main loop and our objective is achieved.

Playing a video media

Now let's play a video. But first, we need to come up with the stream design. The design shown in the following diagram should fulfill our needs:

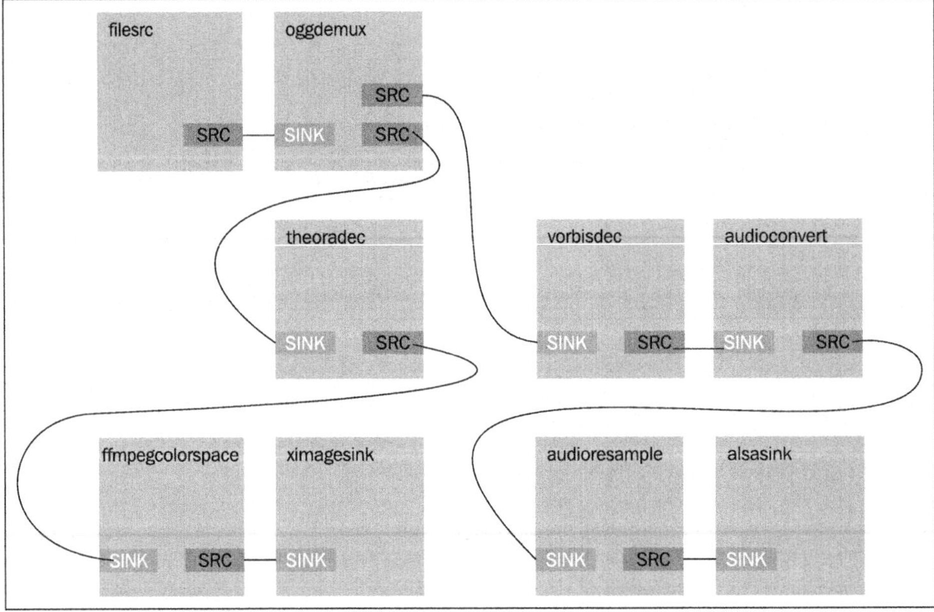

From the preceding diagram, we see that the stream from the file is split into two parts by an **Ogg** demultiplexer. The results are source streams containing both, audio and video. The video stream is passed into a **theora** decoder and a color space converter. This plugin is for decoding video content from the media. After that it is passed to the **ximage** sink. This is for displaying the decoded material to the screen. The audio stream is passed into a **vorbis** decoder and then to the audio converter and the `resampler` element. The **vorbis** plugin is to decode the audio content in the media. After that we pass it to the **alsa** sink, which is for playing the audio into the soundcard.

Time for action – playing video

We will play the `Ap17_spill.ogg` file obtained from Wikipedia. It is an `OggTheora` video stream with audio. Execute the following steps to play this video:

1. Type the following into the command-line terminal:

```
gst-launch-0.10 filesrc location="Ap17_spill.ogg" ! oggdemux
name=demux demux. ! queue ! theoradec ! ffmpegcolorspace
! ximagesink demux. ! queue ! vorbisdec ! audioconvert !
audioresample ! alsasink
```

2. As shown in the following screenshot, a small window will be displayed showing the video being played along with the audio:

What just happened?

The command-line code strictly follows the design shown earlier. We open the `Ap17_spill.ogg` file here:

```
filesrc location="Ap17_spill.ogg" !
```

We create an Ogg demuxer that is connected to `filesrc`, and we name this demuxer as `demux`.

```
oggdemux name=demux demux. !
```

Here, we branch the source of the Ogg demuxer:

```
queue !
```

The first branch is connected to the theora decoder to get the video stream from the theora stream.

```
theoradec !
```

Then we pass it to `ffmpegcolorspace` to get the color space suitable for displaying to the screen:

```
ffmpegcolorspace !
```

Finally, we pass the video stream to `ximagesink` to display it to the screen:

```
ximagesink demux. !
```

We put `demux` with a period to state that this path, which was connected to the element called `demux` ends here.

```
queue !
```

Here, we put another path in the second branch:

```
vorbisdec !
```

In the following line of code, we use the stream to get the audio stream:

```
audioconvert ! audioresample ! alsasink
```

This sequence is similar to what we have seen earlier when we play only the audio stream.

It does not matter which stream you want to put first in the command line, whether it is audio or video, as long as you state the end of the queue with the branch name ending with a period as demonstrated previously.

Have a go hero – defining the audio first

How about giving it a try? Define the audio first in the pipeline, and after that define the video using the command line. There should be no difference in the result though, visually or audibly.

Time for action – programmatically playing the video

Now imagine that we want to use our preceding stream flow design and implement it in our program. The UI of our program can be very simple, just a video box with a **Play/Stop** button below it. Let's do this now:

1. Create a new Vala project, called `video`. This time, let's use the `GtkBuilder` functionality.

2. Edit our `video.ui` file and put a vertical box with two items. For the top item, we put a `DrawingArea` widget and use a button at the bottom. Make sure to have the `DrawingArea` widget expandable.

3. Modify `src/Makefile.am` to contain the following:

```
video_VALAFLAGS =   \
  --pkg gtk+-3.0 --pkg gstreamer-0.10 --pkg gstreamer-
interfaces-0.10 --pkg gdk-x11-3.0
```

4. Modify `configure.ac` to contain the following line:

```
PKG_CHECK_MODULES(VIDEO, [gtk+-3.0 gstreamer-0.10 gstreamer-
interfaces-0.10 gstreamer-plugins-base-0.10 gdk-x11-3.0])
```

5. Include a `video.vala` file, which is available in the code bundle of this book. The main part of the functionalities is shown here:

```
public class Main : GLib.Object
{
  const string UI_FILE = "src/video.ui";

  public Main ()
  {
    Builder builder;

    pipeline = new Pipeline ("video");
    src = ElementFactory.make ("filesrc", "filesrc");
    demux = ElementFactory.make ("oggdemux", "demux");
    queue1 = ElementFactory.make ("queue", "queue1");
    queue2 = ElementFactory.make ("queue", "queue2");
    theoraDecoder = ElementFactory.make ("theoradec", "theora");
    vorbisDecoder = ElementFactory.make ("vorbisdec", "vorbis");
    colorConverter = ElementFactory.make ("ffmpegcolorspace",
"colorspace");
    audioConverter = ElementFactory.make ("audioconvert",
"audio");
    audioResampler = ElementFactory.make ("audioresample",
"resampler");
```

```
    audioSink = ElementFactory.make ("alsasink", "audiosink");
    videoSink = ElementFactory.make ("ximagesink", "videosink");

    pipeline.add_many (src, demux,
                       theoraDecoder, vorbisDecoder,
                       queue1, queue2,
                       colorConverter, audioConverter,
audioResampler,
                       audioSink, videoSink);

    src.link (demux);

    demux.link_many(queue1, queue2);
    demux.pad_added.connect((element, src_pad) => {
      var caps = src_pad.get_caps();
      var name = caps.get_structure(0).get_name();

      Pad sink_pad = null;

      if (name == "video/x-theora") {
          ink_pad = queue1.get_pad("sink");
      } else if (name == "audio/x-vorbis") {
        sink_pad = queue2.get_pad("sink");
      } else {
        return;
      }
      if (sink_pad != null && sink_pad.is_linked() == false) {
        src_pad.link (sink_pad);
      }
    });

    queue1.link_many (theoraDecoder, colorConverter, videoSink);
    queue2.link_many (vorbisDecoder, audioConverter,
audioResampler, audioSink);

    try
    {
      builder = new Builder ();
      builder.add_from_file (UI_FILE);
      builder.connect_signals (this);

      videoArea = builder.get_object ("drawingarea1") as Widget;
      videoArea.draw.connect(() => {
        var xoverlay = videoSink as XOverlay;
        var xid = (ulong)Gdk.X11Window.get_xid(videoArea.get_
window());
        overlay.set_xwindow_id(xid);
```

```
      return false;
    });

    var window = builder.get_object ("window") as Window;
    window.show_all ();
  }
  catch (Error e) {
    stderr.printf ("Could not load UI: %s\n", e.message);
  }

  var bus = pipeline.get_bus ();
  bus.add_signal_watch ();
  bus.message.connect((bus, message) => {

    if (message.type == Gst.MessageType.EOS) {
     stop();
       pipeline.set_state (State.READY);
       reopen();
     }
  });

  playButton = builder.get_object("button1") as Button;
  playButton.clicked.connect(() => {
    if (playing) {
      stop();
    } else {
      play();
    }
  });
  reopen ();
  stop ();

  }

}
```

6. Make sure that we have the `Ap17_spill.ogg` file in our project's folder.

7. Build and run the program. As shown in the following screenshot, we should now be able to play and stop the video, and also can exit the program:

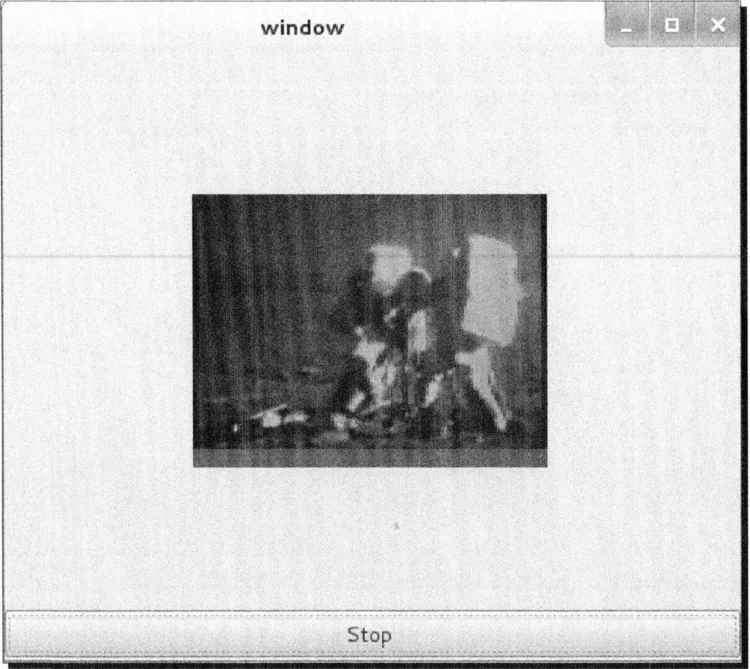

What just happened?

We have several essential parts in this exercise to which we need to pay attention.

The first one is how to connect the audio and video stream sources to the sink in the next element in the queue. We can't link the demultiplexer with the queue before the stream is played. So what we need to do is attach the elements to the `pad_added` signal in the demultiplexer. In this case, the audio and video stream pads are created whenever the stream is played:

```
demux.pad_added.connect((element, src_pad) => {
  var caps = src_pad.get_caps();
  var name = caps.get_structure(0).get_name();

  pad sink_pad = null;
```

What we then do in the signal handler is to check whether the stream contains a video stream (by checking against `video/x-theora`), then we link the pad with the `queue1` element.

```
if (name == "video/x-theora") {
    sink_pad = queue1.get_pad("sink");
}
```

Conversely, if we get the audio stream, we link the pad with `queue2`. Otherwise we do nothing. After this, everything should be connected from the `filesrc` element until `audiosink` and `videosink`, as shown in the following code snippet:

```
else if (name == "audio/x-vorbis") {
    sink_pad = queue2.get_pad("sink");
} else {
    return;
}
if (sink_pad != null && sink_pad.is_linked() == false) {
    src_pad.link (sink_pad);
}
});
```

The next important thing is how to display the video frames. The `ximagesink` sink has its own window to display the video. To attach the video into our `videoArea` widget, we need to hook up the `draw` signal (or any other signal which tells that the widget is ready, which means that the `window` object is valid).

Our handler gets `videoSink` as `XOverlay`, which is a special interface to draw the video frame onto the window we specify. Before doing any drawing, we need to find out the `xid` value, which is the handle number of the window that we want to draw into; this is done using the following code snippet:

```
videoArea.draw.connect(() => {
    var xoverlay = videoSink as XOverlay;
    var xid = (ulong)Gdk.X11Window.get_xid(videoArea.get_window());
    xoverlay.set_xwindow_id(xid);
    return false;
});
```

This window is the `videoArea` widget's X11 window. We first get the `xid` value by calling the `Gdk.X11Window.get_xid` function against our `videoArea` widget. After getting the value of `xid`, we then tell `xoverlay` to use this `xid` value whenever it receives a frame, and render it inside the `videoArea` widget.

Next, our attention turns to how to interact with the stream. When we want to play, obviously we just set the state of the pipeline to PLAYING. When we want to pause, we set it to PAUSE. And when we receive the end of stream notification, or when we close the window, we set it to NULL. After setting it to NULL, we need to again set the location of the `filesrc` element to be able to replay the video.

Summary

In this chapter, we have learned how to play both audio and video files using GStreamer. We also discussed the basics of GStreamer. We know how it works and we know how to wire the elements of GStreamer in order to play our media. We can prototype the stream flow design with command line and then implement it afterwards. Finally, we learned how to put GStreamer together with GTK+ widgets.

Our next stop in *Chapter 8, Playing with Data*, is to play with data. It does not mean data only from databases, but data that comes from various sources.

8
Playing with Data

When we talk about data, it is not only about databases, but data from other sources as well. It is about accessing and manipulating data and presenting them to the users. Better access to data also means better integration, and GNOME is good at this. It provides many APIs to get the job done; we will discuss them in this chapter.

What we want to concentrate on in this chapter is how to get data from multiple sources and how to present it on the screen. To present data on the screen, we will utilize the GTK+ `TreeView` widget. Also, we will introduce **Evolution Data Server** libraries with which we can collect data from address books. To keep the chapter simple, we will only use Seed and Glade.

In this chapter, we will study the following topics in greater detail:

- Presenting data with `TreeView`
- The Evolution Data Server architecture
- Accessing an address book with Evolution Data Server

So let's fetch the data!

Presenting data with TreeView

GTK+ `TreeView` is a widget used to display both the tree and list types of data. The design of the widget uses the **Model-View-Controller (MVC)** design pattern to logically separate the implementation of the data model, how the data is presented, and how the data is accessed and manipulated.

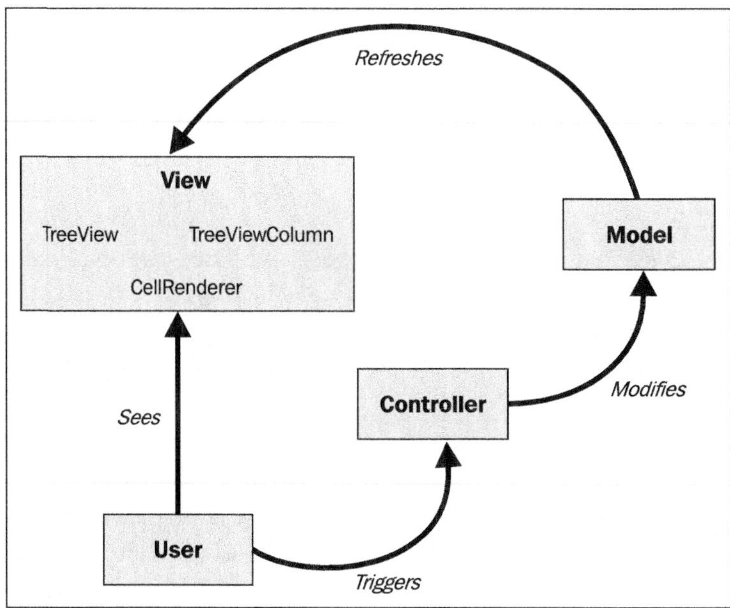

The preceding diagram explains the design pattern visually. To explain this diagram, let's imagine a search engine on the Web. The user, either the end user or a piece of code, triggers something in the controller. In practice, this step could be the end user pressing a **Search** button or a code submitting a search query to the Web, or anything that directly triggers the controller to do something. The controller then modifies the model according to the trigger.

In our search engine story, this could be the search engine on the server. It takes the query, forms them as parameters, and passes them into the model as input. The model then produces new data. This new data replaces and refreshes the presentation on the view object. The user can then view this new presentation. Concretely, the presentation could be the screen that is now displaying the search results.

With this approach, we can have different kinds of presentations while still having the same implementation of the model and controller. In the web browser, our search engine can display detailed results, while in a smartphone, the results can only be displayed in a simple form.

In GTK+, the model is defined in the `TreeModel` interface, which needs to be implemented by the model provider. However, GTK+ provides two simple, ready-to-use models, so we don't need to implement the `TreeModel` interface by ourselves. These models are `ListStore` and `TreeStore`. `ListStore` is used for a simple list data structure while `TreeStore` is used to provide a tree data structure. In the model, we define the columns of the data that we want to keep.

When we want to access the model, we need help from the `Iter` object to iterate the model. The `Iter` object points to a specific record in the data model. We can move this object around while we travel through the data.

Time for action – using TreeView

Suppose that we want to make a simple application that can list data on a table. We also want to remove data from and add new data into it. This can be done by following these steps:

1. Create a new Glade UI file called `treeview.ui`.

2. Insert a window into it.

3. In the window, insert a `Box` control with two items. Make it a vertical box.

4. Place a `ScrollableWindow` window into the upper part of the UI and make it expandable.

5. Put another `Box`, which is capable of containing two items, into the bottom part; this time the box should be a horizontal box.

6. Add two buttons to each column of the vertical box, and name them `btnRemove` and `btnAdd` with **Remove** and **Add** labels respectively.

7. Add a `TreeView` widget (available in **Control and Display**) to the `ScrollableWindow` window.

8. A dialog will pop up asking for the model; press the ellipsis button and click **New**.

9. The model dialog is now automatically filled with `liststore1`.

10. Click on the **Create** button.

11. On the widget list, select **liststore1**.

12. In the **General** tab, rename the selected liststore to `store`.

13. In the **Columns** data below it, click on **<define a new column>**; it will be converted into a text entry of the type `gchararray`.

14. Do it one more time so we will have two entries with the type `gchararray`.

15. Rename the `treeview1` object to `view`.

16. Find the `treeselection1` object under `view` and rename it to `selection`.

17. At the moment, our Glade file should look like the one shown in the following screenshot:

18. Create a new Seed script file named `treeview.js`.

19. Fill it with the following code:

```
#!/usr/bin/env seed

Gtk = imports.gi.Gtk;
GObject = imports.gi.GObject;

Main = new GType({
  parent: GObject.Object.type,
  name: "Main",
  init: function(self) {
    var columns = {
      NAME: 0,
      ADDRESS: 1,
    }

  var ui = new Gtk.Builder()
   this.ui = ui;
   ui.add_from_file("treeview.ui");
   var window = ui.get_object("window1");
   window.resize(300, 400);
   window.show_all();
   window.signal.destroy.connect(Gtk.main_quit);

   this.clients = {};
```

```
var view = ui.get_object("view");
var selection = ui.get_object("selection");
selection.signal.changed.connect(function(s) {
  var btnRemove = ui.get_object("btnRemove");
  btnRemove.sensitive = true;
});


var btnRemove = ui.get_object("btnRemove");
btnRemove.signal.clicked.connect(function() {
  var selection = view.get_selection();
  if (selection) {
    var selected = {};
    var valid = selection.get_selected(selected);
    if (valid && selected.iter) {
      var model = view.get_model();
      model.remove(selected.iter);
    }
  }
});

var btnAdd = ui.get_object("btnAdd");
btnAdd.signal.clicked.connect(function() {
  var selection = view.get_selection();
  if (selection) {
    var selected = {};
    var valid = selection.get_selected(selected);
    if (valid && selected.iter) {
      var model = view.get_model();
      model.insert(selected.iter, 1);
    }
  }
});

column = new Gtk.TreeViewColumn({title:'Name'});
cell = new Gtk.CellRendererText();
cell.editable = true;
column.pack_start(cell);
column.add_attribute(cell, 'text', columns.NAME);
cell.signal.edited.connect(function(obj, path, text) {
  var store = view.get_model();
  var path = new Gtk.TreePath.from_string(path);
  var iter = {};
  store.get_iter(iter, path);
  store.set_value(iter.iter, columns.NAME, text);
});
view.append_column(column);

column = new Gtk.TreeViewColumn({title:'Address'});
```

```
cell = new Gtk.CellRendererText();
cell.editable = true;
column.pack_start(cell);
column.add_attribute(cell, 'text', columns.ADDRESS);
cell.signal.edited.connect(function(obj, path, text) {
  var store = view.get_model();
  var path = new Gtk.TreePath.from_string(path);
  var iter = {};
  store.get_iter(iter, path);
  store.set_value(iter.iter, columns.ADDRESS, text);
});
view.append_column(column);

var store = view.get_model();
var iter = {};
store.append(iter);

store.set_value(iter.iter, columns.NAME, "Robert");
store.set_value(iter.iter, columns.ADDRESS, "North Pole");
  }
});

Gtk.init(Seed.argv);
var main = new Main();
Gtk.main();
```

20. Run the application; we can edit the data by clicking on the field. We can add new rows one after another by selecting one row and clicking **Add**. We can remove a selected row as well. The output is shown in the following screenshot:

What just happened?

In this exercise, we learn about how `TreeView` works. We have `TreeView` as the view, along with two `CellRendererText` widgets and the associated `TreeView` columns. For this model, we use `ListStore`.

We first define the data that we want to maintain. It is a two-column data, with each column having the type string. We use constants to refer to the column number. We use NAME for column number 0 and ADDRESS for column number 1, shown as follows:

```
var columns = {
   NAME: 0,
   ADDRESS: 1,
}
```

We keep the `TreeView` reference in the `view` variable for quick access.

```
var view = ui.get_object("view");
```

We subscribe to the selection's changed signal. Whenever a row is selected, this code will be called. At the moment, it does not have anything useful, but in a real project this could be something such as enabling some buttons, showing a notification, and so on. Following is the selection code:

```
var selection = ui.get_object("selection");
   selection.signal.changed.connect(function(s) {
   var btnRemove = ui.get_object("btnRemove");
   btnRemove.sensitive = true;
});
```

We attach the removing of a record to the **Remove** button's clicked signal in this part of the code:

```
var btnRemove = ui.get_object("btnRemove");
btnRemove.signal.clicked.connect(function() {
```

First, we get the current `selection` object by executing this code:

```
var selection = view.get_selection();
if (selection) {
   var selected = {};
   var valid = selection.get_selected(selected);
```

If the `selection` object is valid, we get the selected row object. If there is a record, the `iter` object inside the selected object will be obtained.

When we get the `iter` object, we can remove the record with this code snippet:

```
var model = view.get_model();
model.remove(selected.iter);
```

Then, we do the same for the **Add** button. But now, instead of removing a record, we insert a new record:

```
var btnAdd = ui.get_object("btnAdd");
btnAdd.signal.clicked.connect(function() {
  var selection = view.get_selection();
  if (selection) {
    var selected = {};
    var valid = selection.get_selected(selected);
    if (valid && selected.iter) {
      var model = view.get_model();
      model.insert(selected.iter, 1);
    }
  }
});
```

Then we set up the columns. Each column is represented with a `TreeViewColumn` widget. Each `TreeViewColumn` is attached with a `CellRenderer` class. Because our data is a plain string, the renderer we use is `CellRendererText`.

```
column = new Gtk.TreeViewColumn({title:'Name'});
cell = new Gtk.CellRendererText();
```

Then, we make the cell editable so we can edit the data, after which we pack it into the column.

```
cell.editable = true;
column.pack_start(cell);
```

We associate the column, cell, and data in our `ListStore` model with the `add_attribute` function. The following code shows that we will modify the `text` property of the `cell` object with the data obtained from column number `0` (which is the value of `columns.NAME`). After everything is set, we append the column into the `view` variable:

```
column.add_attribute(cell, 'text', columns.NAME);
view.append_column(column);
```

Remember in Anjuta we created two columns in the `liststore1` widget so it contains two `gchararray` items? This is to indicate that both the columns are of the type `gchararray` (which is another name for the string). The first column is for holding the `column.NAME` values and the second one for the `column.ADDRESS` values.

Then we connect the edited signal of the cell. What we do in the handler is simply get the new edited text and put it back into our model.

```
cell.signal.edited.connect(function(obj, path, text) {
    var store = view.get_model();
```

We first get the path that is shown in the argument by the `path` variable. We get a path representation that can be interpreted by `ListStore`.

```
var path = new Gtk.TreePath.from_string(path);
var iter = {};
```

In order to set the data, we need to get the `iter` object of the currently edited object. We use the `path` variable and convert it into an `iter` object. After we get the `iter` object, we set the model with the `set_value` function. In `set_value`, we also need to specify the columns that we want to edit.

```
store.get_iter(iter, path);
store.set_value(iter.iter, columns.NAME, text);
```

We add another column for the address; the code for this is the same as the one for the name column.

We add initial data to the model. We add just one line. To add the data, we first need to get the model.

```
var store = view.get_model();
```

Then, we append the `iter` object into the model.

```
var iter = {};
store.append(iter);
```

After this, we put the values using the `iter` object:

```
store.set_value(iter.iter, columns.NAME, "Robert");
store.set_value(iter.iter, columns.ADDRESS, "North Pole");
```

The process of getting and manipulating data seems straightforward. First, we get the model, then the `Iter` object, and then get new values from or add new ones into the model by specifying the column we want to interact with.

Next, instead of using fake data, we use live data by utilizing Evolution Data Server.

The Evolution Data Server (EDS) architecture

EDS abstracts the access and manipulation of an address book, a calendar, and a task. It has a plugin architecture that enables developers to write plugins to access a particular address book, calendar, or task service. An EDS user uses the abstracted API and does not need to know about the details of the service in question. With this approach, GNOME theoretically supports any kind of address book, calendar, or task service. The following diagram briefly shows the structure of the EDS architecture:

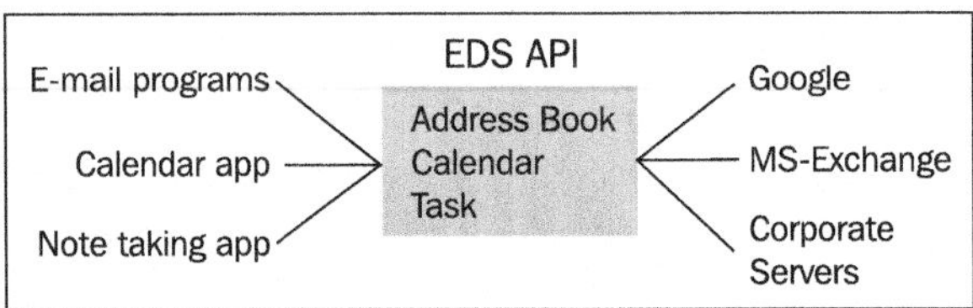

EDS provides a daemon that stays in the memory to serve the users of EDS, which are usually e-mail clients, instant messaging applications, or any applications that need to access data. If the service requires authentication or authorization, GNOME will pop up a dialog so the end user can act upon it, for example, fill in the password, grant access, and so on.

In EDS, an address book has a concept of a data source group, which represents the source of the data, such as a local or remote data source. It is logically represented in the `EBook.SourceGroup` object. Each `SourceGroup` group could have many sources, which represent the actual data source. It is described in the `EBook.Source` object.

Time for action – setting up the address book and the calendar data source

Before you can access the address book and calendar data, we need to set up the data source first. Now we will discuss how to set up a Google account in GNOME. Make sure you already have an active Google account before continuing. Let's see how we can do this:

1. Open **GNOME System Settings**.

2. Open **Online Accounts**.

3. Click on the **+** button in the bottom-left corner of the window.

4. Choose the account type we want to use with GNOME. In this exercise, we choose **Google services**.

5. We will be presented with the login page of the service.

6. Make sure to successfully log in to the service.

7. Grant access to GNOME, notifying it that we want to use this service.

8. After all the online steps have been completed, enable the service we want to use in our computer. In particular, enable the **Contacts** service, which is shown in the following screenshot:

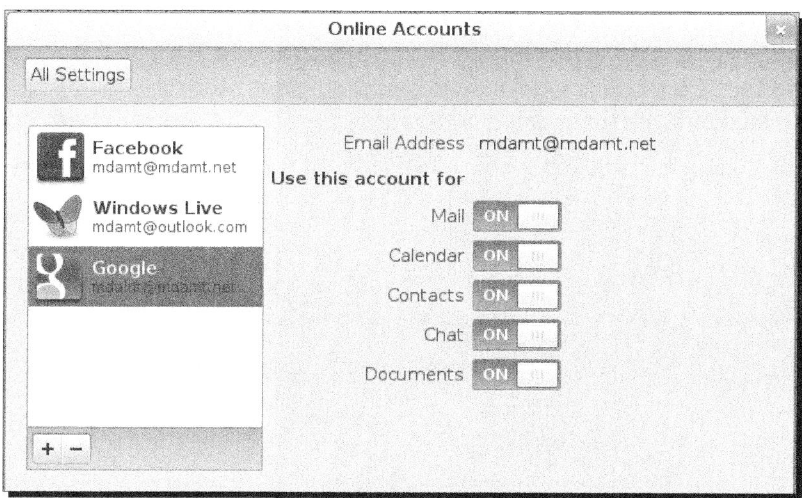

What just happened?

We just connected to our online Google account. It means that the data residing in the Google account is available for us to consume using the GNOME APIs. That is what we are going to do next.

Time for action – accessing the address book

Suppose that we want to create a simple address book program. The data could come from an address book in our local computer or remotely from Google. Follow these steps to do so:

1. Create a new Glade `.ui` file called `address-book.ui`.

2. Add a horizontal box containing two items.

3. Place a `TreeView` widget in the left-hand side of the box. Rename it to `bookView`. When asked for the model, create a new `ListStore` model and rename it to `books`.

4. Rename the `TreeSelection` object, which is created automatically for the `TreeView` widget, to `selection`.

5. Put a `ScrollableWindow` window on the right-hand side of the box.

6. Then, put another `TreeView` widget inside `ScrollableWindow`. Create another `ListStore` model for it and rename it to `contacts`. Rename `TreeView` to `contactView`.

7. Edit the `ListStore` model named `books`. Add two columns inside this model, both with the type `gchararray`.

8. Edit the `ListStore` model named `contact`. Again, add two columns inside the model, both with the type `gchararray`.

9. Our UI design should look similar to the one shown in the following screenshot:

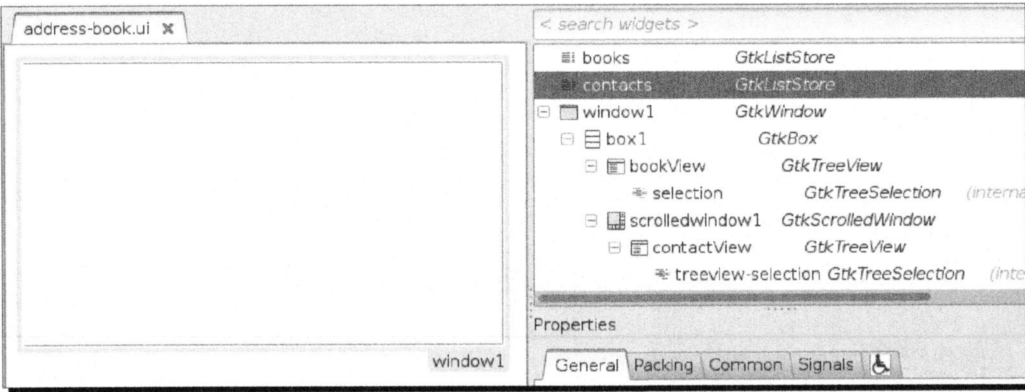

10. Create a new Seed script called `address-book.js`.

11. Following is a block of code that plays a very important part in the execution of the script:

```
Main = new GType({
    parent: GObject.Object.type,
    name: "Main",
    init: function(self) {

      var bookColumn = {
        UID: 0,
        NAME: 1,
      }

      var contactColumn = {
        NAME: 0,
        EMAIL: 1,
      }

      this.listContacts = function(e) {
        var c = {};
```

```
var q = EBook.BookQuery.any_field_contains("");
var r = e.get_contacts_sync(q.to_string(), c, null);
if (r && c && c.contacts && c.contacts.length > 0) {
  var store = self.contact_view.get_model();
  c.contacts.forEach(function(contact) {
    var iter = {};
    store.append(iter);

    var name = contact.full_name;
    if (!name) {
      name = contact.nickname;
    }
    store.set_value(iter.iter, contactColumn.NAME, name);
    store.set_value(iter.iter, contactColumn.EMAIL, contact.
email_1);

  });
  }
}

this.clients = {};

var book_view = ui.get_object("bookView");
var selection = ui.get_object("selection");
selection.signal.changed.connect(function(s) {
  var selected = {}
  s.get_selected(selected);
  var book = selected.model.get_value(selected.iter,
bookColumn.UID);

  var uid = book.value.get_string();
  if (uid == "") {
    return;
  }
  source = self.sources.peek_source_by_uid(uid);
  var e = null;
  if (typeof(self.clients[uid]) !== "undefined") {
    e = self.clients[uid];
    if (e) {
      self.clients[uid] = e;
      self.listContacts(e);
    }
  } else {
    var e = new EBook.BookClient.c_new(source);
    var r = e.open(false, null, function() {
```

```
                    if (e) {
                        self.clients[uid] = e;
                        self.listContacts(e);
                    }
                });
            }

        });

        var cell = new Gtk.CellRendererText();
        var column = new Gtk.TreeViewColumn({title:'Book'});
        column.pack_start(cell);

        column.add_attribute(cell, 'markup', bookColumn.NAME);
        book_view.append_column(column);

        var contact_view = ui.get_object("contactView");
        this.contact_view = contact_view;
        cell = new Gtk.CellRendererText();
        column = new Gtk.TreeViewColumn({title:'Name'});
        column.pack_start(cell);
        column.add_attribute(cell, 'text', contactColumn.NAME);
        contact_view.append_column(column);

        cell = new Gtk.CellRendererText();
        column = new Gtk.TreeViewColumn({title:'E-mail'});
        column.pack_start(cell);
        column.add_attribute(cell, 'text', contactColumn.EMAIL);
        contact_view.append_column(column);


        var s = {};
        var e = EBook.BookClient.get_sources(s);
        this.sources = s.sources;

        var groups = this.sources.peek_groups();
        if (groups && groups.length > 0) {
            var store = book_view.get_model();
            groups.forEach(function(item) {
                var iter = {};
                store.append(iter);

                store.set_value(iter.iter, bookColumn.UID, "");
                store.set_value(iter.iter, bookColumn.NAME, "<b><i>"
+item.peek_name()+ "</i></b>");

                var sources = item.peek_sources();
                if (sources && sources.length > 0) {
```

```
sources.forEach(function(source) {
    store.append(iter);
    store.set_value(iter.iter, bookColumn.UID, source.
peek_uid());
    store.set_value(iter.iter, bookColumn.NAME, source.
peek_name());
    });


        }
    });
}


}
});
```

12. Run the code. The application is executed and a window is displayed, as shown in the following screenshot:

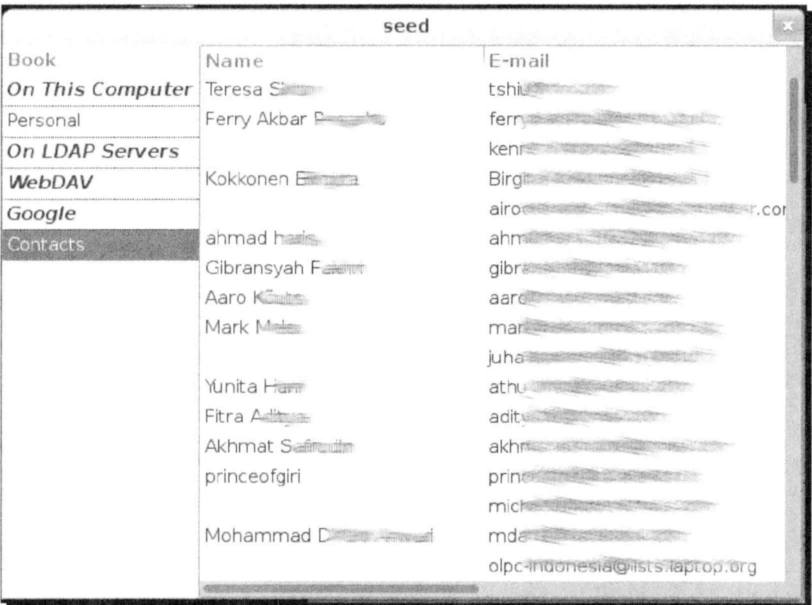

What just happened?

Depending on your settings, the result of our previous exercise might not look the same. (Also pardon the blurry text; they are real e-mail addresses and I want to obfuscate them for privacy reasons.) In the preceding screenshot, EDS returns four sources of address books, namely **On This Computer**, **On LDAP Servers**, **WebDAV**, and **Google**. Out of these sources, only two have the real data; these are **On This Computer** and **Google**. The names of the address books listed in the preceding screenshot are **Personal** and **Contacts**.

When we click on **Contacts**, a list of all the contacts is displayed on the right-hand side of the window. Here we only display two columns, the name and e-mail address.

Let's dig into the source code.

First we define the constants for the columns. Here we have two models, one for address book collection (we call it `books`) and one for contacts collection (we call it `contacts`). Each book has a unique identifier and name. Hence, we use this data for the columns.

```
var bookColumn = {
    UID: 0,
    NAME: 1,
}
```

For the contact, we only display the name and e-mail address, so we will need only two columns.

```
var contactColumn = {
    NAME: 0,
    EMAIL: 1,
}
```

We keep a reference of the `bookView` variable in the `.ui` file and save it in the `book_view` variable in the following line of code:

```
var book_view = ui.get_object("bookView");
```

We also get the `selection` object of the `bookView` variable and put it in the `selection` variable.

```
var selection = ui.get_object("selection");
```

The behavior we want for the selection is that when we select a book, we should get the content of that book. To do that, we need to hook the changed signal to a function, as is shown here:

```
selection.signal.changed.connect(function(s) {
```

What we need to do in the handler first is get the `selected` object from the selection.

```
var selected = {}
s.get_selected(selected);
```

In the `selected` object, we get the `Iter` object, which is kept in the `iter` member. We immediately get the value of column number `0` (which is symbolized with `bookColumn.UID`). The value is in the type string, so we use the `get_string()` function. One specific behavior we set is that whenever the `uid` value is empty, it means that the row does not point to a specific book. It is used by the program to display the address' book source.

```
        var book = selected.model.get_value(selected.iter, bookColumn.
    UID);

        var uid = book.value.get_string();
        if (uid == "") {
            return;
        }
```

If `uid` does have some value, we ask EDS to get `EBook.Source` directly, which is identified by the `uid` value. This will return an `EBook.Source` type that has been saved in the `e` variable.

We keep the sources obtained in the client's cache, so we don't need to reopen the source every time we click on the book. When the cache has the source defined with a `uid` value, we just call the `listContacts` function; otherwise, we need to open it first. After that we will keep it in the cache. Then we list the contents using `listContacts`, as shown in the following code snippet:

```
        source = self.sources.peek_source_by_uid(uid);
        var e = null;
        if (typeof(self.clients[uid]) !== "undefined") {
          e = self.clients[uid];
          if (e) {
            self.clients[uid] = e;
            self.listContacts(e);
          }
        } else {
          var e = new EBook.BookClient.c_new(source);
          var r = e.open(false, null, function() {

            if (e) {
              self.clients[uid] = e;
              self.listContacts(e);
            }
          });
        }

      });
```

Note that we asynchronously open the source by supplying a callback as the argument of the function. With this approach, we can give time for the opening of the source without blocking our application and making it unresponsive to the user. If our source needs to be authorized and needs our attention, a dialog window will pop up at this point.

Here, we define the columns for `bookView`. Visually, we display only a single column, which is the book's title or the book's source group.

```
var cell = new Gtk.CellRendererText();
var column = new Gtk.TreeViewColumn({title:'Book'});
column.pack_start(cell);
```

We use a Pango markup as described in the next part of the code. So we don't use the `text` property of `CellRendererText` but instead use markup and map it to column 1 (which is denoted with `bookColumn.NAME`).

```
column.add_attribute(cell, 'markup', bookColumn.NAME);
book_view.append_column(column);
```

In the following code snippet, we define the columns for the contacts. We have two visual columns, and we'll assign them with the `contactColumn.NAME` and `contactColumn.EMAIL` column names respectively:

```
var contact_view = ui.get_object("contactView");
this.contact_view = contact_view;
cell = new Gtk.CellRendererText();
column = new Gtk.TreeViewColumn({title:'Name'});
column.pack_start(cell);
column.add_attribute(cell, 'text', contactColumn.NAME);
contact_view.append_column(column);

cell = new Gtk.CellRendererText();
column = new Gtk.TreeViewColumn({title:'E-mail'});
column.pack_start(cell);
column.add_attribute(cell, 'text', contactColumn.EMAIL);
contact_view.append_column(column);
```

During initialization, we get the address book's sources with the `get_sources` function. After that, we find the available groups on the system with the `peek_groups` function.

```
var s = {};
var e = EBook.BookClient.get_sources(s);
this.sources = s.sources;

var groups = this.sources.peek_groups();
if (groups && groups.length > 0) {
  var store = book_view.get_model();
```

For each group, we add the book ID and the book name into the table, but we won't fill the `uid` value because we only want to keep the `uid` value of the actual address book source. For the name of the group, we enclose it with a markup of bold and italic style, as shown in the following snippet of code:

```
groups.forEach(function(item) {
    var iter = {};
    store.append(iter);

    store.set_value(iter.iter, bookColumn.UID, "");
    store.set_value(iter.iter, bookColumn.NAME, "<b><i>" +item.peek_
name()+ "</i></b>");
```

Note that we used something that looks like HTML markups in the preceding code snippet. In fact, they are Pango markups, the text rendering engine used in the GNOME framework that is similar to HTML, but with comparatively fewer features. The reason we put the markups here is because we want to style the widget on the presentation layer. Hence, we shouldn't both touch the data and add the style here, but only style it when it is displayed. *However, the previous approach is not correct because we modify the data before putting it into the store.* If we search inside the data, we may not find the data because it is already cluttered with markups. The correct implementation would be to style it in the rendering widget. It means we will no longer be able to use `Gtk.CellRendererWidget`, but we will rather use a custom renderer widget that styles the data before displaying it.

We also try to get the actual address book source for each group with the `peek_sources` function, and put each source that is available in the table. And now we place `uid` in column `0` (`bookColumn.UID`); this is shown in the following code snippet:

```
var sources = item.peek_sources();
if (sources && sources.length > 0) {
    sources.forEach(function(source) {
        store.append(iter);
        store.set_value(iter.iter, bookColumn.UID, source.peek_uid());
        store.set_value(iter.iter, bookColumn.NAME, source.peek_name());
    });
```

Note that column `0` is not visible in the table because we did not add `TreeViewColumn` to it.

What the `listContacts` function does first is prepare the query to the address book. EDS provides the `EBook.BookQuery` object to convey the query to EDS. In the following code snippet, we'll ask EDS to get all the data by creating the query with the `any_field_contains("")` function:

```
this.listContacts = function(e) {
    var c = {};
```

```
var q = EBook.BookQuery.any_field_contains("");
var r = e.get_contacts_sync(q.to_string(), c, null);
if (r && c && c.contacts && c.contacts.length > 0) {
```

The `contacts` member of the object that we passed to `get_contacts_sync` will be populated with the contacts from the address book. For each contact that we get (it is in the form of `EBook.Contact`), we get an interesting property (we want only the `full_name`, nickname, and `email_1` properties) and put it into the model.

```
var store = self.contact_view.get_model();
c.contacts.forEach(function(contact) {
  var iter = {};
  store.append(iter);

  var name = contact.full_name;
  if (!name) {
    name = contact.nickname;
  }
  store.set_value(iter.iter, contactColumn.NAME, name);
  store.set_value(iter.iter, contactColumn.EMAIL, contact.
email_1);

  });
  }
}
```

Have a go hero – saving data to the address book

The previous exercise only displays the contents of the address book. How about making it more advanced by adding an **edit** button?

Whenever we get the edited signal to do this, make sure that the new text is saved back in the `EBook.Contact` structure. When we can call the `e.modify_contact_sync` function, the skeleton could look like this:

```
modifiedContact.full_name = newName;
// and/or
modifiedContact.email_1 = newEmail;
// then save it with
e.modify_contact_sync(modifiedContact, null);
```

We also need to refresh the model by rereading the source.

Summary

The centerpoint of data programming in GNOME is the `TreeView` widgets family. The design of the application should also follow the MVC design pattern of the `TreeView` widget. It is important to keep the model up-to-date, so the user always sees the real data instead of the already obsolete, rendered data. The view is represented primarily by the `TreeViewColumn` object and the `CellRenderer` class. We have many ready-to-use `CellRenderer` classes available in GTK+, but if we need a custom one, we could always make a new one by implementing the interface.

One data source that we examined in this chapter was the EDS. It not only includes the address book but also a calendar, a task, and an e-mail. One prominent application that was created for it was the Evolution program.

Next, we will enable our HTML5 application to be integrated with GNOME 3. Let's see how we will do it in the next chapter.

9
Deploying HTML5 Applications with GNOME

In a mobile world, there is still a debate about whether to develop HTML5 or native applications. People who favor HTML5 will develop an application with HTML5 and then run the application with a UI wrapper written in native code, while the opposite approach is to write the application completely with native code. But how about the desktop world? We will try the HTML5 approach in this chapter, and you can have your own opinion about this debate yourself!

The concept of running HTML5 applications is like running the application in a stripped-down web browser as a wrapper. The UI wrapper for our HTML5 application will be written in Vala, using the GTK+ flavor of the famous WebKit layout engine, which is called **WebKitGTK+**. In this chapter, we will not only learn how to run our HTML5 applications inside a UI wrapper, but will also learn to use GNOME platform as the middleware. Specifically, our topics for this chapter are as follows:

- Embedding WebKit inside our GTK+ application
- Introducing JavaScriptCore
- Interfacing with JavaScriptCore

Let's do this right now!

Before we start

Most of the discussions in this chapter require a moderate knowledge of HTML5, JSON, and common client-side JavaScript programming. One particular exercise uses JQuery and JQuery Mobile to show how a real HTML5 application will be implemented.

Embedding WebKit

What we need to learn first is how to embed a WebKit layout engine inside our GTK+ application. Embedding WebKit means we can use HTML and CSS as our user interface instead of GTK+ or Clutter.

Time for action – embedding WebKit

With WebKitGTK+, this is a very easy task to do; just follow these steps:

1. Create an empty Vala project without GtkBuilder and no license. Name it `hello-webkit`.

2. Modify `configure.ac` to include WebKitGTK+ into the project. Find the following line of code in the file:

```
PKG_CHECK_MODULES(HELLO_WEBKIT, [gtk+-3.0])
```

3. Remove the previous line and replace it with the following one:

```
PKG_CHECK_MODULES(HELLO_WEBKIT, [gtk+-3.0 webkitgtk-3.0])
```

4. Modify `Makefile.am` inside the `src` folder to include WebKitGTK into the Vala compilation pipeline. Find the following lines of code in the file:

```
hello_webkit_VALAFLAGS =  \
        --pkg gtk+-3.0
```

5. Remove it and replace it completely with the following lines:

```
hello_webkit_VALAFLAGS =  \
        --vapidir . --pkg gtk+-3.0 --pkg webkit-1.0  --pkg
libsoup-2.4
```

6. Fill the `hello_webkit.vala` file inside the `src` folder with the following lines:

```
using GLib;
using Gtk;
using WebKit;

public class Main : WebView
{
```

```
public Main ()
{
  load_html_string("<h1>Hello</h1>","/");
}

static int main (string[] args)
{
  Gtk.init (ref args);
  var webView = new Main ();
  var window = new Gtk.Window();
  window.add(webView);
  window.show_all ();

  Gtk.main ();

  return 0;
}
}
```

7. Copy the accompanying `webkit-1.0.vapi` file into the `src` folder. We need to do this, unfortunately, because the `webkit-1.0.vapi` file distributed with many distributions is still using GTK+ Version 2.

8. Run it, you will see a window with the message **Hello**, as shown in the following screenshot:

What just happened?

What we need to do first is to include WebKit into our namespace, so we can use all the functions and classes from it.

```
using WebKit;
```

Our class is derived from the `WebView` widget. It is an important widget in WebKit, which is capable of showing a web page. Showing it means not only parsing and displaying the DOM properly, but that it's capable to run the scripts and handle the styles referred to by the document. The derivation declaration is put in the class declaration as shown next:

```
public class Main : WebView
```

In our constructor, we only load a string and parse it as an HTML document. The string is `Hello`, styled with level 1 heading. After the execution of the following line, WebKit will parse and display the presentation of the HTML5 code inside its body:

```
public Main ()
{
    load_html_string ("<h1>Hello</h1>","/");
}
```

In our `main` function, what we need to do is create a window to put our `WebView` widget into. After adding the widget, we need to call the `show_all()` function in order to display both the window and the widget.

```
static int main (string[] args)
{
    Gtk.init (ref args);
    var webView = new Main ();
    var window = new Gtk.Window();
    window.add(webView);
```

The `window` content now only has a `WebView` widget as its sole displaying widget. At this point, we no longer use GTK+ to show our UI, but it is all written in HTML5.

Runtime with JavaScriptCore

An HTML5 application is, most of the time, accompanied by client-side scripts that are written in JavaScript and a set of styling definition written in CSS3. WebKit already provides the feature of running client-side JavaScript (running the script inside the web page) with a component called **JavaScriptCore**, so we don't need to worry about it.

But how about the connection with the GNOME platform? How to make the client-side script access the GNOME objects? One approach is that we can expose our objects, which are written in Vala so that they can be used by the client-side JavaScript. This is where we will utilize JavaScriptCore.

We can think of this as a frontend and backend architecture pattern. All of the code of business process which touch GNOME will reside in the backend. They are all written in Vala and run by the main process. On the opposite side, the frontend, the code is written in JavaScript and HTML5, and is run by WebKit internally. The frontend is what the user sees while the backend is what is going on behind the scene.

Consider the following diagram of our application. The backend part is grouped inside a grey bordered box and run in the main process. The frontend is outside the box and run and displayed by WebKit. From the diagram, we can see that the frontend creates an object and calls a function in the created object. The object we create is not defined in the client side, but is actually created at the backend. We ask JavaScriptCore to act as a bridge to connect the object created at the backend to be made accessible by the frontend code.

To do this, we wrap the backend objects with JavaScriptCore class and function definitions. For each object we want to make available to frontend, we need to create a mapping in the JavaScriptCore side. In the following diagram, we first map the `MyClass` object, then the `helloFromVala` function, then the `intFromVala`, and so on:

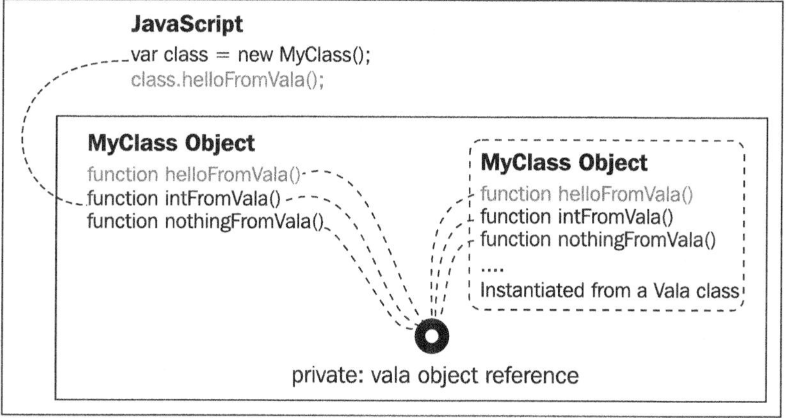

Time for action – calling the Vala object from the frontend

Now let's try and create a simple client-side JavaScript code and call an object defined at the backend:

1. Create an empty Vala project, without GtkBuilder and no license. Name it `hello-jscore`.

2. Modify `configure.ac` to include WebKitGTK+ exactly like our previous experiment.

3. Modify `Makefile.am` inside the `src` folder to include WebKitGTK+ and JSCore into the Vala compilation pipeline. Find the following lines of code in the file:

```
hello_jscore_VALAFLAGS =   \
        --pkg gtk+-3.0
```

4. Remove it and replace it completely with the following lines:

```
hello_jscore_VALAFLAGS =   \
        --vapidir . --pkg gtk+-3.0 --pkg webkit-1.0 --pkg
libsoup-2.4 --pkg javascriptcore
```

5. Fill the `hello_jscore.vala` file inside the `src` folder with the following lines of code:

```
using GLib;
using Gtk;
using WebKit;
using JSCore;

public class Main : WebView
{
  public Main ()
  {
        load_html_string ("<h1>Hello</h1>" +
                    "<script>alert(HelloJSCore.hello())</
script>","/");

        window_object_cleared.connect ((frame, context) => {
                setup_js_class ((JSCore.GlobalContext) context);
        });
  }

  public static JSCore.Value helloFromVala (Context ctx,
        JSCore.Object function,
        JSCore.Object thisObject,
        JSCore.Value[] arguments,
        out JSCore.Value exception) {

        exception = null;

        var text = new String.with_utf8_c_string ("Hello from
JSCore");

        return new JSCore.Value.string (ctx, text);
  }

  static const JSCore.StaticFunction[] js_funcs = {
        { "hello", helloFromVala, PropertyAttribute.ReadOnly },
```

```vala
        { null, null, 0 }
    };

    static const ClassDefinition js_class = {
        0,  // version
        ClassAttribute.None,  // attribute
        "HelloJSCore",  // className
        null,     // parentClass

        null,     // static values
        js_funcs,  // static functions

        null,     // initialize
        null,     // finalize

        null,     // hasProperty
        null,     // getProperty
        null,     // setProperty
        null,     // deleteProperty

        null,     // getPropertyNames
        null,     // callAsFunction
        null,     // callAsConstructor
        null,     // hasInstance
        null     // convertToType
    };

  void setup_js_class (GlobalContext context) {
    var theClass = new Class (js_class);
        var theObject = new JSCore.Object (context, theClass,
context);
        var theGlobal = context.get_global_object ();
        var id = new String.with_utf8_c_string ("HelloJSCore");
        theGlobal.set_property (context, id, theObject,
PropertyAttribute.None, null);
  }

  static int main (string[] args)
  {
    Gtk.init (ref args);
    var webView = new Main ();
    var window = new Gtk.Window();
    window.add(webView);
    window.show_all ();

    Gtk.main ();

    return 0;
  }
}
```

6. Copy the accompanied `webkit-1.0.vapi` and `javascriptcore.vapi` files into the `src` folder. The `javascriptcore.vapi` file is needed because some distributions do not have this `.vapi` file in their repositories.

7. Run the application. The following output will be displayed:

What just happened?

The first thing we do is include the WebKit and JavaScriptCore namespaces. Note, in the following code snippet, that the JavaScriptCore namespace is abbreviated as `JSCore`:

```
using WebKit;
using JSCore;
```

In the `Main` function, we load HTML content into the `WebView` widget. We display a level 1 heading and then call the `alert` function. The `alert` function displays a string returned by the `hello` function inside the `HelloJSCore` class, as shown in the following code:

```
public Main ()
{
  load_html_string("<h1>Hello</h1>" +
          "<script>alert(HelloJSCore.hello())</script>","/");
```

In the preceding code snippet, we can see that the client-side JavaScript code is as follows:

```
alert(HelloJSCore.hello())
```

And we can also see that we call the `hello` function from the `HelloJSCore` class as a `static` function. It means that we don't instantiate the `HelloJSCore` object before calling the `hello` function.

In `WebView`, we initialize the class defined in the Vala class when we get the `window_object_cleared` signal. This signal is emitted whenever a page is cleared. The initialization is done in `setup_js_class` and this is also where we pass the `JSCore` global context into. The global context is where JSCore keeps the global variables and functions. It is accessible by every code.

```
window_object_cleared.connect ((frame, context) => {
                        setup_js_class ((JSCore.GlobalContext)
context);
    });
```

The following snippet of code contains the function, which we want to expose to the client-side JavaScript. The function just returns a `Hello from JSCore` string message:

```
public static JSCore.Value helloFromVala (Context ctx,
        JSCore.Object function,
        JSCore.Object thisObject,
        JSCore.Value[] arguments,
        out JSCore.Value exception) {

    exception = null;

    var text = new String.with_utf8_c_string ("Hello from JSCore");

    return new JSCore.Value.string (ctx, text);
}
```

Then we need to put a boilerplate code that is needed to expose the function and other members of the class. The first part of the code is the `static` function index. This is the mapping between the exposed function and the name of the function defined in the wrapper. In the following example, we map the `hello` function, which can be used in the client side, with the `helloFromVala` function defined in the code. The index is then ended with `null` to mark the end of the array:

```
static const JSCore.StaticFunction[] js_funcs = {
    { "hello", helloFromVala, PropertyAttribute.ReadOnly },
    { null, null, 0 }
};
```

The next part of the code is the class definition. It is about the structure that we have to fill, so that JSCore would know about the class. All of the fields are filled with `null`, except for those we want to make use of. In this example, we use the `static` function for the `hello` function. So we fill the `static` function field with `js_funcs`, which we defined in the preceding code snippet:

```
static const ClassDefinition js_class = {
    0,   // version
    ClassAttribute.None,   // attribute
    "HelloJSCore",   // className
    null,    // parentClass

    null,    // static values
    js_funcs,  // static functions
```

```
        null,      // initialize
        null,      // finalize

        null,      // hasProperty
        null,      // getProperty
        null,      // setProperty
        null,      // deleteProperty

        null,      // getPropertyNames
        null,      // callAsFunction
        null,      // callAsConstructor
        null,      // hasInstance
        null       // convertToType
    };
```

After that, in the the `setup_js_class` function, we set up the class to be made available in the `JSCore` global context. First, we create `JSCore.Class` with the class definition structure we filled previously. Then, we create an object of the class, which is created in the global context. Last but not least, we assign the object with a string identifier, which is `HelloJSCore`. After executing the following code, we will be able to refer `HelloJSCore` on the client side:

```
void setup_js_class (GlobalContext context) {
        var theClass = new Class (js_class);
        var theObject = new JSCore.Object (context, theClass,
context);
        var theGlobal = context.get_global_object ();
        var id = new String.with_utf8_c_string ("HelloJSCore");
        theGlobal.set_property (context, id, theObject,
PropertyAttribute.None, null);
}
```

The real use case of calling Vala code would be more interesting than just calling a static function. Let's see how to call a non-static function from an object created in Vala.

Have a go hero – using a separate HTML file

In our previous section, we put the HTML5 code inside our Vala code. Whenever the code gets lengthier, it will get messier and will be impossible to maintain anymore. How about putting it outside the Vala code, say, in a dedicated file?

Don't continue to our next section just yet before finishing this task!

Time for action – connecting GNOME with client-side JavaScript

Imagine that we want to create a GNOME launcher. We display the available programs in our system with HTML5 and then will be able to launch them. Let us see how this can be done:

1. Create an empty Vala project, without GtkBuilder and no license. Name it `html5-launcher`.

2. Modify `configure.ac` to include WebKitGTK+ and Gee into the project. Find the following line in the file:

```
PKG_CHECK_MODULES(HTML5_LAUNCHER, [gtk+-3.0 ])
```

3. Remove it and replace it completely with the following line:

```
PKG_CHECK_MODULES(HTML5_LAUNCHER, [gtk+-3.0 gee-1.0
webkitgtk-3.0])
```

4. Modify `Makefile.am` inside the `src` folder to include WebKitGKT+, Gio, and JavaScriptCore into the Vala compilation pipeline. Find the following lines of code in the file:

```
html5_launcher_VALAFLAGS =   \
        --pkg gtk+-3.0
```

5. Remove it and replace it completely with the following lines:

```
html5_launcher_VALAFLAGS =   \
        --vapidir . --pkg gee-1.0 --pkg gio-unix-2.0 --pkg gtk+-
3.0 --pkg webkit-1.0 --pkg libsoup-2.4 --pkg javascriptcore
```

6. Fill the `html5_launcher.vala` file inside the `src` folder. For brevity, the shortened content of this file is shown in the following code just to show the important parts of the entire code:

```
public class Main : WebView
{
  public Main ()
  {
    load_uri("file:///%s/index.html".printf(Environment.get_
current_dir()));

    window_object_cleared.connect ((frame, context) => {
                LauncherJSCore.setup_js_class ((JSCore.
GlobalContext) context);
    });
  }
}

// our Vala class
public class Launcher
```

```
  {
    IconTheme icon = null;
    int ICON_SIZE = 80;
    public HashMap<string,DesktopAppInfo> applications {
      get;
      private set;
    }

    public void launch(string name) {
      var app = applications.get(name);
      if (app != null) {
        app.launch(null, new AppLaunchContext());
      }
    }

    public Launcher ()
    {
      icon = IconTheme.get_default ();
      applications = new HashMap<string,DesktopAppInfo>();
      var dir = Dir.open("/usr/share/applications");
      if (dir != null) {
        string entry;
        while (true) {
          entry = dir.read_name();
          if (entry == null) {
            break;
          }
          var appInfo = new DesktopAppInfo.from_filename("/usr/
share/applications/" + entry);
          if (appInfo != null) {
            applications.set(entry, appInfo);
          }
        }
      }
    }

  }

  // Our JSCore wrapper
  public class LauncherJSCore
  {
      public static JSCore.Object js_constructor (Context ctx,
              JSCore.Object constructor,
              JSCore.Value[] arguments,
              out JSCore.Value exception) {

          exception = null;
```

```
        var c = new Class (js_class);
        var newObject = new JSCore.Object (ctx, c, null);

    // register function launch
    var functionName = new String.with_utf8_c_string ("launch");
        var newFunction = new JSCore.Object.function_with_callback
(ctx, functionName, js_launch);
        newObject.set_property (ctx, functionName, newFunction, 0,
null);

    // register function getApplications
    functionName = new String.with_utf8_c_string
("getApplications");
        newFunction = new JSCore.Object.function_with_callback
(ctx, functionName, js_getApplications);
        newObject.set_property (ctx, functionName, newFunction, 0,
null);

        Launcher* launcher = new Launcher ();
        newObject.set_private (launcher);
        return newObject;
    }

    public static JSCore.Value js_getApplications(Context ctx,
      JSCore.Object function,
      JSCore.Object thisObject,
      JSCore.Value[] arguments,
      out JSCore.Value exception) {

        exception = null;

    var launcher = thisObject.get_private() as Launcher;
    StringBuilder json = new StringBuilder("[");

    if (launcher.applications != null) {
      foreach (var key in launcher.applications.keys) {
        var entry = launcher.applications.get(key) as
DesktopAppInfo;
        var name = entry.get_display_name();
        if (entry.get_icon() != null) {
          var icon = launcher.getIconPath(entry.get_icon().to_
string());
          json.append(("{desktop: '%s', name: '%s', icon: '%s'},").
printf (key, name, icon));
        } else {
          json.append(("{desktop: '%s', name: '%s'},").printf (key,
name));
        }
      }
```

```
    }
    if (json.str [json.len - 1] == ',') {
      json.erase (json.len - 1, 1); // Remove trailing comma
    }
    json.append ("]");

    var text = new String.with_utf8_c_string (json.str);
    var obj = ctx.evaluate_script (text, null, null, 0, null);

        return obj;
    }

    public static JSCore.Value js_launch (Context ctx,
            JSCore.Object function,
            JSCore.Object thisObject,
            JSCore.Value[] arguments,
            out JSCore.Value exception) {

        exception = null;

    var launcher = thisObject.get_private() as Launcher;
    if (arguments.length == 1 && arguments[0].is_string(ctx)) {
      var parameter = arguments[0].to_string_copy (ctx, null);
      char buffer[1024];
      parameter.get_utf8_c_string (buffer, buffer.length - 1);
      launcher.launch((string) buffer);
    }
    return new JSCore.Value.undefined (ctx);
    }

    static const ClassDefinition js_class = {
        0,   // version
        ClassAttribute.None,  // attribute
        "Launcher",  // className
        null,     // parentClass

        null,     // static values
        null,     // static functions

        null,     // initialize
        null,     // finalize

        null,     // hasProperty
        null,     // getProperty
        null,     // setProperty
        null,     // deleteProperty

        null,     // getPropertyNames
        null,     // callAsFunction
```

```
        null,    // callAsConstructor
        null,    // hasInstance
        null     // convertToType
    };

    public static void setup_js_class (GlobalContext context) {
    var theClass = new Class (js_class);
        var theConstructor = new JSCore.Object.constructor
(context, theClass, js_constructor);
        var theGlobal = context.get_global_object ();
        var id = new String.with_utf8_c_string ("Launcher");
        theGlobal.set_property (context, id, theConstructor,
PropertyAttribute.None, null);
    }
```

7. Create an HTML5 file with the name of `index.html` and put it in the `src` folder. Fill it with the following lines:

```
<!DOCTYPE HTML>
<html>
<head>
<link rel="stylesheet" href="http://code.jquery.com/mobile/1.1.1/
jquery.mobile-1.1.1.min.css" />
<script src="http://code.jquery.com/jquery-1.7.1.min.js"></script>
<script src="http://code.jquery.com/mobile/1.1.1/jquery.mobile-
1.1.1.min.js"></script>
</head>
<body>
<div data-role="page">
<div data-role="header">
<h1>My Launcher</h1>
</div>
<div data-role="content">
<ul data-role="listview" data-theme="a">
</ul>
</div>

</div>
<script>
$(document).ready(function() {
  var launcher = new Launcher();
  var apps = launcher.getApplications();
  if (apps != null) {
    for (var i = 0; i < apps.length; i ++) {
      var image = $("<img/>").addClass("ui-li-icon").attr("src",
apps[i].icon);
        var link = $("<a/>").attr("href", "#")
```

```
                .text(apps[i].name)
            .attr("data-desktop", apps[i].desktop)
            .addClass("desktop-launcher")
                .append(image)
        var entry = $("<li/>")
                .append(link)
            $("[data-role=listview]").append(entry);
        }
        $("[data-role=listview]").listview('refresh')
    }
    $(".desktop-launcher").click(function() {
        var desktopFile = $(this).attr("data-desktop");
        if (desktopFile) {
            launcher.launch(desktopFile);
        }
    });
});
</script>
</body>
</html>
```

8. Copy the accompanying `webkit-1.0.vapi` and `javascriptcore.vapi` files into the `src` folder.

9. Build and run the application. We should see a launcher as shown in the following screenshot:

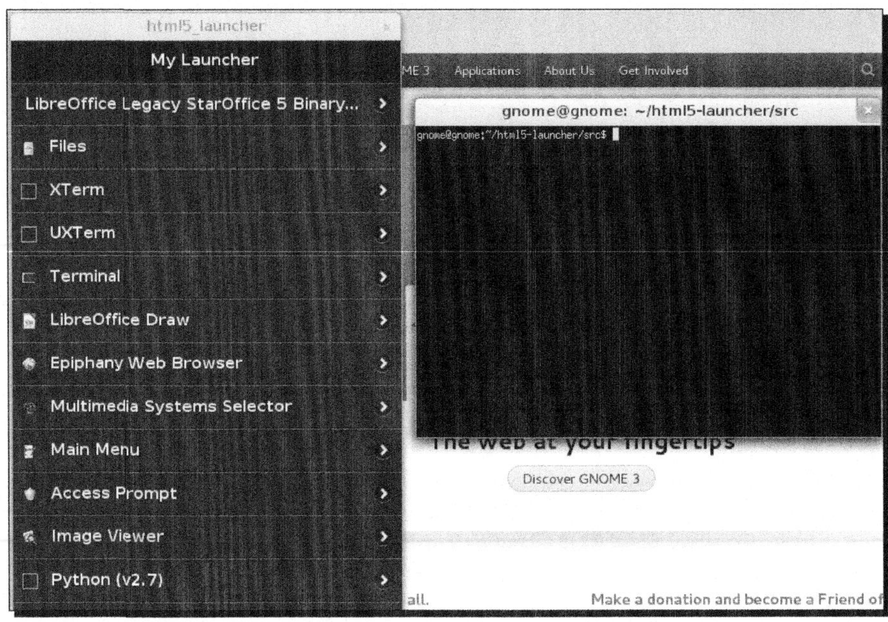

What just happened?

GNOME uses a `freedesktop.org` desktop system. In this system, an application is accompanied with at least one desktop file. This file has a `.desktop` extension and contains information about the application title, icon name, the command which the system must call in order to launch this application, and a set of translations of the application title in many languages when available. What we do in this example is get all the desktop files from the system and display the information contained in them in a menu. And when we click on one of the menu items, our application launches it. The desktop files usually reside in `/usr/share/applications`. So in our simple example, we just get all the files from this folder. Let's see how we do this in detail now.

In this example, we use Gee to make use of the HashMap data structure. This means that we need to include the `Gee` namespace.

```
using Gee;
```

In order to make our Vala code cleaner, we load the HTML5 file from an external file. We also put the object, which needs to be used at the client side, in a separate class, and finally, we put the code needed to set up JSCore in another class. With this separation, our code is better and easy to maintain.

In the constructor of the `Main` class, we load the `index.html` file from the current folder. In real world implementations, the location of the HTML5 file must not be hardcoded and should be flexible. Using a hardcoded location of the file would result in deployment difficulties.

```
public Main ()
{
  load_uri("file:///%s/index.html".printf(Environment.get_current_
dir()));
```

Then, we connect the `LauncherJSCore.setup_js_class` function in the `window_object_cleared` signal.

```
window_object_cleared.connect ((frame, context) => {
            LauncherJSCore.setup_js_class ((JSCore.GlobalContext)
context);
    });
```

Next, we define our Vala class. This class should not use any `JSCore` type system. We call our class `Launcher`.

```
public class Launcher
```

We have a data structure created with a `HashMap` type. It contains the mapping between the desktop filename and the object containing the desktop data structure. The desktop file is represented with the `DesktopAppInfo` object, which is provided by the `Gio` namespace.

```
public HashMap<string,DesktopAppInfo> applications {
  get;
  private set;
}
```

In the `Launcher` constructor, we initialize the `icon` object from `IconTheme` in order to translate the icon name obtained from the `DesktopAppInfo` object into an actual path in the filesystem. We need this because HTML can't display an icon just by its name, but we need to specify the full URI. After this, we initialize the `HashMap` object.

```
public Launcher ()
{
  icon = IconTheme.get_default ();
  applications = new HashMap<string,DesktopAppInfo>();
```

Then we populate the object with all the desktop files found in `/usr/share/applications`. We first create a `Dir` object pointing to the folder mentioned previously, then iterate its `read_name()` function. When the function returns `null`, it means it no longer finds a file and we must exit the `while` loop. If we don't do this, we will end up in an infinite loop and our application would be not responsive. There is no other cure for this than killing the frozen application.

```
var dir = Dir.open("/usr/share/applications");
if (dir != null) {
  string entry;
  while (true) {
    entry = dir.read_name();
    if (entry == null) {
      break;
    }
```

For each filename we get from the `read_name()` function, we must create a `DesktopAppInfo` object of that file. We just instantiate the object by using the `from_filename()` constructor and pass the full path of the desktop file. If the file is not a desktop file, then the instantiation will fail and the value will be `null`. If the value is not `null`, we immediately put the object into the `HashMap` data structure.

```
var appInfo = new DesktopAppInfo.from_filename("/usr/share/
applications/" + entry);
  if (appInfo != null) {
    applications.set(entry, appInfo);
  }
```

Then we prepare a function that does the actual translation of the icon name into the full path of the icon in the filesystem. We use the `lookup_icon()` function and try to find the icon in the current active theme. When we find it, we get the full path of the icon, otherwise we just use the original icon name.

```
public string getIconPath(string name) {
    var i = icon.lookup_icon (name, ICON_SIZE, IconLookupFlags.
GENERIC_FALLBACK);
    if (i != null) {
      return i.get_filename();
    } else {
      return name;
    }
}
```

At last, we have a function to launch an application. What we do first is to get the `DesktopAppInfo` object from the `HashMap` type and call the `launch()` function, which is supplied by `DesktopAppInfo`. For each launched application, we create a new `AppLaunchContext` object, which defines the environment setting of the application.

```
public void launch(string name) {
  var app = applications.get(name);
  if (app != null) {
    app.launch(null, new AppLaunchContext());
  }
}
```

Now, let's shift to our `JSCore` wrapper. The wrapper only contains static functions and by itself is not an object.

```
// Our JSCore wrapper
public class LauncherJSCore
```

The first part of the wrapper is the constructor. This is the constructor of our object whenever we call a new `Launcher` object in our client-side JavaScript. In our constructor, we first create a `JSCore` class based on the class definition we will see later:

```
public static JSCore.Object js_constructor (Context ctx,
        JSCore.Object constructor,
        JSCore.Value[] arguments,
        out JSCore.Value exception) {

    exception = null;
    var c = new Class (js_class);
    var newObject = new JSCore.Object (ctx, c, null);
```

Then, we register the functions that we want to expose to the client side. Here, we register the `launch` and `getApplications` functions. What we do here is to create a `JSCore` string containing the name of the function, then create a `JSCore` object mapped to the function, which we will wrap the Vala function into. In this case, we create a `newFunction` object from the `js_launch` function. Then we use the `set_property()` function to assign the `newFunction` function object with the `functionName` parameter. After this, our function called `launch` is recognized in the `Launcher` object. We need to do this for each function that we want to expose to the client-side JavaScript.

```
// register function helloFromVala
var functionName = new String.with_utf8_c_string ("launch");
    var newFunction = new JSCore.Object.function_with_callback
(ctx, functionName, js_launch);
        newObject.set_property (ctx, functionName, newFunction, 0,
null);
```

Finally, we create and keep the reference of our `Launcher` object and set it as `private` in the `JSCore` object. So, whenever we want to call the Vala function, we just get this object back from the private area and call it from there.

```
Launcher* launcher = new Launcher ();
newObject.set_private (launcher);
return newObject;
    }
```

Let's see each of the wrapping functions we expose to the client-side script. First is the `getApplications()` function.

```
public static JSCore.Value js_getApplications (Context ctx,
    JSCore.Object function,
    JSCore.Object thisObject,
    JSCore.Value[] arguments,
    out JSCore.Value exception) {
```

We set the `exception` value to `null` stating that we don't generate a JavaScript exception.

```
exception = null;
```

As discussed earlier, we can get the Vala object by getting it from the private area with the `get_private()` function and immediately cast it into `Launcher`. Also, we prepare a `StringBuilder` object to keep a JSON representation of the application list. The string is initialized with `[` because we will use JSON as the array of applications. We will concatenate all JSON representations of the desktop files inside this string.

```
var launcher = thisObject.get_private () as Launcher;
StringBuilder json = new StringBuilder ("[");
```

At this point, we must check whether the list's value is `null` or not. If not, we iterate by getting all the keys from the `HashMap` data structure. As we already know, the key contains the name of the desktop file and the value contains the `DesktopAppInfo` object. So, by using the `get()` function in the `HashMap` data structure, we can get the `DesktopAppInfo` object.

```
if (launcher.applications != null) {
    foreach (var key in launcher.applications.keys) {
        var entry = launcher.applications.get(key) as DesktopAppInfo;
```

After we get the `DesktopAppInfo` object, which we put into the entry variable, we get the name of the application with the `get_display_name()` function, and get the icon with the `get_icon()` function. Whenever we can get the actual path of the icon in the filesystem, we create a JSON similar to the following:

```
{desktop: '%s', name: '%s', icon: '%s'}
```

And if we cannot get the actual path of the icon in the filesystem, we create the JSON as shown here:

```
{desktop: '%s', name: '%s'}
```

We do this until all the desktop files are handled and put into the JSON string.

```
        var name = entry.get_display_name();
        if (entry.get_icon() != null) {
            var icon = launcher.getIconPath(entry.get_icon().to_string());
            json.append((("{desktop: '%s', name: '%s', icon: '%s'},").
printf (key, name, icon));
        } else {
            json.append((("{desktop: '%s', name: '%s'},").printf (key,
name));
```

At the end of the loop, we must remove any trailing commas, otherwise the JSCore will fail during the conversion of our JSON string into a `JSCore` object, which we will return in this `JSCore` function.

```
if (json.str [json.len - 1] == ',') {
    json.erase (json.len - 1, 1); // Remove trailing comma
}
```

We terminate the string with `]`, which marks the end of the array.

```
json.append("]");
```

Afterwards, we convert the JSON string into a `JSCore` string. Then convert the JSON string into a `JSCore` object with the `evaluate_script()` function. Finally, we return that object.

```
var text = new String.with_utf8_c_string (json.str);
var obj = ctx.evaluate_script (text, null, null, 0, null);


return obj;
```

The next one is the `launch()` function. In this function, we have an `arguments` parameter in our JavaScript code, which can simply be obtained from the `arguments` parameter in this `JSCore` function. If the `arguments` parameter's `length` property is equal to `1` and the content of the `arguments` variable is a string, then we can say that this is a valid call to this function. In this case, we just call the `launch()` function in the `launcher` object and pass the contents of the `arguments` variable to the function. But before doing so, we need to convert the string coming from the `arguments` variable, that is, the `JSCore` string, into the C string, which is recognized by the Vala function by using the `get_utf8_c_string()` function.

```
public static JSCore.Value js_launch (Context ctx,
        JSCore.Object function,
        JSCore.Object thisObject,
        JSCore.Value[] arguments,
        out JSCore.Value exception) {

    exception = null;

var launcher = thisObject.get_private () as Launcher;
if (arguments.length == 1 && arguments[0].is_string(ctx)) {
  var parameter = arguments[0].to_string_copy (ctx, null);
  char buffer[1024];
  parameter.get_utf8_c_string (buffer, buffer.length - 1);
  launcher.launch((string) buffer);
}
```

In case the call is invalid, then we just return an `undefined` value to the caller.

```
return new JSCore.Value.undefined (ctx);
```

And the following code contains our `JSCore` class definition structure. We fill everything with `null`, except the name of the class with the `Launcher` value and the constructor field pointing to the `js_constructor` function, which we discussed earlier.

```
static const ClassDefinition js_class = {
    0,   // version
    ClassAttribute.None,   // attribute
    "Launcher",   // className
    null,      // parentClass
```

```
        null,     // static values
        null,     // static functions

        null,     // initialize
        null,     // finalize

        null,     // hasProperty
        null,     // getProperty
        null,     // setProperty
        null,     // deleteProperty

        null,     // getPropertyNames
        null,     // callAsFunction
        null,     // callAsConstructor
        null,     // hasInstance
        null      // convertToType
    };
```

At last, the following code snippet shows our `setup_js_class` function, which is called from the `WebView` widget explained earlier. Here, we create an `JSCore` object constructor that points to our `js_constructor` function. Then, we connect the constructor object with the `Launcher` name in the global context. So, whenever the code at the client side mentions `new Launcher()`, the constructor will be called.

```
public static void setup_js_class (GlobalContext context) {
    var theClass = new Class (js_class);
        var theConstructor = new JSCore.Object.constructor (context,
    theClass, js_constructor);
        var theGlobal = context.get_global_object ();
        var id = new String.with_utf8_c_string ("Launcher");
        theGlobal.set_property (context, id, theConstructor,
PropertyAttribute.None, null);
    }
```

We will not go too deep into the `index.html` file, but just look at the following lines of code:

```
var launcher = new Launcher();
var apps = launcher.getApplications();
```

These are the lines that actually call our wrapped Vala code. Nice, isn't it?

> Actually, this HTML-based launcher was really implemented for GNOME. Manokwari. This is a desktop shell for GNOME 3 and is developed with the techniques that we just discussed. Check it out at `http://manokwari.blankonlinux.or.id` and study the source code.

Have a go hero – where to put index.html

It would be nice if we can put the `index.html` file in a different folder that does not contain the `html5-launcher` executable file, for example, if you not only have HTML files, but also CSS, image files, and other files as well. What we can do here is to put a string constant where we can put these assets into and deploy them nicely in the real environment. During development, we can use `src/` or some other folder, but while deploying them, we can use a different folder, for example, `/usr/share/html5-launcher/`.

Summary

In this chapter, we learned how to create an application written in HTML5 that can also communicate with the GNOME platform underneath by utilizing JSCore. To display an HTML5 page, we use the WebKit's `WebView` widget. When there is no communication with the main process, we can display any HTML5 page only by using this widget.

Then we added a business process in our Vala code. We connected the objects created in the Vala code with the client-side JavaScript code, which is defined in the HTML5 page. Unfortunately, we need to use Boilerplate code to start with, and fill the code with our implementation. We need to wrap every function that we want to expose to the client-side code with the `JSCore` function.

With this approach, we can create a full HTML5 application without a web server and do the business process inside our Vala code. This does not stop here as it is only limited by your imagination. For example, if you find that a certain HTML5 feature is not supported by GtkWebKit, you can create your own extension with the same API using Vala.

We will learn how to integrate our application with the GNOME desktop in the next chapter.

10
Desktop Integration

One of the signs that an application is a good application is that it integrates nicely with the platform. Integration means that it can access the platform seamlessly without re-implementing the features just to fake the look and feel instead it gets the features directly from the platform.

In this chapter, the context of the platform is the GNOME desktop. This is one of the central points in the GNOME platform, hence it needs a dedicated chapter. Our main goal is to learn how to utilize some of the the desktop features, namely the session management, launcher, keyring, and notification system. Specifically, this is what we are going to discuss:

- Talking with the GNOME session management
- Launcher installation
- Storing secret data to GNOME Keyring
- The notification system
- Let's start by studying the D-Bus, one of our tools to get the integration done nicely

Talking to each other with D-Bus

D-Bus is an **interprocess communication (IPC)** and a **remote procedure call (RPC)** system used by `freedesktop.org` desktop implementations. GNOME is one of the implementers of this software. D-Bus makes it possible for the applications to talk to each other. It uses a bus system where a party can post a command or query on a bus, and the other parties which listen to the bus can take action upon the requested command. It has three separate channels: **system bus**, **session bus**, and **private bus**.

System bus is dedicated for system-wide messages, such as creating a user and hardware notifications. The bus is run by the system and every D-Bus-aware application run by any user in the system may listen and react to the bus. The second type is the session bus, which is run by the user of the running desktop. Every application which is run by the same user in the same session may listen and react to the bus. The third one is the private bus, which is a point-to-point bus and only the connected parties can talk to each other.

Each application can establish a connection to the bus. Each connection has a name which looks like an inverted internet domain name, for example, `org.gnome.SettingsDaemon.Power`. The application then can expose some services in the bus with an identifier called path. The path looks like a filesystem path, for example, `/org/gnome/SettingsDaemon/Power`.

The application can either expose the services according to a common interface, for example, the `org.freedesktop` interfaces or provide its own interfaces. An interface is exactly like an API that must be implemented properly according to the specification, both by the publisher and by the user of the interface.

Concretely, an application can post a message containing a command to the bus by specifying the connection name and path of the recipient. The application which owns the connection name and exposes the specified path would then react and reply with another message if necessary, depending on the interface.

In another case, an application could also broadcast a message that a signal has been emitted with a specified path. Another application which is interested in the signal can just tap the bus, listen for the emission, and perform something upon receiving the signal.

D-Bus is one of the primary tools to achieve a very good integration with the GNOME desktop. Many features available in the platform are accessible using D-Bus. To get an intuition on how D-Bus helps the integration with GNOME desktop, let's try to listen to the D-Bus session.

You can find more information about D-Bus here:
`http://www.freedesktop.org/wiki/Software/dbus.`

Time for action – listening to D-Bus

To see what is going on over the D-Bus session bus, let's try this experiment:

1. Open the terminal.

2. Type `dbus-monitor` and hit *Enter*.

3. Our screen would be then full of messages coming from D-Bus. Try to increase the sound volume, or access a GNOME main menu, or activate an application. Each of your actions would be broadcasted on the bus.

What just happened?

The `dbus-monitor` command listens to whatever is posted to the session bus. If you are using a laptop computer and it is charging, you may see something like this:

```
signal sender=:1.6 -> dest=(null destination) serial=192 path=/org/
gnome/SettingsDaemon/Power; interface=org.freedesktop.DBus.Properties;
member=PropertiesChanged
    string "org.gnome.SettingsDaemon.Power"
    array [
       dict entry(
          string "Tooltip"
          variant                string "Laptop battery 1 hour 10 minutes
until charged (44%)"
       )
    ]
    array [
    ]
```

The output says that it is displaying a `PropertiesChanged` signal in the `org.freedesktop.DBus.Properties` interface. According to the interface, the signal has three arguments: a string, an array, and another array. This particular signal is exposed in the `/org/gnome/SettingsDaemon/Power` path and broadcasted to everybody. It sends `org.gnome.SettingsDaemon.Power` in the first argument, an array containing a dictionary record, and an empty array.

If we are interested in what is happening on the system bus, give the system argument.

Pop quiz – a good example application?

Q1. With the previous data being posted all the time to the bus, what would be the best example of an application that is suitable to consume the data?

1.   A battery system tray applet

2.   A battery checker application

The GNOME session manager

The GNOME session manager is responsible for a user's desktop environment session. It runs the startup applications and the desktop shell, enables a user to log out, and shut down the computer. The application can even ask the manager to cancel the logout or shutdown. For example, when a user wants to log out but there is an application that has an unsaved document, the logout can be stopped temporarily until the user saves the document or explicitly quits the application.

The session also keeps track of the user's presence, whether the user is available, busy, idle, or invisible. The user can also set a text as the presence status.

Time for action – talking to the session manager

Let's now try to talk to the session manager:

1. Create a script called `session.js`, (available in the source code distribution). The important parts are as follows:

```
var SessionManagerInterface = {
  name: "org.gnome.SessionManager",
  methods: [
      { name: 'CanShutdown', inSignature: '', outSignature: 'b' },
      { name: 'Logout', inSignature: 'u', outSignature: '' },
      { name: 'Shutdown', inSignature: '', outSignature: '' },
      { name: 'Inhibit', inSignature: 'susu', outSignature: 'u' },
      { name: 'Uninhibit', inSignature: 'u', outSignature: '' }
  ]
}

Presence.prototype = {
  _init: function() {
    DBus.session.proxifyObject(this,
        'org.gnome.SessionManager',
        '/org/gnome/SessionManager/Presence');
  }
}

var PresenceInterface = {
  name: "org.gnome.SessionManager.Presence",
  methods: [
      { name: 'SetStatus', inSignature: 'u', outSignature: '' },
      { name: 'SetStatusText', inSignature: 's', outSignature: '' },
  ]
}
```

```
Main = new GType({
  parent: GObject.Object.type,
  name: "Main",
  init: function(self) {
    DBus.proxifyPrototype(SessionManager.prototype,
SessionManagerInterface);
    DBus.proxifyPrototype(Presence.prototype, PresenceInterface);
    this.manager = new SessionManager();
    this.presence = new Presence();
    ...

    var combo = ui.get_object("presenceStatus");
    cell = new Gtk.CellRendererText();
    combo.pack_start(cell);
    combo.add_attribute(cell, "text", 1);

    combo.signal.changed.connect(function(s) {
      var selected = {}
      s.get_active_iter(selected);
      var id = s.model.get_value(selected.iter, 0);
      self.presence.SetStatusRemote(id.value.get_int());
    });

    var textStatus = ui.get_object("textStatus");
    textStatus.signal.changed.connect(function(b) {
      self.presence.SetStatusTextRemote(textStatus.text);
    });

    var logout = ui.get_object("logOut");
    logout.signal.clicked.connect(function(b) {
      self.manager.LogoutRemoteSync(0);
    });

    var shutdown = ui.get_object("powerOff");
    shutdown.signal.clicked.connect(function(b) {
      self.manager.ShutdownRemoteSync();
    });

    var inhibit = ui.get_object("inhibit");
    inhibit.signal.toggled.connect(function(b) {
      if (inhibit.active == 1) {
        inhibit.label = "Uninhibit";
        var window = ui.get_object("window1");
        var xid = window.get_window().get_xid();
        self.inhibitCookie = self.manager.InhibitRemoteSync(applic
ationId,
```

```
          xid,
          "I forbid you to logout",
          1);

      } else {
        self.manager.UninhibitRemoteSync (self.inhibitCookie);
        inhibit.label = "Inhibit";
      }
    });
    window.show_all ();
  }
});
```

2. Alternatively, create a Vala project with GtkBuilder support, and name it
    `session-vala`.

3. Find this line in `src/Makefile.am`.

```
session_vala_VALAFLAGS =   \
        --pkg gtk+-3.0 --pkg gdk-x11-3.0
```

4. Edit it to be like this:

```
session_vala_VALAFLAGS =   \
        --pkg gtk+-3.0
```

5. Create `src/session_vala.vala` with the most important parts as shown in the
    following code:

```
using GLib;
using Gtk;

[DBus (name = "org.gnome.SessionManager")]
interface SessionManager : GLib.Object {
    public abstract bool can_shutdown () throws IOError;
    public abstract void logout (uint32 mode) throws IOError;
    public abstract void shutdown () throws IOError;
    public abstract uint32 inhibit (string appId, uint32 xid,
string reason, uint32 flags) throws IOError;
    public abstract void uninhibit (uint32 cookie) throws IOError;
}

[DBus (name = "org.gnome.SessionManager.Presence")]
interface Presence: GLib.Object {
    public abstract void set_status_text (string text) throws
IOError;
    public abstract void set_status (uint32 mode) throws IOError;
}
```

```vala
public class Main : Object
{
  ...

  public Main ()
  {
      manager = Bus.get_proxy_sync (BusType.SESSION,
        "org.gnome.SessionManager",
        "/org/gnome/SessionManager");

      presence = Bus.get_proxy_sync (BusType.SESSION,
          "org.gnome.SessionManager",
        "/org/gnome/SessionManager/Presence");

    ...
    var combo = builder.get_object ("presenceStatus") as ComboBox;
    var cell = new CellRendererText ();
    combo.pack_start (cell, true);
    combo.add_attribute (cell, "text", 1);

    combo.changed.connect ((object) => {
      TreeIter iter;
      object.get_active_iter (out iter);
      Value value;
      object.model.get_value (iter, 0, out value);
      presence.set_status (value.get_int ());
    });

    var textStatus = builder.get_object ("textStatus") as Entry;
    textStatus.changed.connect (() => {
      presence.set_status_text (textStatus.text);
    });

    var logout = builder.get_object ("logOut") as Button;
    logout.clicked.connect (() => {
      manager.logout (0);
    });

    var shutdown = builder.get_object ("powerOff") as Button;
    shutdown.clicked.connect (() => {
      manager.shutdown ();
    });

    var inhibit = builder.get_object ("inhibit") as ToggleButton;
    inhibit.toggled.connect ((object) => {
      if (object.active == true) {
        object.label = "Uninhibit";
```

```
          var window = builder.get_object("window1") as Window;
          var xid = Gdk.X11Window.get_xid(window.get_window());
          cookie = manager.inhibit("MyApplication",
            (uint32) xid,
            "I forbid you to logout",
            1);
        } else {
          manager.uninhibit(cookie);
          object.label = "Inhibit";
        }
      });


    }


  }
```

6. Create a UI with Glade, call it `session.ui`.

7. Put **Entry**, **ComboBox**, and a set of buttons. The first button is **ToggleButton** and the rest are plain buttons.

8. Give the name `textStatus` to **Entry**, `presenceStatus` to **ComboBox**, `inhibit` to **ToggleButton**, and **logOut** and **powerOff** names to the rest of the **Button** objects respectively.

9. In **ComboBox**, create a new model by clicking on the ellipsis button, and call it as `liststore1`.

10. Following the steps we learned when we did the interaction with data source in *Chapter 8, Playing With Data*, put two fields in `liststore1`. The first data is an integer, which is noted as **gint** and the second one is string, which is **gchararray**.

11. Prefill `liststore1` with these data pairs:

```
0 Available
1 Invisible
2 Busy
3 Idle
```

12. Back to the **presenceStatus** widget, set the **Active** item with 0 value.

13. Save the UI and run the application. We should see the following screenshot:

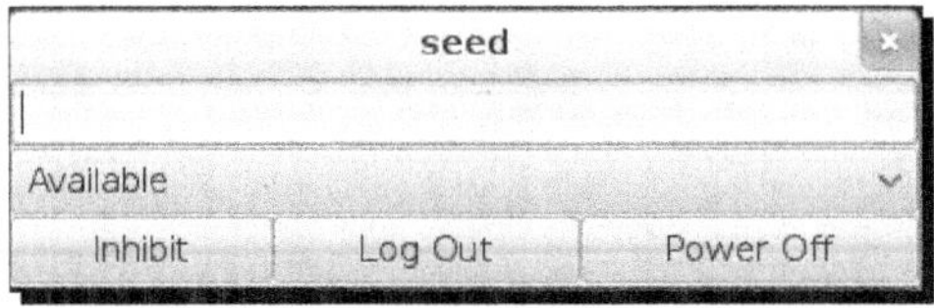

14. We can put a status text by entering text into the textbox. We can change the status of presence by selecting it from the combobox. If we press the **Log Out** button, the session will be closed as soon as we agree to log out, and the same with the **Power Off** button, with the difference that **Power Off** will turn off the computer. If we activate the inhibit button, the logout and power off action will be cancelled.

What just happened?

What we did was, we interacted with the GNOME session manager using the D-Bus API. Our first step is to create a proxy object. What this object does is to act as a bridge to the D-Bus API. So instead of calling the real D-Bus API, which is inaccessible in Seed, we call it through a proxy.

To prepare a proxy, we simply create a JavaScript object with a prototype. We define an initialization function in the object, which in turn calls the `DBus.session.proxifyObject` function. This function creates the connection between the JavaScript function with the D-Bus function calls.

In this experiment, we access two sets of API from the session manager. The first one is `SessionManager` and the second one is `Presence`. This means that we would have two proxy objects installed in our application.

The first proxy is created by specifying the connection name, which is `org.gnome.SessionManager` and the path where the functions are defined and exposed, which is `/org/gnome/SessionManager`.

```
function SessionManager() {
  this._init();
}


SessionManager.prototype = {
  _init: function() {
    DBus.session.proxifyObject(this,
      'org.gnome.SessionManager',
      '/org/gnome/SessionManager');
  }
}
```

After that, we define the interface that we want to map with this object. The interface lists all methods, signals, and properties from the D-Bus world, which we want to access. For our purpose in this example, we only define the connection name and the methods. Note that we have `inSignature` and `outSignature` in the method descriptions. `inSignature` denotes the parameters which we pass into the function and `outSignature` denotes the variables which are returned by the function.

```
var SessionManagerInterface = {
  name: "org.gnome.SessionManager",
  methods: [
    { name: 'CanShutdown', inSignature: '', outSignature: 'b' },
    { name: 'Logout', inSignature: 'u', outSignature: '' },
    { name: 'Shutdown', inSignature: '', outSignature: '' },
    { name: 'Inhibit', inSignature: 'susu', outSignature: 'u' },
    { name: 'Uninhibit', inSignature: 'u', outSignature: '' }
  ]
}
```

Based on the previous description, we have five functions, `CanShutdown`, `Logout`, `Shutdown`, `Inhibit` and `Uninhibit`. These are the functions defined in the `org.gnome.SessionManager` connection.

Not all functions exposed in the connection need to be defined in our proxy. We only need to define the functions that we want to use.

The parameters are passed as a single string, where each character denotes the variable type according to the D-Bus convention. The following table lists the types as copied from the D-Bus specification Version 0.19:

Conventional name	Code	Description
INVALID	0 (ASCII NUL)	Not a valid type code, used to terminate signatures.
BYTE	121 (ASCII "y")	8-bit unsigned integer.
BOOLEAN	98 (ASCII "b")	Boolean value, 0 is FALSE and 1 is TRUE. Everything else is invalid.
INT16	110 (ASCII "n")	16-bit signed integer.
UINT16	113 (ASCII "q")	16-bit unsigned integer.
INT32	105 (ASCII "i")	32-bit signed integer.
UINT32	117 (ASCII "u")	32-bit unsigned integer.
INT64	120 (ASCII "x")	64-bit signed integer.

Conventional name	Code	Description
UINT64	116 (ASCII "t")	64-bit unsigned integer.
DOUBLE	100 (ASCII "d")	IEEE 754 double.
STRING	115 (ASCII "s")	UTF-8 string (*must* be valid UTF-8). Must be null terminated and contain no other null bytes.
OBJECT_PATH	111 (ASCII "o")	Name of an object instance.
SIGNATURE	103 (ASCII "g")	A type signature.
ARRAY	97 (ASCII "a")	An array.
STRUCT	114 (ASCII "r"), 40 (ASCII "("), 41 (ASCII ")")	Struct, type code 114 "r", is reserved for use in bindings and implementations to represent the general concept of a struct, and must not appear in signatures that are used on D-Bus.
VARIANT	118 (ASCII "v")	Variant type (the type of the value is part of the value itself).
DICT_ENTRY	101 (ASCII "e"), 123 (ASCII "{"), 125 (ASCII "}")	Entry in a dict or map (array of key-value pairs). Type code 101 "e" is reserved for use in bindings and implementations to represent the general concept of a dict or dict entry, and must not appear in signatures used on D-Bus.
UNIX_FD	104 (ASCII "h")	Unix file descriptor.
(reserved)	109 (ASCII "m")	Reserved for a "maybe" type compatible with the one in GVariant, and must not appear in signatures used on D-Bus until specified here.
(reserved)	42 (ASCII "*")	Reserved for use in bindings/implementations to represent any *single complete type*, and must not appear in signatures used on D-Bus.
(reserved)	63 (ASCII "?")	Reserved for use in bindings/implementations to represent any basic type, and must not appear in signatures used on D-Bus.
(reserved)	64 (ASCII "@"), 38 (ASCII "&"), 94 (ASCII "^")	Reserved for internal use by bindings/implementations, and must not appear in signatures used on D-Bus. GVariant uses these type codes to encode calling conventions.

The second proxy object is for the Presence API. The API is used for setting the status, both textual and numeric. The numeric status corresponds to the following constants:

- 0 is for available
- 1 is for invisible
- 2 is for busy
- 3 is for idle

> The complete specification of the API can be read at `http://people.gnome.org/~mccann/gnome-session/docs/gnome-session.html`.

The API is defined in the `org.gnome.SessionManager.Presence` connection.

```
Presence.prototype = {
  _init: function() {
    DBus.session.proxifyObject(this,
      'org.gnome.SessionManager',
      '/org/gnome/SessionManager/Presence');
  }
}
```

The interface is shorter, as we only need two functions, `SetStatus` for the numerical status and `SetStatusText` for the textual status.

```
var PresenceInterface = {
  name: "org.gnome.SessionManager.Presence",
  methods: [
    { name: 'SetStatus', inSignature: 'u', outSignature: '' },
    { name: 'SetStatusText', inSignature: 's', outSignature: '' },
  ]
}
```

After we map the functions with the proxy objects, we can't just call the function as we normally do. Seed adds `Remote` and `RemoteSync` as a postfix to all the functions that we defined in the interface in the setup process. So, what our application does is it calls the function name appended with `Remote` or `RemoteSync`. The `RemoteSync` version is the synchronous call while the `Remote` call is the asynchronous version of the function.

The setup process is done when we call the `proxifyPrototype` functions as we do here:

```
    DBus.proxifyPrototype(SessionManager.prototype,
SessionManagerInterface);
    DBus.proxifyPrototype(Presence.prototype, PresenceInterface);
```

It means that based on the interface defined in the interface object, Seed would populate the `Remote` and `RemoteSync` function calls in the prototype. As we learned in *Chapter 3, Programming Languages*, in JavaScript we can add functions as members of an object.

Next, we initialize some variables to be an instance of the newly created proxy objects:

```
this.manager = new SessionManager();
this.presence = new Presence();
```

In our previous experience of handling a data source in *Chapter 8, Playing With Data*, we used a ListStore as a model to keep our data. Now, we do it again. But instead of using a TreeView, here we have a ComboBox. The ComboBox also uses the MVC design pattern and uses the ListStore as the model. Same with TreeView, we need a renderer to actually display the data on the screen. Again, we use `CellRendererText` to do this task as shown in the following code snippet:

```
var combo = ui.get_object("presenceStatus");
cell = new Gtk.CellRendererText();
combo.pack_start(cell);
combo.add_attribute(cell, "text", 1);
```

After that, we connect the `changed` signal of the ComboBox to a handler. In this handler, what we do is to get the current `Iter` object of the ComboBox, get the integer value of the `iter` object, and call `SetStatusRemote` of the `Presence` proxy object. As we discussed previously, the `SetStatusRemote` function in Seed code is actually the `SetStatus` function in the D-Bus side. We pass an integer in `SetStatusRemote`, this matches with the value of `u` that we defined in the `SetStatus` function's `inSignature` member of the interface object.

```
combo.signal.changed.connect(function(s) {
  var selected = {}
  s.get_active_iter(selected);
  var id = s.model.get_value(selected.iter, 0);
  self.presence.SetStatusRemote(id.value.get_int());
});
```

Then, we connect the changed signal of the `textStatus` widget, and upon receiving the signal we call the `SetStatusTextRemote` function. We pass `textStatus.text`, which is a string, and it matches with the `s` value `inSignature` of the `SetStatus` function we defined in the interface object.

```
var textStatus = ui.get_object("textStatus");
textStatus.signal.changed.connect(function(b) {
  self.presence.SetStatusTextRemote(textStatus.text);
});
```

The next widget on our list is the `logOut` widget. We handle the `clicked` signal by calling `LogoutRemoteSync` by passing a `0` value into it. In the GNOME Session Manager documentation, `0` means that we simply want to log out. `1` means that the logout process is done without prompting the user. Finally, a value of `2` means that the logout process is forcefully done, without prompt and ignoring any inhibitors.

```
var logout = ui.get_object("logOut");
logout.signal.clicked.connect(function(b) {
    self.manager.LogoutRemoteSync(0);
});
```

Next one is the `powerOff` widget. When this button is pressed, what we want is to initiate the shutdown process. To do this, we call the `ShutdownRemoteSync` function:

```
var shutdown = ui.get_object("powerOff");
shutdown.signal.clicked.connect(function(b) {
    self.manager.ShutdownRemoteSync();
});
```

Finally, we need to handle the `inhibit` ToggleButton. We handle the two states of the button, when it is active and when it is in normal state. In the active state, we change the label to `Uninhibit` to show that the behavior has now changed, and we ask `SessionManager` to register ourselves as the inhibitor. When there is an inhibitor, any logout process will be cancelled. To do this, we call `InhibitRemoteSync`. The return value is a cookie which we must pass to `inhibit`. We use this cookie when calling `UninhibitRemoteSync` in the opposite state of the ToggleButton. After calling this, the logout process would be normal again.

```
var inhibit = ui.get_object("inhibit");
inhibit.signal.toggled.connect(function(b) {
    if (inhibit.active == 1) {
        inhibit.label = "Uninhibit";
        var window = ui.get_object("window1");
        var xid = window.get_window().get_xid();
        self.inhibitCookie = self.manager.InhibitRemoteSync(application
Id,
            xid,
            "I forbid you to logout",
            1);

    } else {
        self.manager.UninhibitRemoteSync(self.inhibitCookie);
        inhibit.label = "Inhibit";
    }
});
```

Now let's inspect the Vala code. How it works is the same with the Seed code, but take a look at how we call the D-Bus functions. First, we need to create the interface of the classes and methods that we want to use.

We have a `DBus` attribute mentioned, followed with the name of the connection:

```
[DBus (name = "org.gnome.SessionManager")]
```

Then we define the interface and derive `GLib.Object` so that we can also handle signals. For each method, we convert the original function name, which is written in camel case (the first character of each word is written in uppercase and the words are concatenated together without any delimiters), into lowercase words joined together with underscores. For example, the `CanShutdown` function must be converted to `can_shutdown`. Each method must be declared to throw the `IOError` exception, and the arguments are written in Vala style using Vala-native data types.

```
interface SessionManager : GLib.Object {
    public abstract bool can_shutdown () throws IOError;
    public abstract void logout (uint32 mode) throws IOError;
    public abstract void shutdown () throws IOError;
    public abstract uint32 inhibit (string appId, uint32 xid, string
reason, uint32 flags) throws IOError;
    public abstract void uninhibit (uint32 cookie) throws IOError;
}
```

We declare all interfaces first before using them, so the `Presence` interface and `SessionManager` must be declared as shown here:

```
[DBus (name = "org.gnome.SessionManager.Presence")]
interface Presence: GLib.Object {
    public abstract void set_status_text (string text) throws IOError;
    public abstract void set_status (uint32 mode) throws IOError;
}
```

Then we need to create the proxy objects of these interfaces. We use `get_proxy_sync`, mapping the connection names and the paths of these interfaces. If the results are not null, then they are ready to use.

```
manager = Bus.get_proxy_sync (BusType.SESSION,
    "org.gnome.SessionManager",
    "/org/gnome/SessionManager");

presence = Bus.get_proxy_sync (BusType.SESSION,
    "org.gnome.SessionManager",
    "/org/gnome/SessionManager/Presence");
```

At this point, the `manager` and `presence` objects should be already connected to the D-Bus objects.

Compared with the Seed counterpart, calling the methods in Vala is simpler. One can just call the function name directly and pass the arguments if any. For example, the `shutdown` function can be called using just the following code snippet:

```
manager.shutdown();
```

Have a go hero – checking all nulls

As discussed previously, all proxy objects are not guaranteed to be connected to D-Bus. For example, when a service provider of a certain connection or path is not installed, then the connection will fail and the variable value will be null.

Go ahead, revisit our code and check on every occurrence of the proxy objects. If the value is not null, the code can go forward; but if it is null, we need to do something. Think of a good strategy for handling this case.

Launcher

Launcher is the place where a user runs an application by clicking on its icon. In GNOME Shell the launcher is accessible in the **Applications** tab, in the **Activities** menu. The applications are listed categorically, showing the icons, the title, and the descriptions of the application. The title and the descriptions are nicely localized. The applications can also be filtered by searching.

In the previous version of GNOME or in the GNOME Fallback mode, the launcher is in the GNOME panel. The applications are also listed categorically and the title and the descriptions are also localized.

We have seen the way to list the applications in *Chapter 9, Deploying HTML5 Applications with GNOME*, although not exactly in the same order with GNOME Shell or GNOME panel. The essential part of the experiment was to load the information contained in the desktop files. So, in order to make an application's icon appear in the launcher, we need to create a desktop file for it.

Time for action – putting our application in the launcher

Now let's try to create a launcher for our previous application:

1. Rename `session.js` as `session-tester` (without any extension).

2. Modify the UI loader part to open `/usr/share/session-manager-test/session.ui`, and modify the following line:

```
ui.add_from_file("session.ui");
```

3. Modify it to:

```
ui.add_from_file("/usr/share/session-manager-test/session.ui");
```

4. Prepare a new text file, name it as `session-manager-test.desktop`, and fill it with the following code:

```
[Desktop Entry]
Name=Session Manager Test
Comment=Testing the interaction with GNOME session manager
OnlyShowIn=GNOME;
Exec=session-tester
Icon=help-browser
StartupNotify=true
Terminal=false
Type=Application
Categories=GNOME;GTK;Settings
```

5. Install the UI file into the `/usr/share/session-manager-test` directory (create the directory if you have not done so!), the desktop file to `/usr/share/applications`, and the `session-tester` script into `/usr/bin`.

6. Open the **Activities** menu in GNOME Shell, navigate through the **Applications** tab, and look for **Session Manager Test**, you'll find it!

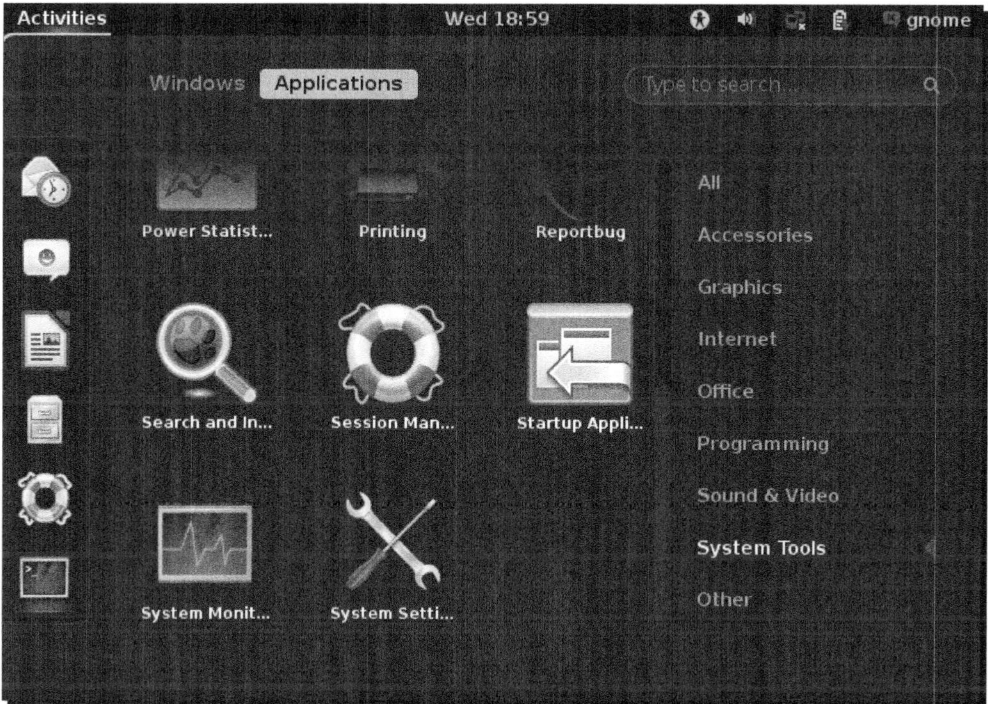

What just happened?

What we did was a simple modification to the script to load the UI file in the system-wide configuration. This process must be done in all deployments of our applications, but this is a pretty bad example because we hardcode the path of the UI file. One way to avoid hardcoding the path is to keep a configuration file. Revisit *Chapter 4, Using GNOME Core Libraries*, to access the configuration system.

Next, we created a desktop file. It is started with the following line:

```
[Desktop Entry]
```

Then, we specify the name of the application. The following is the text which will be displayed in the launcher:

```
Name=Session Manager Test

Comment=Testing the interaction with GNOME session manager
```

`OnlyShowIn` defines the launcher in which this application would appear. If, for example, we add Unity, the application would only appear in Unity and GNOME.

```
OnlyShowIn=GNOME;
```

Next, we define the name of the executable. This is the name of the application that we install into `/usr/bin`.

```
Exec=session-tester
```

Then, we define the icon which is used in the launcher. Here, we just steal an icon from the `help-browser` application. In real applications, we should provide our own icon.

```
Icon=help-browser
StartupNotify=true
```

After that, we specify that we don't need a terminal to run our application. If we provide, for example, bash script; we may need to ask the terminal to open it if there is no hashbang or missing the executable permission.

```
Terminal=false
```

Next, we define our application as, of course, `Application`:

```
Type=Application
```

Finally, we tell the launcher that our application should fall into these categories. In the launcher, we can simply see our application reside in **System Tools** which maps to `Settings`.

```
Categories=GNOME;GTK;Settings
```

The launcher normally listens for any changes that we did in all files in `/usr/share/applications`. So whenever we put a new file or modify the existing one, the changes will automatically be seen almost instantly in the launcher, so we don't need to restart the desktop.

You can find the formal specification of the contents of desktop files at `http://standards.freedesktop.org/desktop-entry-spec/latest/index.html`.

GNOME keyring

Many use cases of real-life applications involve storing passwords, secret data, or keys. Implementing the storage for this kind of data is hard and requires special skills in the security field. GNOME Keyring is the secret data storage infrastructure available on the GNOME platform. Applications that use GNOME Keyring can save passwords, secret data, or keys in the keyring and retrieve them later when needed.

The keyring is protected and associated with the user account. It can be configured so that whenever a user logs in to the system, the keyring is automatically available to the application and when the user logs out, the keyring is also closed. Otherwise, the keyring can be opened using a password.

The keyring has an accompanying application called **Seahorse**. It is an application which can display the stored secret data within the user's session. The integration which we aim for is not to replace Seahorse, but just to keep the data secure in the keyring. However, we could still inspect the data using Seahorse.

Time for action – storing passwords securely

Unfortunately, we will do this only with Vala, as `gir-1.2` which is required by Seed doesn't include the necessary function to store the password easily.

1. Create a new empty Vala object without GtkBuilder, let's call it `keyring`.

2. Open `configure.ac` and find this line: `PKG_CHECK_MODULES(KEYRING, [gtk-3.0 ])`. Modify the whole line to look like the following code:

   ```
   PKG_CHECK_MODULES(KEYRING, [gnome-keyring-1 ])
   ```

3. Open `src/Makefile.am` and find the following line:

   ```
   keyring_SOURCES = \
       keyring.vala config.vapi

   keyring_VALAFLAGS =  \
       --pkg gtk+-3.0
   ```

4. Modify the whole line to look like the following:

```
keyring_SOURCES = \
  keyring.vala config.vapi gnome-keyring.vapi

keyring_VALAFLAGS =  \
  --pkg gnome-keyring-1
```

5. Create a new file in the `src/` directory, call it `gnome-keyring.vapi`, and fill it with the following lines:

```
[CCode (cprefix = "GnomeKeyring", lower_case_cprefix = "gnome_
keyring_")]
namespace GnomeKeyringOverrides {
[Compact]
public struct PasswordSchemaAttribute {
  public unowned string name;
   public GnomeKeyring.AttributeType type;
     }

     [Compact]
     [CCode (cheader_filename = "gnome-keyring.h")]
     public struct PasswordSchema {
             public GnomeKeyring.ItemType item_type;
             [CCode(array_length = false)]
             public PasswordSchemaAttribute[] attributes;
     }
     [CCode (cheader_filename = "gnome-keyring.h")]
     public static void* store_password (GnomeKeyringOverrides.
PasswordSchema schema,
string? keyring, string display_name, string password, owned
GnomeKeyring.OperationDoneCallback callback, ...);

     [CCode (cheader_filename = "gnome-keyring.h")]
     public static void* find_password (GnomeKeyringOverrides.
PasswordSchema schema,
owned GnomeKeyring.OperationGetStringCallback callback, ...);
}
```

6. Open `src/keyring.vala` and use the following code:

```
using GnomeKeyring;

public class Main : Object
{
  private const GnomeKeyringOverrides.PasswordSchema secretData =
{
    ItemType.GENERIC_SECRET,
    {
```

```vala
      { "name", AttributeType.STRING },
      { null, 0}
    }
  };

  public void returning_password_callback(Result result, string?
password) {
    if (result == Result.OK) {
      stdout.printf ("Password is: %s\n", password);
    } else {
      stdout.printf ("Failed, code: %d\n",(int) result);
    }
  }

  public void store_password_callback(Result result) {
    if (result == Result.OK) {
      GnomeKeyringOverrides.find_password (
        secretData,
      returning_password_callback,
        "name", "myuser",
      null);
    } else {
      stdout.printf ("Failed, code: %d\n",(int) result);
    }
  }

  public Main ()
  {
    GnomeKeyringOverrides.store_password (
        secretData,
      null,
        "My Application Password",
        "this-is-a-password",
        store_password_callback,
        "name", "myuser",
      null);
  }

  static int main (string[] args)
  {

    var app = new Main ();

    var loop = new MainLoop();
        loop.run ();
    return 0;

  }
}
```

7. Build the application, but don't run it just yet!

8. Open the **Activities** menu in GNOME Shell, find the **Seahorse** application, and run it. You should see some entries inside (or even empty), but no entry with the name **My Application Password**. Exit Seahorse.

9. Run our application, it will display the following:

```
Password is: this-is-a-password
```

10. It keeps running, but after a while you can kill it by pressing the *Ctrl + C* keys combination.

11. Run Seahorse again, we should see an entry called **My Application Password**. If we click it, we should be able to see the password, which is **this-is-a-password**.

What just happened?

What we did was we saved a user password into the GNOME Keyring system. This password can be recovered later when we need it, as demonstrated by the application in the previous section. Do you use the "remember password" feature in a web browser? When we use this feature, the browser prefills the password field with the saved password. But instead of keeping the password to ourselves, we store this in GNOME Keyring.

Unfortunately, the Vala function and class mapping of GNOME Keyring distributed in many popular distributions have wrong information, so we can't use them as it is. In *Chapter 9, Deploying HTML5 Applications with GNOME*, we tried to replace the original `.vapi` file with a custom `.vapi` file. But now, we put an override file which fixes the incorrect information rather than replacing the whole file. The override file, which we call `gnome-keyring.vapi` is included in the build phase as shown in point 4 of our previous action in the *Time for action – storing passwords securely* section.

The content of the override is the functions and class member that replace the original version, which was wrongly written. Here, we have the overrides for the `store_password` and `find_password` functions, and the `PasswordSchema` structure. We can't just replace the original version, but we need to use a different namespace. In this example, we use the `GnomeKeyringOverrides` namespace.

So whenever we want to use the original version, we use `GnomeKeyring`, and when we want to use the overridden version, we use the `GnomeKeyringOverrides` namespace.

Before using the `store_password` and `find_password` functions, we need to define the structure of the data that we want to keep. In the following code snippet, we describe a structure which we call `secretData`. The data only has one field, which we call `name`. What we want to do with this data is that we want to store a password associated with a name. We end the structure with a pair of `null` and `0` as the end-of-structure mark.

```
private const GnomeKeyringOverrides.PasswordSchema secretData = {
  ItemType.GENERIC_SECRET,
  {
    { "name", AttributeType.STRING },
    { null, 0}
  }
};
```

In the previous example, we use the asynchronous version of the store and find password functions. It means that when we call this function, it returns from the function immediately. We process the success of the function in another callback function. If we choose the synchronous version (the function names end with the `sync` postfix) and there is something heavy running in the GNOME Keyring side, our application could freeze until the operation is completed; but this won't happen with the asynchronous calls.

As said, we need to prepare a couple of callback functions. The first one is for the `find_password` function. We get the result in the `result` variable, and the password in the `password` variable. Note the question mark in the type definition of password which means that the content may be null. This is true whenever the result is not the value of `Result.OK`. The function is used to just simply print the password or the error code when it fails. In real applications, this should inject the returned password into a field or some other element which requires the password content.

```
public void returning_password_callback(Result result, string?
password) {
    if (result == Result.OK) {
      stdout.printf ("Password is: %s\n", password);
    } else {
      stdout.printf ("Failed, code: %d\n",(int) result);
    }
}
```

Then we have the callback for the `store_password` function. It checks the `result` value, and if it is a successful one, we just try to get the password with the `find_password` function. In real applications, this could just simply show a notification that the password has been saved or just quietly do something else.

```
public void store_password_callback(Result result) {
    if (result == Result.OK) {
      GnomeKeyringOverrides.find_password (
        secretData,
      returning_password_callback,
        "name",  "myuser",
      null);
    } else {
      stdout.printf ("Failed, code: %d\n",(int) result);
    }
}
```

In main function, we simply store the **this-is-a-password** password in an area called **My Application Password**. We associate the password with the `myuser` string. In real applications, the association could be extended. For example, for a network password, the additional data needed could be extended to the server name, port number, service path, and so on. We end the function with `null` to mark it as the end of the data. If we have the extended data structure, we should keep passing the needed data as the parameter of the function, according to the order defined in the structure, and end it with `null`.

```
public Main ()
{

    GnomeKeyringOverrides.store_password (
```

```
      secretData,
   null,
     "My Application Password",
     "this-is-a-password",
     store_password_callback,
     "name", "myuser",
   null);
}
```

Notification system

An application may need to inform users about an event which is happening. When the application is active and the user is currently using it, the information may be simply displayed inside the application. But what happens if the application is currently running but stays in the background or is being minimized? The user would not be able to see the information. This is not good, especially when the piece of information is a very important one. For this purpose we should use the notification system, which is available to users at all times.

GNOME has **libnotify** as its notification system. The main process runs as a **daemon**, a program that never quits and only exits when the desktop is closed. It listens to all application requests to display the notifications. Upon receiving the request, it displays the notification text at the bottom of the screen. `Application` simply uses the library to send the notification to the daemon.

Time for action – sending notifications

Let's now try to send some notification:

1. Create a new Seed script called `notification.js`.

2. Fill it with the following code:

```
#!/usr/bin/env seed

GLib = imports.gi.GLib;
Notify = imports.gi.Notify;
GObject = imports.gi.GObject;

Main = new GType({
  parent: GObject.Object.type,
  name: "Main",
  init: function() {
    Notify.init('Test Application');
    var n = new Notify.Notification({
```

```
        summary: 'This is a notification text',
        body: 'This is a longer version of the notification text',
        });
    n.add_action('ok-button', 'OK', function() { n.close()});
    n.show();
  }
});

var main = new Main();
var context = GLib.main_context_default();
var loop = new GLib.MainLoop.c_new(context);
loop.run();
```

3. Run it. Note that the notification text is truncated. It is shown momentarily at the bottom of the screen and if we move our mouse close to the text, the container of the text will expand, showing all the portions of the text. It will also display the **OK** button. But as soon as we move out from the area, the text will disappear. If we do not press the **OK** button, the notification will stay at the bottom-right corner of the screen.

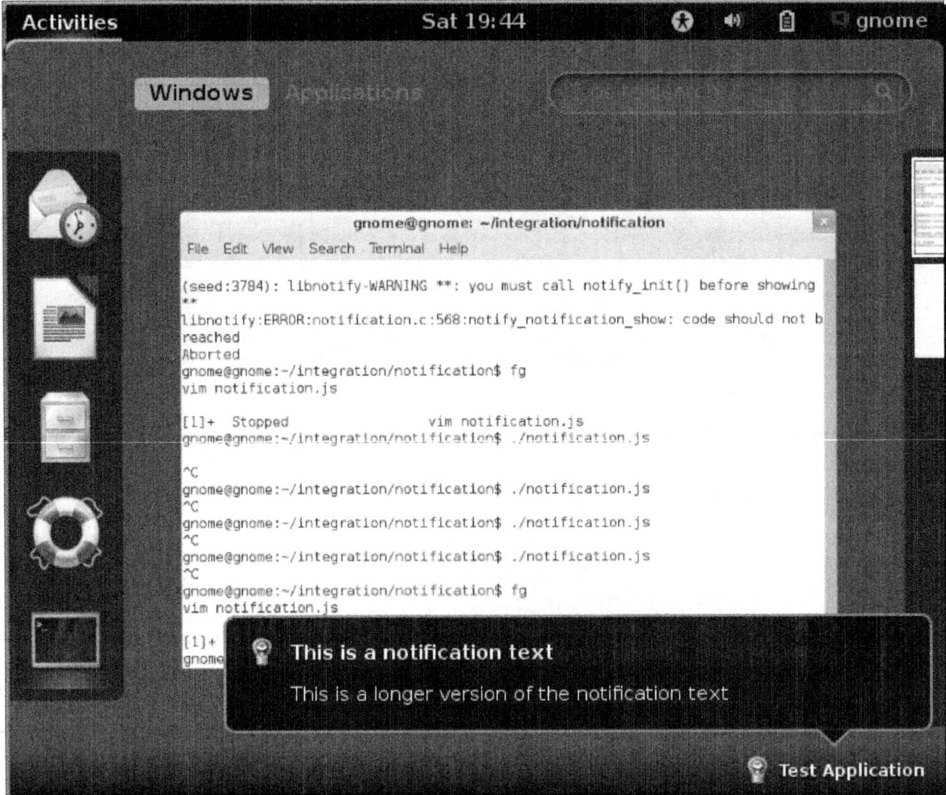

What just happened?

What we did was just a simple function call to `libnotify`. First we need to declare it by performing an import from `Notify`:

```
Notify = imports.gi.Notify;
```

Before calling any function from `libnotify`, we must call the `init` function. Otherwise no other function can be called successfully.

```
Notify.init('Test Application');
```

Then we create a new notification object. One object can hold one notification text. We set the text, the summary, and the body in the constructor. The `summary` section is the short text that would appear initially on the screen. The `body` section is the longer text that is displayed by placing the mouse cursor inside the notification area. With Seed, we could pass these texts in an object.

```
var n = new Notify.Notification({
  summary: 'This is a notification text',
  body: 'This is a longer version of the notification text',
});
```

Then we add an `OK` button. We simply close the notification whenever the button is clicked. The action is attached with an anonymous function as defined here.

```
n.add_action('ok-button', 'OK', function() { n.close()});
```

When we want to show the notification, we can just call the `show` function:

```
n.show();
```

Our notification would remain in the notification area—even when our program is closed—until the **OK** button is pressed.

Have a go hero – displaying an icon

Let's try to display an icon inside our notification. It's very easy to do, we could just put an icon name in the `icon` field of the object we pass in the constructor.

Summary

In this chapter we have learned about integration to some important parts of the desktop, namely the session management, launcher, keyring, and notification system. We introduced ourselves to D-Bus. Then we discussed about accessing the features using the D-Bus API as well as the usual library API.

We now know that we can create an application which can initiate a logout or shutdown process and we also know how to inhibit the Session Manager from continuing the process. We know how to make our application visible in the launcher by installing the desktop file into the `/usr/share/applications` directory. We learned how to store sensitive data into the keyring and retrieve it when we need it. Finally we discussed how to display a notification that is displayed by the desktop. With these experiences, we can leverage our applications to be fully integrated with the GNOME desktop.

We also learned the trick to overcome wrong `.vapi` supplied by many popular distributions by creating an override file.

The next chapter discusses the aspects that we have to pay attention to when our application goes global. So if we want our application to be successful on an international level, we must not miss it.

11
Making Our Applications Go International

GNOME has a very good track record as far as internationalization is concerned (often abbreviated as i18n), which is a method of designing applications that can be adapted in various languages and regional settings without any engineering changes. Since its early versions, GNOME already supported many languages and regions. This provides us with a good choice to also make our applications ready to be deployed anywhere in the world.

This chapter is very important if we aim to distribute our applications in countries outside the United States. Why? Because, by default, GNOME (and other subsystems) uses English as the interface language and uses the U.S. date, time, number, and monetary formats. When we target our market outside the U.S., we need to follow the steps discussed in this chapter. Specifically, this chapter is about understanding the following topics:

- Locale introduction
- Bootstrapping an i18n infrastructure
- Translating the UI text
- The localization process

Now, let's start!

Understanding locale

Internally, GNOME uses the **Portable Operating System Interface (POSIX)** locale system to make i18n work. A **locale** contains a set of cultural parameters written in a specified script in a particular variant of a language spoken in a certain territory. The parameters include the character set used in the locale, the language code, and the presentation of date and time, number, currency, address, telephone, and measurement.

Each locale is identified with a locale code. This code is defined in the following format:

```
language[_territory][.codeset][@modifier]
```

For example, the locale of the Aceh language spoken in Indonesia, which is written in the Jawi script in a UTF-8 character set, is coded as `ac_ID.UTF-8@Jaw`. The parts in square brackets are sometimes omitted when it is less ambiguous. The language part of the code is coded in ISO-639, the territory is coded in ISO-3166, and the script is coded in ISO-15924 standards.

Each parameter can have a different locale assigned to it. For example, we can use a fully Dutch-translated desktop, but use a Western Arabic numeric format and U.S. measurement and monetary settings. However, GNOME only provides limited settings to reduce confusion.

The settings are applied to the system usually when the user logs in to the desktop. If the user did not choose a locale during installation, the system usually uses a C locale (also known as the POSIX locale). POSIX itself is an international standard issued by IEEE for maintaining compatibility between operating systems. The standard includes the POSIX locale, which is the base locale that then can be extended to support other cultural preferences.

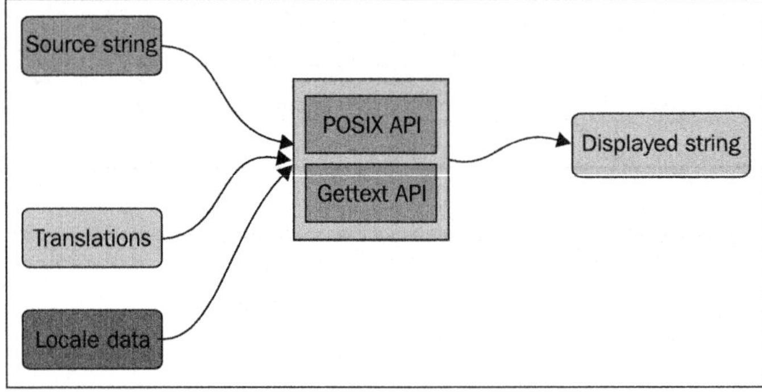

The preceding diagram shows an illustration on how an application uses a locale. On the right-hand side we have a collection of data. **Source string** is the text from the source code, which is intended to be shown in the application, be it a label text, a header, a caption of an image, an information text, and so on. **Translations** are a set of translations of the source string in many human languages and dialects, such as U.S. English, British English, Indonesian, Japanese, and so on. **Locale data** affects the formatting (for example, the number and the date presentation) and the content of the text (such as displaying the day of the week in the target language). The source string is then passed into the API in the middle and then transformed into the final string, which is then displayed on the right-hand side.

Translations and locale data should be prepared for all target market areas of the application. They may be missing. In this case, the source string is displayed without any transformation, meaning whatever is written in the source code will be displayed without any translations or formatting changes.

Time for action – getting the available locales

We can see a list of the available locales on our system easily. This should be our first command, which we must master in order to make our life easier later when we need to debug why our application can't get translated. Let's see how to do this:

1. Open a terminal.

2. Run the following command:

    ```
    locale -a.
    ```

3. We will be presented with a list of the locales available in our system (the actual output in your own computer may vary). Here is a sample list:

    ```
    C
    C.UTF-8
    en_US.utf8
    POSIX
    ```

What just happened?

In the previous list, we see that we have four locales installed in the system. We have C, both in Universal Character Set and UTF-8, POSIX, and English-US in UTF-8 locales. It means that we can only have four different translations of an application. C and POSIX usually are not used at all for translations and are only used by the source language, which is the language used in the source code (the human language used in the textual presentation, not the programming language). With this fact, it means that we can only have one translation, which is the English-US.

The character set affects how the data is presented on the screen, in the storage, and during data transfers. It is a mapping between an integer number, called a **code point**, to a character, the presentation of a letter, number, symbol, and many other types of characters. GNOME uses UTF-8 internally, so we will stick to this character set.

Have a go hero – exploring the locale parameters

Try to run `locale` without any parameter to see all the locale parameters. The parameters are affected by setting the locale environment variables (prefixed with `LC_`). Can you somehow guess which parameter is represented by which variable?

Time for action – adding a locale

If you only see English-US in the available locale list, let's add a locale to the system. If you see a locale other than English-US, you can skip this action. Let's add an Indonesian locale with an Indonesian territory, so the code for it is `id_ID`. Of course, you can use a different locale depending on your preference.

1. Edit the `/etc/locale.gen` file as a superuser.

2. Find a line that shows `id_ID.UTF-8`.

3. Remove the comment mark, which is the hash mark in front of the line.

4. Save the file.

5. Open a terminal and run the `sudo locale-gen` command.

6. Depending on the content of the `/etc/locale.gen` file, the output may vary. But if you only uncomment Indonesian and English-US, then you will see the following output:

   ```
   Generating locales (this might take a while)...
     en_US.UTF-8... done
     id_ID.UTF-8... done
   Generation complete.
   ```

7. To check whether our command has succeeded, let's type `locale -a` in the terminal again.

8. We should see the `id_ID.utf-8` locale in the list, as shown here:

   ```
   C
   C.UTF-8
   en_US.utf8
   id_ID.utf8
   POSIX
   ```

What just happened?

The locale information for many cultures already exists within the system. However, they are still in the textual form and not enabled. What we did with the `locale-gen` command was generate the binary representation and enable the locales that are listed without a comment in the `/etc/locale.gen` file. With this command, it is enabled system wide. Hence, we need a root privilege and we used `sudo` to accomplish the task (note that `locale -a` does not need this privilege).

Time for action – getting different outputs with different locales

Ok, so now that we have a locale other than English-US, what's next? Let's start with a very simple one, the date program.

1. Open a terminal.

2. Type the following:

    ```
    LC_ALL=C date
    ```

3. See the output, as shown here:

    ```
    Sun Oct 28 15:41:38 EET 2012
    ```

4. Then type the following command (don't forget to change `id_ID.utf8` to the locale that you have enabled previously).

    ```
    LC_ALL=id_ID.utf8 date
    ```

5. Check the output; it will be similar to the one shown here:

    ```
    Min Okt 28 15:41:45 EET 2012
    ```

What just happened?

In this action, we configured the settings manually by using the `LC_ALL` environment variable. By setting the `LC_ALL` variable to any locale identifier, the POSIX system would immediately use the specified locale to transform the output of the application. As mentioned earlier, the system has many parameters that we can set. The `LC_ALL` variable is the magic parameter that sets all of the parameters with a single value.

Actually, the output of the date program is purely date and time data. So, the parameter affected is `LC_TIME`.

Have a go hero – using a bogus local identifier

As we can see, the output is translated into Indonesian just after we set the locale. Try to provide any bogus locale identifier (or try to make a typo!) and you will see that it no longer works. Also, if you have other locales installed, try them all!

i18n in a Vala project

To make i18n work in Vala, there are several steps needed to be done. Let's create a Vala project and do the i18n steps one by one.

Time for action – bootstrapping the infrastructure

The first thing we need to do is prepare the build infrastructure. This step is quite tricky because if you miss even a single detail, you could get lost for hours trying to find out why everything does not work. But don't be afraid, let's jump into the freezing water and get a fish out of it!

1. Create a Vala project with GtkBuilder support; let's call it `hello-i18n`.

2. Edit the `configure.ac` file and alter this file by referencing the following code. What you need to do is insert the highlighted lines between the lines that are not highlighted. If you worry about not getting it properly, you can just copy and paste the whole file.

```
AC_INIT(hello_i18n, 0.1)
AC_CONFIG_HEADERS([config.h])
AM_INIT_AUTOMAKE([1.11])
AM_SILENT_RULES([yes])
AC_PROG_CC

LT_INIT
IT_PROG_INTLTOOL()

AH_TEMPLATE([GETTEXT_PACKAGE], [Package name for gettext])
GETTEXT_PACKAGE=hello-i18n

AC_DEFINE_UNQUOTED([GETTEXT_PACKAGE], ["$GETTEXT_PACKAGE"],
                   [The domain to use with gettext])
AC_SUBST(GETTEXT_PACKAGE)
AM_GLIB_GNU_GETTEXT

PACKAGE_LOCALE_DIR=[${datadir}/locale]
AC_SUBST(PACKAGE_LOCALE_DIR)

dnl Check for vala
AM_PROG_VALAC([0.10.0])

dnl Development mode
AC_ARG_ENABLE(development,
```

```
    AS_HELP_STRING([--enable-development],[enable development
mode]),
      enable_development="$enableval",
          enable_development=no)
if test "x$enable_development" = "xyes"; then
  DEVELOPMENT_MODE="yes"
fi

AC_SUBST(DEVELOPMENT_MODE)
AH_TEMPLATE([DEVELOPMENT_MODE], [Whether in development mode or
not])
AC_DEFINE_UNQUOTED([DEVELOPMENT_MODE], ["$DEVELOPMENT_MODE"],
                   [Development mode])

PKG_CHECK_MODULES(HELLO_I18N, [gtk+-3.0 ])

AC_OUTPUT([
Makefile
src/Makefile
po/Makefile.in

])
```

3. Create a folder named `po` in the top folder of the project.

4. Create a new file called `POTFILES.in` inside the `po` folder; fill this file with the following code:

    ```
    [type: gettext/glade] src/hello_i18n.ui
    ```

5. Also create a new file called `LINGUAS` inside the `po` folder; fill this file with the language code that we want to support. To continue with the previous example, let's add Indonesian into the file by adding the following:

    ```
    id
    ```

6. If you are using another locale, you can just put the language code, not the whole locale identifier.

7. We need to set up an initial translation template inside this new folder. We need to open a terminal and run the following command inside the `po` folder:

    ```
    intltool-update --pot
    ```

8. The result of this command is a file called `hello-i18n.pot`. This is an empty translation file and we will use this as the base of the translation.

9. Duplicate the `hello-i18n.pot` file by copying it and naming it `id.po`. Again, if you are using a different language, adjust the filename to reflect the code of the language. The `.po` extension marks it as a portable object file, a translation file format that is very popular in the open source world. For now, keep the `id.po` file as it is, we will use it later.

10. Edit `Makefile.am` in the top folder; alter its content by referring to the following code. Only the parts that are highlighted were added or modified from the original generated file:

```
    SUBDIRS = src po

hello_i18ndocdir = ${prefix}/doc/hello_i18n
hello_i18ndoc_DATA = \
   README\
   COPYING\
   AUTHORS\
   ChangeLog\
   INSTALL\
   NEWS

EXTRA_DIST = \
   $(hello_i18ndoc_DATA) \
   intltool-extract.in \
   intltool-merge.in \
   intltool-update.in


DISTCLEANFILES = \
   intltool-extract \
   intltool-merge \
   intltool-update \
   po/.intltool-merge-cache \
   $(NULL)

# Remove doc directory on uninstall
uninstall-local:
   -rm -r $(hello_i18ndocdir)
```

11. Edit the `src/config.vapi` file and add this line to the namespace:

```
public const string DEVELOPMENT_MODE;
```

12. Edit `src/Makefile.am` and append `--Xcc='--include config.h'` to the `hello_i18n_VALAFLAGS` declaration so that the entire code will look like the following:

```
hello_i18n_VALAFLAGS =   \
   --pkg gtk+-3.0 --Xcc='--include config.h'
```

13. Still in the same file, insert `-include config.h` into the `AM_CPPFLAGS` declaration, so that the entire code declaration will look like the following:

```
AM_CPPFLAGS = \
    -DPACKAGE_LOCALE_DIR=\""$(localedir)"\" \
    -include config.h \
    -DPACKAGE_SRC_DIR=\""$(srcdir)"\" \
    -DPACKAGE_DATA_DIR=\""$(pkgdatadir)"\" \
    $(HELLO_I18N_CFLAGS)
```

14. Edit `src/hello_i18n.vala` and add the following code in the `main` function:

```
    if (Config.DEVELOPMENT_MODE == "yes") {
      Intl.bindtextdomain(Config.GETTEXT_PACKAGE, "src/po");
    } else {
      Intl.bindtextdomain(Config.GETTEXT_PACKAGE, Config.PACKAGE_
LOCALE_DIR);
    }

    Intl.bind_textdomain_codeset(Config.GETTEXT_PACKAGE, "UTF-8");
    Intl.textdomain(Config.GETTEXT_PACKAGE);
```

15. Configure the project by clicking **Configure Project...** in the **Build** menu, and in the upcoming dialog window add `--enable-development` in **Configure Options**.

16. Let's build the project.

17. We won't see anything particular in this first step, but our build should be successful.

What just happened?

We had to do the infrastructure setup by ourselves as Anjuta does not do this for us. What we did was basically set the autotools to include gettext and intltool into the build pipeline. **Gettext** is a library that helps us to translate our applications into the target's local languages, and **intltool** is a library that helps prepare the data required for the translation system.

We also prepared the basic folder for the translation files. This `po` folder will contain translations of the UI texts. For now, though, it has nothing useful.

The other important thing we did was to add the code configuration filesystem. In `configure.ac`, we specify `GETTEXT_PACKAGE` and `DEVELOPMENT_MODE` to be configurable by the code. What we did was insert the following lines:

```
AH_TEMPLATE([DEVELOPMENT_MODE], [Whether in development mode or not])
AC_DEFINE_UNQUOTED([DEVELOPMENT_MODE], ["$DEVELOPMENT_MODE"],
                   [Development mode])
```

The result is a file called `config.h` that will be generated when building the application, and these two variables would be available in that file. Then, the source code (`config.vapi` and the generated C-language code) would be able to access the values. We will discuss this further in the next action.

Last but not least, we put translation initialization steps in the main function.

```
if (Config.DEVELOPMENT_MODE == "yes") {
  Intl.bindtextdomain(Config.GETTEXT_PACKAGE, "src/po");
} else {
  Intl.bindtextdomain(Config.GETTEXT_PACKAGE, Config.PACKAGE_LOCALE_
DIR);
}

Intl.bind_textdomain_codeset(Config.GETTEXT_PACKAGE, "UTF-8");
Intl.textdomain(Config.GETTEXT_PACKAGE);
```

The `bindtextdomain` function sets the lookup folder of the translation catalog (in Gettext terms, it is called **domain**) to point to the specified folder. The catalog's name and the folder are specified in the arguments. A catalog contains mapping between the source language (usually written in English) and the target language. The function basically tells us that the translations are available in the folder, and the files to look at have the names as specified by the catalog name.

We have two branches in this part depending on the `DEVELOPMENT_MODE` value. If it is in the `DEVELOPMENT_MODE` mode, the translations are set to be in the `src/po` folder, otherwise it is set to the system folder (usually `/usr/share/locale`). The `DEVELOPMENT_MODE` value itself is set when we pass `–enable-development` in the project configuration.

The `bind_textdomain_codeset` part tells that we are using a UTF-8 character set. And finally, `textdomain` attaches the catalog into the current process, so any gettext function after this initialization assumes that the catalog would be in use.

These are all the steps that we have to follow to have multilingual support in our applications. But no worries, you only need to do this once, during the start of the development.

One important thing is that we must remove `--enable-development` from the project's configuration dialog, because with this flag set, the code will look for the translation in the source code tree, and not in the system.

Time for action – creating a UI

After the infrastructure is ready, now let's move on and create the UI.

1. Open the `hello_i18n.ui` file.

2. Put a **Box** widget and split it into five items.

3. In the first four items, put five **Label** controls inside each of the items.

4. For the last item, put a **Button** control.

5. Edit the labels. For each label, assign a text from the following list:

```
This is a label
Today's date is %x
The price is %^=#6n
The weight is %.3f %s
```

6. For the button, set `See you later` as the text.

7. When editing the labels, press the ellipsis button that is on the right-hand side of the textbox. We will be presented with the following dialog:

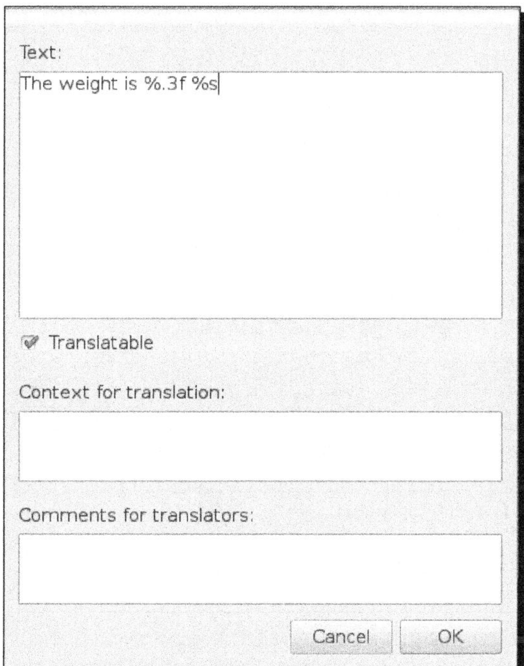

8. For all the labels (including the button's label), make sure the **Translatable** checkbox is checked. This is essential, because without this, we can't have our application translated at all.

9. Modify the `hello_i18n.vala` file to look like the following code snippet:

```vala
using GLib;
using Gtk;

public class Main : Object
{
  /*
    * Uncomment this line when you are done testing and building a
tarball
    * or installing
  */
//const string UI_FILE = Config.PACKAGE_DATA_DIR + "/" + "hello_
i18n.ui";
const string UI_FILE = "src/hello_i18n.ui";
  /* ANJUTA: Widgets declaration for hello_i18n.ui - DO NOT REMOVE
*/
  Builder builder = null;

  public Main ()
  {
    try
    {
      builder = new Builder ();
      builder.add_from_file (UI_FILE);
      builder.connect_signals (this);

      var window = builder.get_object ("window") as Window;
      /* ANJUTA: Widgets initialization for hello_i18n.ui - DO NOT
REMOVE */
      window.show_all ();
    }
    catch (Error e) {
      stderr.printf ("Could not load UI: %s\n", e.message);
    }

    var b = builder.get_object ("button1") as Button;
    b.clicked.connect(()=>{
      Gtk.main_quit();
    });

    var dateData = new Date();
```

```vala
char buffer[100];
    Time t = Time.local (time_t ());

    var date = builder.get_object ("label_date") as Label;
t.strftime (buffer, date.label);
date.label = (string) buffer;

var priceData = 9.99;
var price = builder.get_object ("label_price") as Label;
Monetary.strfmon(buffer, price.label, priceData);
price.label = (string) buffer;

weak string measurement = LangInfo.get_info(LangInfo.Item.
MEASUREMENT);
bool metric = (measurement[0] == 1);

var weightData = 11.24;
var weight = builder.get_object ("label_weight") as Label;
weight.label = weight.label.printf(metric ? weightData :
weightData * 2.20462, metric ? "Kg" : "Lb");

  }

  [CCode (instance_pos = -1)]
  public void on_destroy (Widget window)
  {
    Gtk.main_quit();
  }

  static int main (string[] args)
  {
    Gtk.init (ref args);
    if (Config.DEVELOPMENT_MODE == "yes") {
      Intl.bindtextdomain(Config.GETTEXT_PACKAGE, "src/po");
    } else {
      Intl.bindtextdomain(Config.GETTEXT_PACKAGE, Config.PACKAGE_
LOCALE_DIR);
    }
    Intl.bind_textdomain_codeset(Config.GETTEXT_PACKAGE, "UTF-8");
    Intl.textdomain(Config.GETTEXT_PACKAGE);

    var app = new Main ();

    Gtk.main ();

    return 0;
  }
}
```

10. If you notice in the preceding code block, we need the `LangInfo.get_info` and `Monetary.strfmon` functions that are not available anywhere in the system. Actually, we wrap the original `nl_langinfo` and `strfmon` values from `glibc` in the two files we need to add, that is, `langinfo.vapi` and `monetary.vapi`. So first, let's create a new empty file and name it `langinfo.vapi` and fill it with the following code:

```
[CCode (cprefix = "", lower_case_cprefix = "", cheader_filename =
"langinfo.h")]
public class LangInfo {
        public enum Item
           {
    [CCode (cname="_NL_MEASUREMENT_MEASUREMENT")]
      MEASUREMENT
   }

   [CCode (cname="nl_langinfo")]
   public static weak string get_info (Item type);

 }
```

11. Next, create an empty `monetary.vapi` file and fill this file with the following code:

```
[CCode (cprefix = "", lower_case_cprefix = "", cheader_filename =
"monetary.h")]
public class Monetary {

   public static ssize_t strfmon(char[] s, string format, double
data, ...);

 }
```

12. Edit `src/Makefile.am` and add `monetary.vapi` and `langinfo.vapi` into the `hello_i18n_SOURCES` declaration, so that the code will be as follows:

```
hello_i18n_SOURCES = \
   hello_i18n.vala config.vapi monetary.vapi langinfo.vapi
```

13. Rebuild and run the application. We should see the following window:

What just happened?

The important part in this action is to make the labels translatable. This will enable intltool to pick up the text in the `hello_i18n.ui` file.

The next important things are the (re) introduction of the `Monetary.strfmon` and `LangInfo.get_info` functions. `Monetary.strfmon` is a wrapper of the `strfmon` function and is used to format monetary data as a string. The monetary data should be displayed completely with the currency symbol according to the locale. This function is wrapped by providing a `.vapi` file stating the corresponding C header filename and the function name, which we wrap. In this case, it is a straightforward wrapping, which means the original function's name (`strfmon`) is the same as the wrapper function's name (also called `strfmon`).

Then, we have the `LangInfo.get_info` function, which is a wrapper of the `nl_langinfo` function. This function takes a locale setting item and converts that into a pointer or a string. A locale item is an item that describes a particular locale setting in a locale file. In this case, we wrap two parts. The first is the locale item, which we wrap as an enumeration and name it `Item`. We only need the `LC_MEASUREMENT` item, so we only wrap it inside the enumeration. If you need other items, you can wrap and put it in the enumeration as well. The enumeration order is no longer important as we directly map the `enum` member with the actual C-language `enum` member by using the following code:

```
[CCode (cname="_NL_MEASUREMENT_MEASUREMENT")]
MEASUREMENT
```

This means that `LangInfo.MEASUREMENT` in Vala is exactly the same as `_NL_MEASUREMENT_MEASUREMENT` in C.

After that, we wrap the `wrap nl_langinfo` function as `LangInfo.get_info`.

```
[CCode (cname="nl_langinfo")]
public static weak string get_info (Item type);
```

We opt to use `get_info` rather than `nl_langinfo`, because a wrapper with a `nl_` prefix makes no sense here in Vala; so, `get_info` reflects what the function does. We use the `weak` keyword in the function to denote that the returned string should not be managed by Vala.

Time for action – translating UI texts

The next step is to actually translate the UI text. We will see how to extract the texts from the UI file and translate them.

1. Go to the `po` folder using a terminal.

2. Update the `id.po` file, which we duplicated from the first part of the action, by typing the following command:

```
intltool-update id
```

3. From the **GNOME Activities** menu, launch the **Gtranslator** program.

4. During the first launch, we need to fill the profile. Provide a name to the profile and fill your name and e-mail address. The next window will ask you about the language properties that you are going to translate into. Make sure the language code is correct (refer to ISO-639). Enter **UTF-8** and **8bit** as the character set and transfer the encoding values respectively. **Team email** is the e-mail address used by the translators of this language. The **Plural forms** option determines how a word should use its plural form. In the Indonesian language, the number of plurals is two, and a word should use the plural form when the count of the object referred by the word is greater than one. Hence we choose the option **nplurals=2; plural=(n>1)**. For the Indonesian language, it would look like this:

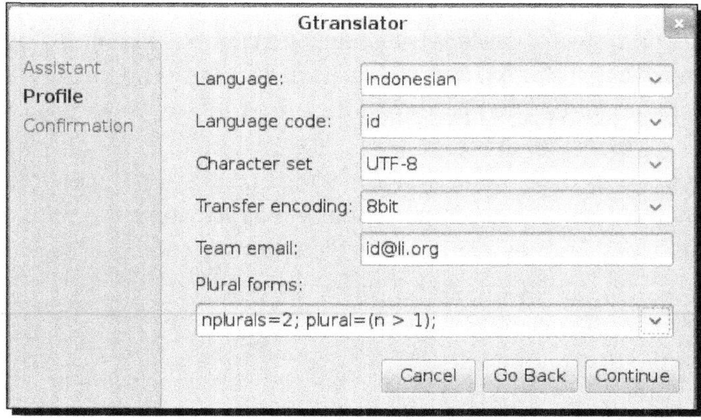

5. Click **Continue**, finish the setup of **GTranslator**, and go ahead and open the `id.po` file using its menu.

6. After this file is opened, we are now ready to translate. Click on each text in the list and enter its translation in the **Translated** textbox. All formatting marks such as `%x`, `%s`, and others must not be modified or changed by translators except when it is requested to do so (for example, when adjusting the date format). The order of the appearance of these formats must not be changed as well.

7. Translate the text by referring to the following translation table:

Original text	Translated text
This is a label	**Ini adalah label**
Today's date is %x	**Tanggal hari ini adalah %x**
The price is %^=#6n	**Harganya %^=#6n**
The weight is %.3f %s	**Beratnya %.3f %s**
See you later	**Sampai jumpa**

8. Save the file.

9. Rebuild our application.

10. In the terminal, create a `po` folder inside the `src` folder. Inside the `po` folder, create an `id` folder. After that, create the `LC_MESSAGES` folder inside `id`. So, altogether we should have a new folder called `src/po/id/LC_MESSAGES`.

11. Then rename the `id.gmo` file, which was produced after the rebuild, to `hello-i18n.mo` into the folder we created in the previous step. Notice the `hello-i18n` name must be exactly the same as the value of the `GETTEXT_PACKAGE` variable, which we set earlier.

12. Go to the top folder of the project by using the terminal and run the application with the Indonesian language, as shown here:

```
LANGUAGE=id LC_ALL=id_ID.utf8 src/hello-i18n
```

13. The application window should look like the one shown in the following screenshot. Be amazed!

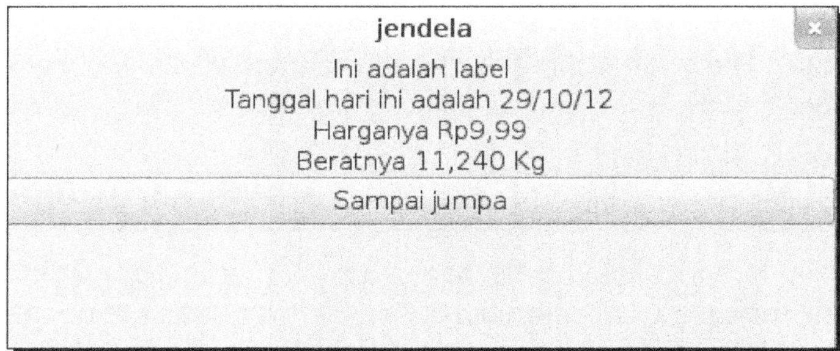

What just happened?

This part is where the UI text is generated and translated. The resulting `.po` files are then taken to the translators' hand and then into the translation queue. This must be done whenever we update any text in the source code. This is exactly done by just entering the following command:

```
intltool-update id
```

Note that this will only update the `id.po` file; any remaining files must be updated individually. What this command actually does is it extracts new text from the files stated in the `POTFILES` file and merges them with the existing `id.po` file. If there is an ambiguity, the translator would be notified in **GTranslator** by being shown the text in a fuzzy state. The translator can then fix this issue by providing a new translation for those fuzzy texts.

After all the strings inside the `.po` files are translated, all translated `.po` files must be returned back to the `po` folder. We then perform a build here. Actually, what the build does is it simply issues the following command:

```
msgfmt -cv id.po -o id.gmo
```

This step converts `id.po` from a text form to `id.gmo` in a binary form. The application can only take the binary form, hence we need this step. The `bindtextdomain` function in the application sets the folder to the `src/po/` folder whenever we are in the development mode. Actually, it will look for the binary `.gmo` files in the `src/po/<language-code>/` `LC_MESSAGES` folder. The language code is the code specified in the LANGUAGE environment variable. If this variable is not specified, it will look for the language code in the LANG, `LC_MESSAGES`, and at last `LC_ALL` variables consecutively.

The command we execute to run the application is as follows:

```
LANGUAGE=id LC_ALL=id_ID.utf8 src/hello-i18n
```

This sets the `bindtextdomain` function to look for the translation in `src/po/id/LC_MESSAGES` (because the LANGUAGE variable is set to `id`) and otherwise use `id_ID.utf8` as the locale setting. The result is that the UI texts are translated to Indonesian, and the monetary, number, and measurement parameters are also set to Indonesian.

Have a go hero – installing another locale

If you have another locale installed to try, here is a good chance. For example, try to set `LC_MEASUREMENT` to `en_US.utf8` (United States), `LC_MONETARY` to `de_DE.utf8` (German), and `LC_TIME` to `ar_SA.utf8` (Saudi Arabia). Would you be able to get an output similar to the one shown in the following screenshot?

The localization process

From the actions we did, we know that we need a process to do the localization. **Localization** (often abbreviated as **L10n**) is a further step after internationalization. It is where the actual work specific to the target market area is done. We need this process as it involves the translators who usually can't even build the application.

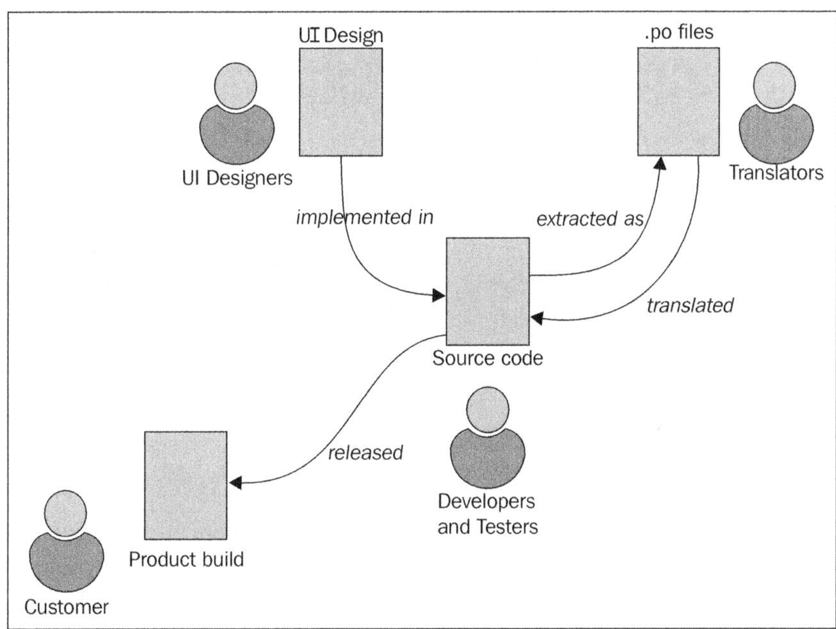

The previous diagram shows a very simplified L10n process. The source code is produced by the developers according to the UI design. The design could be in formal documents or mockups. During the development, the developers add text into the source code and UI files. These texts are then extracted to `.po` files for each language of the target markets.

Here, the translators own the files until they are fully translated. The translated files are then handed over back to the developers. The developers and testers could make a build to test. Whenever a milestone is due, the product build is created along with the translation and delivered to the customer.

We need to set up a good infrastructure to make our life easier. The whole scenario described previously should be done in an automated way, so no delay should be produced between the steps.

In reality, before a build is delivered to the customer, a series of tests with each locale must be carried out thoroughly. Most of the time, the translators could easily get lost without a context while translating the UI text. This error can be minimized by using comments in the translation file; however, there is another issue that makes the test important. This is about how the text is displayed. There must be a check to find whether they are truncated in the translation or not. If it is, then check whether an engineering process must be carried out (for example, to resize the text size) or the translator must figure out an alternative translation. The tester should also check whether the text is rendered correctly or not. If the target market involves countries with Asian languages, or languages that are written in both the left and right direction, then the test must be carried out even more carefully.

Summary

This chapter discussed about preparing our application to be both internationalized and localized. The difference between the two is that the i18n part makes sure that our software is capable of displaying multilingual and multicultural information, whereas L10n is the actual effort to deliver the language and culture settings into the application. In short, i18n makes our software L10n ready.

We started the chapter by introducing ourselves with locale. We now know how to get the list of available locales in our system as well as how to enable a locale.

Then, using a Vala project, we learned to bootstrap the i18n architecture. This process must be done during the initial stage of a project. After that, we learned how to prepare the source code to get the UI text translated and were exposed to some of the i18n functions to get time, monetary, and measurement data to be localized. Then, we learned how the translators work with the translation files.

Finally, we discussed an example of the L10n process. This example can be adjusted depending on how the organization arranges the engineering process.

In the next chapter, we will discuss about quality control in our application. We will apply the best practices in software engineering in a GNOME way.

12
Quality Made Easy

Software quality is not checked before releasing the product into the market. It is done way before that. Many software developers even check the quality before a single piece of code is written. Tested, well-written, and well-kept code along with a set of well-defined rules together are the essentials for software development. How to do this all in the GNOME development environment? Let's find out.

Unit testing, among other testing required for a software, is sometimes tricky to write. This chapter will concentrate on performing unit tests. We will use the testing framework provided by GLib, GTK+, and Gdk. In this chapter, we use command lines intimately instead of Anjuta so that we can get the intuition on how to automate the testing easily. For the actions, we will use old code from previous chapters and add unit testing to them.

Specifically we will dig out:

- The concept of unit testing
- Stubbing library
- Testing GUI modules

Now, let's get rolling.

Reasons for performing unit testing

Unit tests are localized and are specific tests carried out for a specific object in our source code. We need to make sure that the test really tackles each of the functionalities. To do unit testing, we simply do the following:

- Test each function.

- Test each branch in the function; for example, if the function contains `if` and `else` statements, or `switch` and `case` statements.

- The previous rules are to make sure that we cover all places in the source code so that there are no surprises, especially a bad one, waiting for us when we deliver the program to the customer.

- To test the functions, we need to pass data in the argument list. We should craft the data and, if necessary, repeat the test using different sets of data to make sure the second rule is fulfilled.

- Unit testing should be performed whenever a piece of code is written. Many software developers use the **Test-Driven Development (TDD)** methodology by creating the unit tests even before they write the code! This has an advantage in that we would know what to expect from the code so that we can focus on what the function should deliver. This is especially important when we write libraries, so we know exactly what the API looks like and how to use them, by creating the unit test first.

- Unit testing must be deterministic, meaning that we must know exactly what the output is by giving a certain input. To achieve this, the data we inject into the testing must not be random and the behavior of the API we use also must be deterministic.

Time for action – creating our first unit test

For our first action, let's revisit our old code where we have our first encounter with Vala, the `hello-vala` program from the *Getting to know Vala* section in *Chapter 3, Programming Languages*. We have two objects, `Book` and `Bookstore`, which we will create unit tests for.

1. Let's reopen the `hello_vala.anjuta` file from Anjuta.

2. Open the `configure.ac` file in the top directory of the project. Find the output section as shown in the following code:

```
AC_OUTPUT([
Makefile
src/Makefile
tests/Makefile
])
```

3. Make changes as shown in the following code:

```
AC_OUTPUT([
Makefile
src/Makefile
tests/Makefile
])
```

4. Open the `Makefile.am` file in the top directory of the project and find the
`SUBDIRS` section.

```
SUBDIRS = src
```

5. Make changes as shown in the following code:

```
SUBDIRS = src tests
```

6. Create a directory called `tests` in the top directory.

7. Create a new `Makefile.am` file inside the `tests` directory and fill it with this code:

```
AM_CPPFLAGS = \
    -DPACKAGE_LOCALE_DIR=\""$(localedir)"\" \
    -DPACKAGE_SRC_DIR=\""$(srcdir)"\" \
    -DPACKAGE_DATA_DIR=\""$(pkgdatadir)"\" \
    $(HELLO_VALA_CFLAGS) \
    $(atk_CFLAGS) \
    $(gee-1.0_CFLAGS)

AM_CFLAGS =\
    -Wall\
    -g

TESTS=test_book test_bookstore

check_PROGRAMS = test_book test_bookstore

test_book_SOURCES = \
    test_book.vala ../src/book.vala

test_book_VALAFLAGS =   \
    --pkg gtk+-3.0 \
    --pkg gee-1.0

test_book_LDFLAGS = \
    -Wl,--export-dynamic

test_book_LDADD = $(HELLO_VALA_LIBS) \
    $(atk_LIBS) \
    $(gee-1.0_LIBS)
```

```
test_bookstore_SOURCES = \
  test_bookstore.vala ../src/book.vala ../src/bookstore.vala

test_bookstore_VALAFLAGS =   \
  --pkg gtk+-3.0 \
  --pkg gee-1.0

test_bookstore_LDFLAGS = \
  -Wl,--export-dynamic

test_bookstore_LDADD = $(HELLO_VALA_LIBS) \
  $(atk_LIBS) \
  $(gee-1.0_LIBS)
```

8. Create a new Vala code called `test_book.vala` inside the `tests` directory. Fill it with this code:

```
public class TestBook {
  static void test_isbn ()
  {
    var b = new Book("1", "title");
    assert(b.isbn == "1");
  }

  static void test_title ()
  {
    var b = new Book("1", "title");
    assert(b.title == "title");
  }

  static void test_add_author()
  {
    var b = new Book("1", "title");
    b.addAuthor("author1");
    b.addAuthor("author2");
    b.addAuthor("author3");
    assert(b.authors.size == 3);
  }

  static int main (string[] args)
  {
    Test.init (ref args);

    Test.add_func ("/test-isbn", test_isbn);
    Test.add_func ("/test-title", test_title);
    Test.add_func ("/test-add-author", test_add_author);
```

```vala
        Test.run ();

        return 0;
    }
}
```

9. Create a new Vala file called `test_bookstore.vala` and also put it inside the `tests` directory. Copy this code into that file:

```vala
public class TestBookStore {
  static void test_add_stock()
  {
    var b = new Book("1", "title");
    var s = new BookStore(b, 1.0, 12);
    s.addStock(13);
    assert(s.getStock() == 25);
    assert(s.isAvailable() == true);
  }

  static void test_remove_stock()
  {
    var b = new Book("1", "title");
    var s = new BookStore(b, 1.0, 12);
    s.addStock(13);
    s.removeStock(10);
    assert(s.getStock() == 15);
    assert(s.isAvailable() == true);
  }

  static void test_stock_alert()
  {
    var b = new Book("1", "title");
    var s = new BookStore(b, 1.0, 12);
    var alert_emitted = false;

    s.stockAlert.connect(() => {
      alert_emitted = true;
    });

    s.removeStock(1);
    assert(alert_emitted == false);
    s.removeStock(10);
    assert(alert_emitted == true);
  }

  static void test_price_alert()
  {
```

```
        var b = new Book("1", "title");
        var s = new BookStore(b, 1.0, 12);
        var alert_emitted = false;

        s.priceAlert.connect(() => {
          alert_emitted = true;
        });

        s.setPrice(2.5);
        assert(alert_emitted == false);
        s.setPrice(0.5);
        assert(alert_emitted == true);
    }

    static int main (string[] args)
    {
        Test.init (ref args);

        Test.add_func ("/test-add-stock", test_add_stock);
        Test.add_func ("/test-remove-stock", test_remove_stock);
        Test.add_func ("/test-stock-alert", test_stock_alert);

        Test.run ();

        return 0;
    }
}
```

10. Open `src/book.vala` and find this piece of code in the file:

```
private string title;
private string isbn;
private ArrayList<string> authors;
```

11. Replace the previous code with this:

```
    internal string title;
    internal string isbn;
    internal ArrayList<string> authors;
```

12. In the project's top directory, issue this command on a terminal:

```
./autogen.sh
```

13. Make sure everything still works fine by building the project and typing the following command:

```
make all
```

14. Build and run the unit tests by issuing this command:

```
make check
```

15. Make sure you see an output that looks similar to these lines:

```
/test-isbn: OK
/test-title: OK
/test-add-author: OK
PASS: test_book
/test-add-stock: OK
/test-remove-stock: OK
/test-stock-alert: OK
PASS: test_bookstore
==================
All 2 tests passed
==================
```

What just happened?

Wow! That was a busy action, wasn't it?

The end result is that we have unit tests checking the validity of our code by showing the test paths and test results. We saw from the previous section that we got all OKs from all of our test paths. It also had a statistic of the tests.

What we did first was we prepared the autotools infrastructure by modifying `configure.ac` and `Makefile.am` and then created a new `Makefile.am` file in the `tests` directory. We introduced the `tests` directory both into the `output` section of `configure.ac` and the `SUBDIRS` section of `Makefile.am`. Without these, the `tests` directory is unknown to the autotools and the rest of the build infrastructure.

Then we have the test files. In `Makefile.am`, we have these lines:

```
TESTS=test_book test_bookstore

check_PROGRAMS = test_book test_bookstore
```

These tell the autotools that we have two programs, which are test programs; they are `test_book` and `test_bookstore`. The first line makes the autotools run the specified programs when we issue the `make check` command. The second line tells the autotools to create binaries with the specified names.

Then we have sections for both `test_book` and `test_bookstore`. The interesting part of the section for `test_book` is this:

```
test_book_SOURCES = \
  test_book.vala ../src/book.vala
```

It tells autotools that the source code files for the `test_book` program are `test_book.vala` and `book.vala`, which are inside the `../src/` directory. The same goes for the `test_bookstore` program. It is a common practice to compile together the source code being tested and the unit test.

Now let's see how a unit test is written. First, take a look at `test_book.vala`.

```
public class TestBook {
```

For each unit test, we have a class that tests a particular object. We name the class by prepending the word `Test` before the name of the object. In this case we have a `Book` object, so our unit test's name is `TestBook`. It is a plain class.

Then, we define the tests that we want to carry out against the object we want to test in `static` functions. The functions are `static` because in the unit test we will not instantiate the object of the `test` class.

One test should test all relevant cases. In our first test, we want to test whether the ISBN is correctly set. Here, we create the `Book` object with the ISBN value of 1, and we test it with the `assert` function to check whether the `isbn` member really has a value of 1.

```
static void test_isbn ()
{
  var b = new Book("1", "title");
  assert(b.isbn == "1");
}
```

We might think that this is rather silly. Why would we want to check the obvious like this? For our human eyes, we think this kind of check would always pass. But believe me, when our code becomes larger and larger, and when we intentionally or accidentally make any slight changes in the code, it could make this test fail. To emphasize my argument, let's see the actual code of `book.vala`:

```
public Book(string isbn, string title) {
  this.isbn = isbn;
  this.title = title;
  authors = new ArrayList<string>();
}
```

Our code in the test checked the `isbn` member immediately after instantiating the object. Imagine that we somehow modify the constructor to look like this:

```
public Book(string isbn, string title) {
   isbn = isbn;
   title = title;
   authors = new ArrayList<string>();
}
```

Note that we may accidentally remove `this` from the previous lines. The code still runs, but the result is wrong. Without the test, we could overlook this and what we end up with is some unhappy customer calling to say that our program produces bad calculations! Now, really try to make the previous error and run `make check` again. We will be notified immediately, as you can see from the following screen output:

```
/test-isbn: **

ERROR:test_book.c:100:test_book_test_isbn: assertion failed: (g_strcmp0
(_tmp1_, "1") == 0)

/bin/bash: line 5:  9305 Aborted                 ${dir}$tst

FAIL: test_book

/test-add-stock: OK

/test-remove-stock: OK

/test-stock-alert: OK

PASS: test_bookstore

====================

1 of 2 tests failed

====================
```

We see from this that the `test_isbn` function correctly points out the error just as we expected. Now, imagine again that we don't have `test_isbn`.

We use `assert` to check the truth value of the expression we pass into the function. The `assert` function will terminate the program immediately when the value is not `true`, and we know that something is wrong when this happens.

We needed to modify the `Book` class so that it looks like this:

```
internal string title;
internal string isbn;
internal ArrayList<string> authors;
```

We changed all private members to `internal`. Vala opens the internal members of all the classes in the same package. It means our unit test can access the member directly. Otherwise, our unit test would not be able to access, for example, the `authors` member. This is a quite annoying limitation as Vala does not have anything analogous to friend classes in C++ where we can keep the member as private yet allow the friend classes to still access them.

Next in line, we have a test to check the title value.

```
static void test_title ()
{
    var b = new Book("1", "title");
    assert(b.title == "title");
}
```

It works the same as the `test_isbn` test. Then we have a test to check whether the `addAuthor` function works as it should.

```
static void test_add_author()
{
    var b = new Book("1", "title");
    b.addAuthor("author1");
    b.addAuthor("author2");
    b.addAuthor("author3");
    assert(b.authors.size == 3);
}
```

Here, we check the `authors` array list. It should have a value of 3 after adding three authors into the `Book` object with the `addAuthor` function. In the `Book` object, we don't have anymore functions that need to be tested. The rest of the functions only output data to the screen. So, let's move on to the `main` function of the unit test.

```
static int main (string[] args)
{
    Test.init (ref args);
```

We can see that we first call the `Test.init` function. This is the initialization function from the `GLib.Test` class.

Then we register all the functions that we defined previously and assign them with test paths. Test path is a hypothetical name that we want to route the actual test function to. The `GLib.Test` class requires that each function be represented by a test path. Then we call the `Test.run` function to run all the paths starting from the root path. The root path is just like the root directory, the top-most path in the hierarchy.

```
    Test.add_func ("/test-isbn", test_isbn);
    Test.add_func ("/test-title", test_title);
```

```
Test.add_func ("/test-add-author", test_add_author);

Test.run ();

return 0;
```


In some cases we need to check the actual value that we put into a data structure, such as the `authors` array list in the `Book` class. In `test_add_author`, we only checked the length of the array but we did not check the actual value. The check is even required when we craft the data structure by ourselves or when the data structure is complex; for example, when the order of data after insertion is important. We could also check this by using more than one data set.

Now imagine that we have our own data structure; so now it is your task to check whether the data we enter is really entered as it should be.

Stubbing our tests

In our code, sometimes we use an external library that may give nondeterministic behavior, which is bad for unit testing. To avoid this, we use a **stubbing** technique. This technique involves creating a new library that mimics the function and API of the original library. In our unit test, we use this new fake library instead of the original library so that we can control the output of the API we use in our code.

Now, let's bring back the `core_settings` project from *Chapter 4, Using GNOME Core Libraries*. It is an experiment of getting and setting GSettings with some value.

1. Open the project with Anjuta.

2. Prepare the infrastructure just as we did in our previous action, that is, create the `tests` directory and introduce it to `configure.ac` and `Makefile.am` in the top directory of the project.

3. Then, we need to make changes to the `CoreSettings` class. The original code has the main function inside the same file with the `CoreSettings` class. We need to split these two.

4. What we need to do is adjust `src/Makefile.am`. Modify the file specifically in the `SOURCES` section. This is the code in the file:

```
core_settings_SOURCES = \
    core_settings.vala config.vapi
```

We need to change it to this:

```
core_settings_SOURCES = \
  core_settings.vala main.vala config.vapi
```

5. Then, we modify `src/core_settings.vala` to this:

```
using GLib;
public class CoreSettings : Object
{
  Settings settings = null;
  public CoreSettings ()
  {
    settings = new Settings("org.gnome.desktop.background");
  }

  public string get_bg()
  {
    if (settings == null) {
      return null;
    }

    return settings.get_string("picture-uri");
  }

  public void set_bg(string new_file)
  {
    if (settings == null) {
      return;
    }
    if (settings.set_string ("picture-uri", new_file)) {
      Settings.sync ();
    }
  }

}
```

6. Then we create a new file called `src/main.vala`, which contains the original main function. But now, let's put it inside a dedicated class called `Main`.

```
public class Main {
  static int main (string[] args)
  {
    var app = new CoreSettings ();
    stdout.printf("%s\n", app.get_bg());
    app.set_bg ("http://www.gnome.org/wp-content/themes/gnome-grass/images/gnome-logo.png");
    return 0;
  }
}
```

7. After the splitting, we move on to the `tests` directory. First, create `Makefile.am` inside it. Use this code for the file:

```
AM_CPPFLAGS = \
   -DPACKAGE_LOCALE_DIR=\""$(localedir)"\" \
   -DPACKAGE_SRC_DIR=\""$(srcdir)"\" \
   -DPACKAGE_DATA_DIR=\""$(pkgdatadir)"\" \
   $(CORE_SETTINGS_CFLAGS)

AM_CFLAGS =\
   -Wall\
   -g

TESTS=test_settings

check_PROGRAMS = test_settings

test_settings_SOURCES = \
   ../src/core_settings.vala test_settings.vala stub/gsettings.vala

test_settings_VALAFLAGS =  \
   --pkg gee-1.0

test_settings_LDFLAGS = \
   -Wl,--export-dynamic

test_settings_LDADD = $(CORE_SETTINGS_LIBS)
```

8. Next, create a new file called `test_settings.vala` in the `tests` directory.

```
public class TestSettings {
  static void test_set_get()
  {
    var s = new CoreSettings();
    s.set_bg("test123");
    assert (s.get_bg() == "test123");
  }

  static int main (string[] args)
  {
    Test.init (ref args);

    Test.add_func ("/test-set-get", test_set_get);

    Test.run ();

    return 0;
  }
}
```

9. After that, create a directory called `stub` inside the `tests` directory.

10. Then, create a new file called `gsettings.vala` inside the `stub` directory. Use this code for the file:

```
using Gee;

public class Settings : Object {
  HashMap<string,string> map;

  [CCode(cname="g_settings_new")]
  public Settings(string s) {
     map = new HashMap<string,string>();
  }

  [CCode(cname="g_settings_sync")]
  public static void sync() {
     /* do nothing */
  }

  [CCode(cname="g_settings_set_string")]
  public bool set_string(string key,  string value) {
     map.set(key,  value);
     return true;
  }

  [CCode(cname="g_settings_get_string")]
  public string get_string(string key) {
     return map.get(key);
  }
}
```

11. Rebuild the project by calling this command from the terminal:

```
./autogen.sh
```

12. Finally, execute this command:

```
make check
```

13. Make sure the test passes perfectly, showing the following message:

```
/test-set-get: OK
PASS: test_settings
=============
1 test passed
```

What just happened?

After we built the infrastructure, we split the code into two parts, the `CoreSettings` and `Main` classes. This is essentially because we can't have more than one `main` function in a program, one from the code and one from the test. The other and more important reason is that the class we want to test contains the code that belongs to the class and nothing else. With that in place, we have a clean and organized code and it would be easier to trace when something bad happens.

We fix this by putting the original main function into its own file with its own class. We also rename the original `Main` class to `CoreSettings` to really reflect what it does (using `Settings` from GNOME's core libraries).

Then we put the test file inside the `tests` directory. We also created a new subdirectory called `stub`, inside the `tests` directory. In it, we have the `gsettings.vala` file. The file contains an imitation of the `GSettings` class. The stub contains only the functions that we really use in the code. We should not implement other functions that we do not use.

In our case here, we implement `GSettings` with a hash map implementation from `Gee`:

```
using Gee;
public class Settings : Object {
  HashMap<string,string> map;
```

The constructor is used in the code, hence we need to implement it. Inside, we initialize the hash map. The argument is not important, so we don't need to keep it anywhere. Stubbing in Vala is very tricky. This is because the functions used by Vala codes are actually the generated C functions. So, even if we have exactly the same class and function names in the stub with the original library, the generated class and function names are no longer the same in the generated C file. The discrepancies in the class and function names in the stub will not be taken into use by the test program.

To overcome this problem, we need to tell Vala to generate the names that are identical to the stubbed library. We use the `CCode` attribute just before the class or function declaration in the Vala code. In our experiment, we have this attribute followed immediately by the constructor.

```
[CCode (cname="g_settings_new")]
public Settings (string s) {
  map = new HashMap<string,string>();
}
```

This makes sure that Vala will generate the `g_settings_new` C function from the `Settings` constructor.

We use the `Settings.sync` function in the code, so we need to define the `sync` function. According to the GSettings API reference, the function is static so we need to create the same.

```
[CCode(cname="g_settings_sync")]
public static void sync() {
   /* do nothing */
}
```

We need to create the function, even if we don't need the functionalities. If we skip this, the compilation will fail because Vala won't find the `sync` function in `gsettings.vala` and it will not try to resolve the name from the original library.

After that, we create the `set_string` function. In this function, we simply wrap the hash map and insert the `key` and `value` pairs into the map:

```
[CCode(cname="g_settings_set_string")]
public bool set_string(string key, string value) {
   map.set(key, value);
   return true;
}
```

The same goes with `get_string`. Note that we must use the `CCode` attribute and define the required C function name.

```
[CCode(cname="g_settings_get_string")]
public string get_string(string key) {
   return map.get(key);
}
}
```

Now let's take a look at the test code:

```
public class TestSettings {
  static void test_set_get()
  {
     var s = new CoreSettings();
     s.set_bg("test123");
     assert (s.get_bg() == "test123");
  }
```

Based on the `CoreSettings` class' code, we only need to test the `set_bg` and `get_bg` functions. There is no other function that offers functionalities in the class. So we straightaway implement the `main` function.

```
static int main (string[] args)
{
  Test.init (ref args);
  Test.add_func ("/test-set-get", test_set_get);
  Test.run ();
  return 0;
}
}
```

There we initialize the `Test` framework, add the test path, and run the test. Wait, where is our stub used? Let's revisit `tests/Makefile.am` and unveil the mystery. Take a look at the SOURCES section:

```
test_settings_SOURCES = \
  ../src/core_settings.vala test_settings.vala stub/gsettings.vala
```

It says that Vala must compile these three files together at the same time. Our test code does not have any reference to GSettings, only our source code in `core_settings.vala` does. So, if we take a look at `core_settings.vala`, we see:

```
public CoreSettings ()
{
  settings = new Settings ("org.gnome.desktop.background");
}
```

What it does is it actually instantiates the `settings` object from `gsettings.vala` instead of GSettings, and here what it does is it calls `get_string` from `gsettings.vala`:

```
public string get_bg()
{
  if (settings == null) {
    return null;
  }

  return settings.get_string ("picture-uri");
}
```

The key to stubbing is to produce exactly the same API with the library we use. When building, we compile the code, the tests, and the stub together. Otherwise, either Vala will complain about using the wrong API or even if the build is successful, our stub will not get called.

Testing GUI modules

What we have done so far is straightforward testing of functions, which gives a result based on the value we pass into the arguments. GUI modules, however, expect input from user behavior, such as the click of a mouse, typing of the keyboard, and other such instances. More generally, they react by giving a certain output based on one or more events.

When testing GUI modules, we will no longer be able to use the methods we learnt previously. When testing GUI modules we must have the following aspects handled:

- Setting the environment to prepare the GUI test application
- Initialization of the graphical framework
- Emitting and handling the UI events
- Event loop management

We will discuss these now.

Time for action – testing a GTK+ module

Let's take our old `custom_composite` Vala project and put a unit test in it.

1. As usual, let's create the `tests` directory and include it in `configure.ac` and `Makefile.am` in the top directory.

2. Split the code into two parts. Use this code in `custom_window.vala`:

```vala
using GLib;
using Gtk;

public class CustomWindow : Window
{
  Entry entry;
  Box box;
  public signal void search_updated(string value);

  void show_search_box() {
    entry.show();
    entry.has_focus = true;
  }

  void hide_search_box() {
    entry.hide();
  }
```

```vala
  public override void add(Widget widget) {
    if (widget != box) {
      box.pack_start(widget, true, true);
    } else {
      base.add(widget);
    }
  }

  public CustomWindow ()
  {
    box = new Box(Orientation.VERTICAL, 0);
    entry = new Entry();
    box.pack_start (entry, false, true);
    box.show();

    add(box);

    key_release_event.connect((event) => {
      search_updated(entry.text);
      return false;
    });

    key_press_event.connect((event) => {
      if (!entry.get_visible()) {
        show_search_box();
      }
      return false;
    });
  }
}
```

3. Use this one for the `main` class:

```vala
using GLib;
using Gtk;

public class Main {
  static int main (string[] args)
  {
    Gtk.init (ref args);
    var window = new CustomWindow();
    var label = new Label("This is a text");

    window.add(label);
    window.resize(400,400);
    window.search_updated.connect((value) => {
      label.set_text("Searching for keyword " + value);
```

```
        });

        label.show();
        window.show();
        Gtk.main ();

        return 0;
    }
}
```

4. Then, modify the `Makefile.am` file to include both the implementation class and the main class.

```
custom_composite_SOURCES = \
    custom_composite.vala main.vala config.vapi
```

5. Next, let's create `Makefile.am` for the tests:

```
AM_CPPFLAGS = \
    -DPACKAGE_LOCALE_DIR=\""$(localedir)"\" \
    -DPACKAGE_SRC_DIR=\""$(srcdir)"\" \
    -DPACKAGE_DATA_DIR=\""$(pkgdatadir)"\" \
    $(CUSTOM_COMPOSITE_CFLAGS)

AM_CFLAGS =\
     -Wall\
     -g

TESTS=test_custom_window
check_PROGRAMS = test_custom_window

test_custom_window_SOURCES = \
    ../src/custom_composite.vala test_custom_window.vala

test_custom_window_VALAFLAGS =  \
    --pkg gtk+-3.0

test_custom_window_LDFLAGS = \
    -Wl,--export-dynamic

test_custom_window_LDADD = $(CUSTOM_COMPOSITE_LIBS)
```

6. Create a new file called `test_custom_window.vala` inside `tests` and use this code:

```
using Gtk;

public class TestCustomWindow {

    static void process_events()
    {
```

```
      while (Gtk.events_pending ()) {
        Gtk.main_iteration_do(true);
      }
  }

  static void test_initial_child ()
  {
    var window = new CustomWindow();
    var child = window.get_child () as Box;
    window.show_now();

    assert (child != null);
    window.destroy ();
  }

  static void test_child_visibility ()
  {
    var window = new CustomWindow();
    var child = window.get_child () as Box;
    window.show_now();

    var entry_is_found = false;
    var children = child.get_children ();
    if (children != null && children.nth(0) != null) {

      var entry = children.nth_data(0) as Entry;

      assert (entry != null);
      assert (entry.visible == false);

      Gdk.test_simulate_key (window.get_window (), 1, 1, Gdk.
Key.a, 0, Gdk.EventType.KEY_PRESS);
      Gdk.test_simulate_key (window.get_window (), 1, 1, Gdk.
Key.a, 0, Gdk.EventType.KEY_RELEASE);

      process_events (); // Process events

      assert (entry.visible == true);

      entry_is_found = true;
    }

    assert (entry_is_found);
    window.destroy ();
  }

  static void test_search_updated ()
  {
```

```
      var window = new CustomWindow();
      window.show_now();
      var search_updated_was_emitted = false;
      var search_updated_was_correct = false;

      window.search_updated.connect ((text) => {
        search_updated_was_emitted = true;
        if (text == "a") {
          search_updated_was_correct = true;
        }
      });

      Gdk.test_simulate_key (window.get_window (), 1, 1, Gdk.Key.a,
  0, Gdk.EventType.KEY_PRESS);
      Gdk.test_simulate_key (window.get_window (), 1, 1, Gdk.Key.a,
  0, Gdk.EventType.KEY_RELEASE);

      process_events (); // process events

      assert (search_updated_was_emitted);
      assert (search_updated_was_correct);
      window.destroy ();
    }

  static int main (string[] args)
  {
    Gtk.test_init (ref args);

    Test.add_func ("/test-search-updated", test_search_updated);
    Test.add_func ("/test-initial-child", test_initial_child);
    Test.add_func ("/test-child-visibility", test_child_
  visibility);

    Idle.add (() => {
      Test.run ();
      Gtk.main_quit ();
      return true;
    });

    Gtk.main ();

    return 0;
  }
}
```

7. Rebuild the project by using this command:

```
./autogen.sh
```

8. Set up the environment for the GUI initialization by issuing the following command:

```
export DISPLAY=:0
```

This only needs to be done once when we first run any GUI tests. This is needed when you run the test in the terminal console. If you run the test directly inside GNOME, you don't need this.

9. On running the test you will see a window flashing for a moment before the test ends. Type the following command in the shell to run the test:

```
make check
```

10. Make sure all the tests are passed successfully.

```
/test-search-updated: OK
/test-initial-child: OK
/test-child-visibility: OK
PASS: test_custom_window
=============
1 test passed
=============
```

What just happened?

Now we just directly concentrate on how the unit test is done.

Let's see what the `CustomWindow` class does:

- It is a window and creates a text entry inside
- A window can only take one child and this should not remove the text entry
- It emits the `search_updated` signal whenever the user presses a key in the window

This is the base of our strategy to create unit tests.

For our first test, we check whether the constructor creates the `Box` object as the placeholder for the `Entry` and other widgets correctly.

```
static void test_initial_child ()
{
  var window = new CustomWindow ();
  var child = window.get_child () as Box;
  window.show_now ();
```

```
    assert (child != null);
    window.destroy ();
}
```

Here, we simply check whether the constructor has the `Box` object. This test is a straightforward test.

In the next test we check the visibility of the text entry. Initially, the text entry must be hidden, and after we press any key, the entry must be visible.

```
static void test_child_visibility ()
{
    var window = new CustomWindow();
    var child = window.get_child () as Box;
    window.show_now();
```

Here, we call `show_now` in order to display the window immediately. If we use `show`, the showing may be deferred until other events are processed.

```
    var entry_is_found = false;
    var children = child.get_children ();
    if (children != null && children.nth(0) != null) {

        var entry = children.nth_data(0) as Entry;
```

Next, we try to get the text entry. The entry is the first child of the window, so we use the `nth_data` method and pass `0` to denote the element at index `0`.

```
        assert (entry != null);
        assert (entry.visible == false);
```

We use `Entry` to cast the returned widget as an `Entry` widget. By using this cast, it will return `null` if the widget returned is not an `Entry` widget. Here, we check whether the `entry` variable is really a type of an `Entry` widget by comparing it with the `null` value. If it succeeds, we continue checking whether the visibility is set to `false` because we want to make sure that the initial visibility for the entry must be `false`.

```
    Gdk.test_simulate_key (window.get_window (), 1, 1, Gdk.Key.a, 0,
Gdk.EventType.KEY_PRESS);
    Gdk.test_simulate_key (window.get_window (), 1, 1, Gdk.Key.a, 0,
Gdk.EventType.KEY_RELEASE);
```

Then we simulate a key press followed with a key release by using `test_simulate_key` from the `Gdk` class. We send these events to the `window` object. The function requires `Gdk.Window`, so we use `get_window` to pass `Gdk.Window` from the `window` object. The usage of `show_now` for showing the `window` object is essential here, because if we use `show` and the showing is not yet performed, then the `get_window` function will return `null` and our test will fail.

We can use any location of the press and release events. Here, we use the (1,1) coordinate. The key we send is the *a* key, so we use `Gdk.Key.a` without any other key modifier. We send the press event first and then follow it with a release event.

```
        process_events (); // Process events
        assert (entry.visible == true);

        entry_is_found = true;
    }
    assert (entry_is_found);
    window.destroy ();
}
```

Just after we send the key, we need to process the pending events by calling the `process_events` function. Then after that, we can check the visibility. Without calling `process_events`, the key events may not be processed by the system so the visibility of the `entry` object has not changed yet. We then destroy the window afterwards.

Here is what the `process_events` function does:

```
static void process_events()
{
    while (Gtk.events_pending ()) {
      Gtk.main_iteration_do(true);
    }
}
```

It basically processes any pending events in the queue. When it finds them, it simply executes the main loop by calling `main_iteration_do` and we allow GTK+ to complete the operation even when it is blocking by providing the `true` argument.

Next, we check whether the signal is emitted properly with the correct value.

```
static void test_search_updated ()
{
    var window = new CustomWindow ();
    window.show_now ();
    var search_updated_was_emitted = false;
    var search_updated_was_correct = false;

    window.search_updated.connect ((text) => {
      search_updated_was_emitted = true;
      if (text == "a") {
        search_updated_was_correct = true;
      }
    });
```

Here, we connect the `search_updated` signal. We record the success of the handler with a local variable. We check whether the text from the signal is a, which is the key event that we send into the window.

```
        Gdk.test_simulate_key (window.get_window (), 1, 1, Gdk.Key.a, 0,
    Gdk.EventType.KEY_PRESS);
        Gdk.test_simulate_key (window.get_window (), 1, 1, Gdk.Key.a, 0,
    Gdk.EventType.KEY_RELEASE);

        process_events (); // process events
```

After we send the key events, we call `process_events`. This is to make sure that our signal handler is called so that we can assert the result.

```
        assert (search_updated_was_emitted);
        assert (search_updated_was_correct);
        window.destroy ();
```

In our `main` function, we first call the `Gtk.test_init` function. This is to set up the environment to be suitable for testing. Next, we add the test paths.

```
    static int main (string[] args)
    {
        Gtk.test_init (ref args);

        Test.add_func ("/test-search-updated", test_search_updated);
        Test.add_func ("/test-initial-child", test_initial_child);
        Test.add_func ("/test-child-visibility", test_child_visibility);
```

We still need `Gtk.main` to get the GTK+ system up and running. When we run the test outside GNOME, we need to run the X11 server and set up the environment so that the test can run. We do this by setting the `DISPLAY` environment variable to our X11 display number. Typically the value is `:0`. This is a bit of a cumbersome setup especially if we do the test remotely.

However, once it is running, we need to ensure that our tests are run. To do this, we need to set up an idle handler. Inside the handler we simply run the test and then exit the GTK+ system.

```
        Idle.add (() => {
            Test.run ();
            Gtk.main_quit ();
            return true;
        });

        Gtk.main ();
```

Have a go hero – adding missing tests

In our previous test, we only checked for the existence of the `Box` object inside the `window` object. We missed another essential test to check:

+ Whether `Entry` is really created
+ Whether `Entry` can coexist when we add a new widget into the `window` object.

Figure it out and let's create some tests!

Summary

We have now seen how to do unit testing in our GNOME code. The most tricky part for a beginner is mainly to figure out the tests that must be written. We have to discuss this by first identifying the functionalities provided by the code that we want to test. Then we narrow down to each existing branch in the code by giving different arguments so that the code path will be visited in all cases.

We know that we must create a deterministic test and we realize that the library (or even our own code) we use may give nondeterministic behavior. To solve this problem, we need to create a stub for each library, which potentially gives nondeterministic values. We also need to do stubbing when the library we use is too complex or requires a heavy setup when we run the unit test.

Finally, we know how to test our GUI modules by using GTK+'s own initialization function. We also need to process all pending events before asserting something. We also learnt that we need to use the `show_now` function to get the Gdk window immediately set up.

The tests we wrote must be run on every change we make to the code. This is to make sure that we will not see regressions in the code. Many software developers run the test before they send the code to the source code repository and they set up a nightly test by running all test cases in the suite.

In our final chapter, we will learn how to do two big projects, a browser and a twitter client. We will use all of our techniques that we learnt in the previous chapters, so brace yourself!

13
Exciting Projects

After spending so much time learning how to develop not so useful applications, it is time to move on to the next level. Now we will develop a web browser and a Twitter client. The applications we are going to make are simple yet useful. You can also use them as the basis for enhanced versions, if you decide to make them.

In this chapter, we will revisit most of the topics we have learnt so far, but with adding complexities and exploring them in more depth. Specifically, we will obtain more knowledge in these areas:

◆ Implementing a web browser using WebKitGTK

◆ Doing path hardcoding using the configure script

◆ Developing a multiscript Seed application

So, let's start with our first project.

Part I – web browser

The first application we will develop is a web browser. We aim for a basic browser that is simple enough to develop. The browser includes a set of navigation buttons and the ability to open pages from the Internet.

To make the whole development easier, we create a mockup version of our browser. This is simply a drawing showing how our web browser will look. Based on this mockup, we will derive a UI layout, done in the Anjuta/Glade tool.

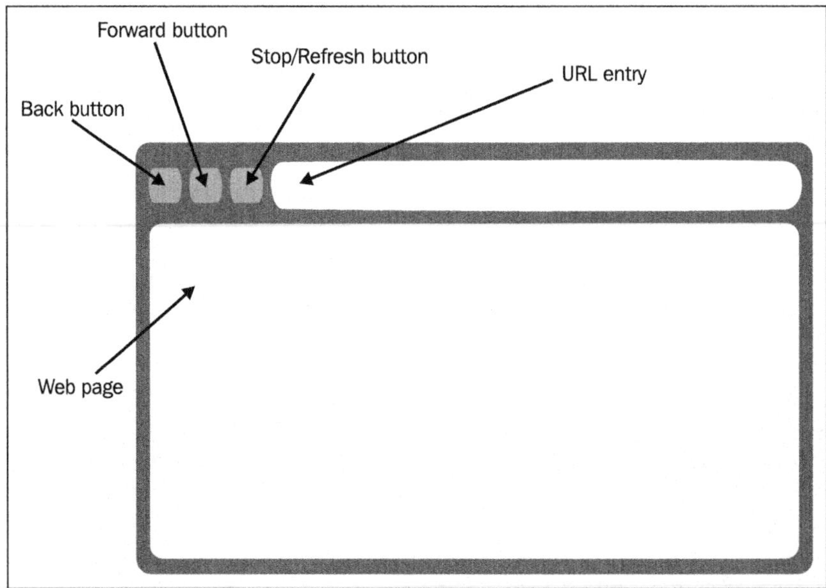

First, let's familiarize ourselves with the structure of the UI of our browser. The main window is split into two parts. The area which displays the web page occupies most of the window area. The top-most part is used by the navigation buttons and the URL entry.

The navigation buttons are independent buttons and represent the back, forward, and stop/reload actions, respectively. There is an additional button hidden beside the URL entry, which is the go button. The button is shown when the URL entry is being filled in.

That's it; it's just as simple as that. By the way, in GUI design terminology, the UI hosting the navigation buttons and the URL entry is called **chrome**.

Time for action – designing our UI

Now let's fire up Anjuta and design our UI. A Glade designer does not have GtkWebUI in its palette, so here is what we are going to do:

1. Create a new Vala project and call it `web-browser`. Use GtkBuilder for the UI.
2. Open `web_browser.ui` with Glade designer by just double-clicking the file in the **Project** dock.
3. Put a vertical `Box` object in the window with two items.

4. Put another `Box` object, this time a horizontal one, on the top part of the vertical `Box` object, leaving the bottom part empty. Split the horizontal `Box` object into five elements by filling the **Number of elements** option with 5.

5. Put a **button** on each empty box element, except the third one. On each button, activate the **Stock button** option and fill it with `gtk-go-back`, `gtk-go-forward`, `gtk-refresh`, and `gtk-ok  stock` buttons on each **button** respectively.

6. Give the buttons names, use `btn_back`, `btn_forward`, `btn_refresh`, and `btn_go`. Put the name in each **Name** option of the button.

7. Put an `Entry` object on the third empty **box** and give `url_entry` as its name. Go to the **Packing** tab and make sure the **Expand** option is set to **Yes**.

8. Put a **Scrolled Window** object (it's in the **Containers** section) into the bottom empty box. Make sure the **Expand** option is set to **Yes**.

9. Set both the **Horizontal Scrollbar Policy** and **Vertical Scrollbar Policy** values to **Never**.

10. We should have the UI file ready and it should look like this:

What just happened?

What we did was create the UI layout for our web browser. As we can see, it is a straightforward translation from the mockup. One thing is still missing though; the web page area is still empty. However, we have `ScrolledWindow` as the container for the `WebView` object later. The objective of using the `ScrolledWindow` container is to make sure that the window is not resizing depending on the content because the sizing is already handed over to `ScrolledWindow`. We disable the scroll bars on vertical and horizontal axes because `WebView` already handles the scroll bars on its own.

Browser interaction

Now let's inspect the interaction design of our browser. At the initial stage, we have an idle browser, having all navigation buttons disabled and the URL entry empty. At this point, our web view only contains the **Welcome** text (or the translated word of **Welcome** if it is localized to another language). The next possible move by the user is to fill in the URL entry.

When a user starts to type something, the go button appears. All navigation buttons are still disabled as we don't have any content displayed. Then, either the user keeps typing or decides to complete the process by clicking on the go button. When this happens, the web view starts to load the requested URL.

When the page is being loaded, the refresh button changes itself into a stop button. When the user presses this button, the loading is immediately stopped, cancelling everything. Then the stop button changes back into the refresh button. Either way, the browser stays at the idle state.

Whenever the user continues to interact with the loaded web page, the navigation button's states are updated accordingly. If the browser can go back, it means the back button is active. Same thing happens with the forward button.

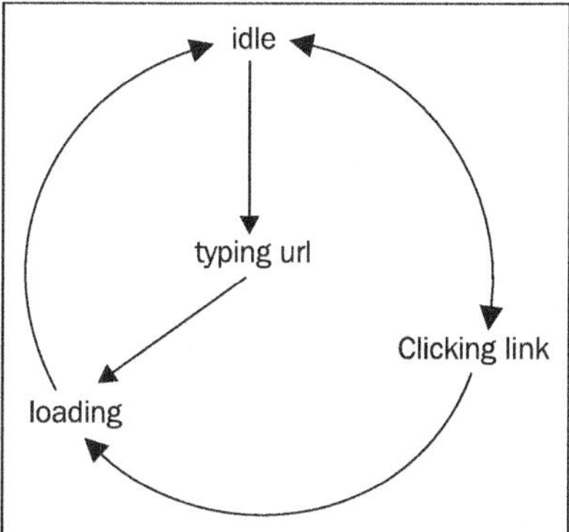

Based on the previous description, we have four states which are applied to our browser. It is **idle** when it waits for the user to start the interaction. Then it is in the **typing url** state when the user starts to type something. Another possibility is to enter the **Clicking link** state whenever the user clicks on any link on a page. After that, the state is in the **loading** state when some page is being loaded. The final state would be the idle state again.

With this design in our hands now, we are ready to implement the code.

Time for action – preparing the build infrastructure

Let's now modify the project we created earlier and improve it with **i18n** (**internationalization**) and test the build infrastructure:

1. Modify the `configure.ac` file and make it look like this:

```
AC_INIT(web_browser, 0.1)
AC_CONFIG_HEADERS([config.h])
AM_INIT_AUTOMAKE([1.11])
AM_SILENT_RULES([yes])
AC_PROG_CC

LT_INIT
IT_PROG_INTLTOOL()
```

```
AH_TEMPLATE([GETTEXT_PACKAGE], [Package name for gettext])
GETTEXT_PACKAGE=web-browser

AC_DEFINE_UNQUOTED([GETTEXT_PACKAGE], ["$GETTEXT_PACKAGE"],
                   [The domain to use with gettext])
AC_SUBST(GETTEXT_PACKAGE)
AM_GLIB_GNU_GETTEXT


dnl Check for vala
AM_PROG_VALAC([0.10.0])

dnl Development mode
AC_ARG_ENABLE(development,
  AS_HELP_STRING([--enable-development],[enable development
mode]),
    enable_development="$enableval",
       enable_development=no)
if test "x$enable_development" = "xyes"; then
  DEVELOPMENT_MODE="yes"
  PACKAGE_LOCALE_DIR=[${PWD}/locale]
  PACKAGE_UI_DIR=[${PWD}/src]
else
  PACKAGE_LOCALE_DIR=[${datadir}/locale]
  PACKAGE_UI_DIR=[${datadir}/web-browser]
fi

AC_SUBST(PACKAGE_LOCALE_DIR)
AC_SUBST(PACKAGE_UI_DIR)
AH_TEMPLATE([PACKAGE_UI_DIR], [Location of the .ui file])
AC_DEFINE_UNQUOTED([PACKAGE_UI_DIR], ["$PACKAGE_UI_DIR"],
                   [Location of the .ui file])

AC_SUBST(DEVELOPMENT_MODE)
AH_TEMPLATE([DEVELOPMENT_MODE], [Whether in development mode or
not])
AC_DEFINE_UNQUOTED([DEVELOPMENT_MODE], ["$DEVELOPMENT_MODE"],
                   [Development mode])

PKG_CHECK_MODULES(WEB_BROWSER, [gtk+-3.0 webkitgtk-3.0])
PKG_CHECK_MODULES(TEST_WEB_BROWSER, [gtk+-3.0 ])

AC_OUTPUT([
Makefile
src/Makefile
tests/Makefile
po/Makefile.in
])
```

2. Modify the `Makefile.am` file, and fill it with this:

```
SUBDIRS = src tests po

web_browserdocdir = ${prefix}/doc/web_browser
web_browserdoc_DATA = \
  README\
  COPYING\
  AUTHORS\
  ChangeLog\
  INSTALL\
  NEWS

EXTRA_DIST = \
  $(web_browserdoc_DATA)
  intltool-extract.in \
  intltool-merge.in \
  intltool-update.in

DISTCLEANFILES = \
  intltool-extract \
  intltool-merge \
  intltool-update \
  po/.intltool-merge-cache \
  $(NULL)

# Remove doc directory on uninstall
uninstall-local:
  -rm -r $(web_browserdocdir)
```

3. Modify the `src/Makefile.am` file, and use this whole file:

```
uidir = $(PACKAGE_UI_DIR)
ui_DATA = web_browser.ui

AM_CPPFLAGS = \
  -DPACKAGE_LOCALE_DIR=\""$(localedir)"\" \
  -DPACKAGE_SRC_DIR=\""$(srcdir)"\" \
  -DPACKAGE_DATA_DIR=\""$(pkgdatadir)"\" \
  $(WEB_BROWSER_CFLAGS)

AM_CFLAGS =\
   -Wall\
   -g

bin_PROGRAMS = web_browser
```

```
web_browser_SOURCES = \
   main.vala web_browser.vala config.vapi

web_browser_VALAFLAGS =   \
   --vapidir . \
   --pkg gtk+-3.0 \
   --pkg webkit-1.0   \
   --pkg libsoup-2.4 \
   --Xcc='--include config.h'

web_browser_LDFLAGS = \
   -Wl,--export-dynamic

web_browser_LDADD = $(WEB_BROWSER_LIBS)


EXTRA_DIST = $(ui_DATA)

# Remove ui directory on uninstall
uninstall-local:
   -rm -r $(uidir)
   -rm -r $(pkgdatadir)
```

4. Create the po directory.

5. Add po/POTFILES.in with this content:

   ```
   [type: gettext/glade] src/web_browser.ui
   src/web_browser.vala
   ```

6. Add po/POTFILES.skip with this content:

   ```
   src/web_browser.c
   tests/web_browser.c
   ```

7. Add the po/LINGUAS file and fill it with the language code that we support,
   for example to support the Indonesian language, we put:

   ```
   id
   ```

8. Populate the translation template by running this command inside the po directory:

   ```
   intltool-update -pot
   ```

9. Copy the resulting web-browser.pot to id.po (or any other file, depending on
   the content of the LINGUAS file) and revisit *Chapter 11, Making Our Applications
   Go International*, on how to handle the po file.

10. Create the tests directory.

11. Add `tests/Makefile.am` **using this content:**

```
AM_CPPFLAGS = \
  -DPACKAGE_LOCALE_DIR=\""$(localedir)"\" \
  -DPACKAGE_SRC_DIR=\""$(srcdir)"\" \
  -DPACKAGE_DATA_DIR=\""$(pkgdatadir)"\" \
  -I. \
  $(WEB_BROWSER_CFLAGS)

AM_CFLAGS =\
   -Wall\
   -g

TESTS=test_web_browser
check_PROGRAMS = test_web_browser

test_web_browser_SOURCES = \
  ../src/config.vapi webkit.vala ../src/web_browser.vala test_web_
browser.vala

test_web_browser_VALAFLAGS =  \
  --pkg gtk+-3.0 \
  --Xcc='--include config.h'

test_web_browser_LDFLAGS = \
  -Wl,--export-dynamic

test_web_browser_LDADD = $(TEST_WEB_BROWSER_LIBS)
```

12. Add `tests/test_web_browser.vala` **and fill it with this code:**

```vala
using Gtk;

public class TestWebBrowser {

  static void process_events()
  {
    while (Gtk.events_pending ()) {
      Gtk.main_iteration_do(true);
    }
  }
  static int main (string[] args)
  {
    Gtk.test_init (ref args);

    Idle.add (() => {
      Test.run ();
      Gtk.main_quit ();
      return true;
```

```
        });

        Gtk.main ();

        return 0;
    }
}
```

13. Add `tests/webkit.vala` and use this content:

```vala
using Gtk;

[CCode (lower_case_cprefix = "webkit_")]
namespace WebKit {

    [CCode (cheader_filename="webkit/webkit.h")]
    public class WebFrame : Object {
    }

    [CCode (cheader_filename="webkit/webkit.h")]
    public class WebView : Viewport {

        public WebView() {
        }

        [CCode (cname="webkit_web_view_load_string")]
        public void load_string (string content, string mime, string
encoding, string base_uri) {
        }

    }
}
```

14. Put the `webkit-1.0.vapi` file which accompanies this book into the `src` directory.

15. Use the following code for the `src/web_browser.vala` file:

```vala
using GLib;
using Gtk;
using WebKit;

public class WebBrowser : Object
{
    internal Builder builder = null;
    WebView view = null;
    const string UI_FILE = Config.PACKAGE_UI_DIR + "/" + "web_
browser.ui";

    public WebBrowser ()
    {
```

```
      Gtk.Settings.get_default ().gtk_button_images = true;
      try
      {
        builder = new Builder ();
        builder.add_from_file (UI_FILE);

        view = new WebView();
        view.load_string("<h1>" + _("Welcome") + "</h1>", "text/
html", "UTF-8", "/");
        var box = builder.get_object ("webhost") as Container;
        box.add(view);

        var window = builder.get_object ("window") as Window;
        window.show_all ();

        window.destroy.connect(() => {
          Gtk.main_quit();
        });

      }
      catch (Error e) {
        stderr.printf (_("Could not load UI: %s\n"), e.message);
      }
    }
  }
```

16. Create `src/main.vala` and use this content:

```
using GLib;
using Gtk;

public class Main : Object
{
  static int main (string[] args)
  {
    Gtk.init (ref args);
    var app = new WebBrowser ();
    Gtk.main ();
    return 0;
  }
}
```

17. Modify `src/config.vapi` to look like this:

```
[CCode (cprefix = "", lower_case_cprefix = "", cheader_filename =
"config.h")]
namespace Config {
  public const string DEVELOPMENT_MODE;
```

```
public const string GETTEXT_PACKAGE;
public const string SPRITE_DIR;
public const string BACKGROUND_DIR;
public const string PACKAGE_DATA_DIR;
public const string PACKAGE_UI_DIR;
public const string PACKAGE_LOCALE_DIR;
public const string PACKAGE_NAME;
public const string PACKAGE_VERSION;
public const string VERSION;
}
```

18. Build using the `--enable-development` option by running:

```
./autogen.sh --enable-development
```

19. Alternatively, put the option in the **Configure Options** field in the **Configure Project...** submenu in the **Build** menu.

20. Go to the console and type this command:

```
make check
```

21. You should check this output to see whether the unit tests pass or not.

22. You should also be able to run the application and it should display this UI without any possible interaction except closing it.

What just happened?

Wow, that was a somewhat heavy series of actions, wasn't it?

We have just set up the build infrastructure which includes i18n and unit testing. We left the functionalities unimplemented. We also kept the implementation minimal, just enough to get the build process successful. Now let's take a look at this more closely.

The first thing we did was to set up the `configure.ac` file. It is quite similar to what we had in the previous chapters, but there are a couple interesting new things introduced here. Here is the first one:

```
dnl Development mode
AC_ARG_ENABLE(development,
  AS_HELP_STRING([--enable-development],[enable development mode]),
    enable_development="$enableval",
        enable_development=no)
if test "x$enable_development" = "xyes"; then
  DEVELOPMENT_MODE="yes"
  PACKAGE_LOCALE_DIR=[${PWD}/locale]
  PACKAGE_UI_DIR=[${PWD}/src]
else
  PACKAGE_LOCALE_DIR=[${datadir}/locale]
  PACKAGE_UI_DIR=[${datadir}/web-browser]
fi
```

This snippet shows the addition of the `--enable-development` option to the `configure` script. It looks pretty familiar except that we added the definition of `PACKAGE_LOCALE_DIR` and `PACKAGE_UI_DIR`. The values of these variables depend on the addition or omission of the `--enable-development` option from the parameter of the `configure` script. `PACKAGE_LOCALE_DIR` holds the location of the `LOCALE` directory as we have discussed in *Chapter 11, Making Our Applications Go International*. `PACKAGE_UI_DIR` holds the location of the `.ui` file.

This is a very good improvement compared to our approach in previous chapters regarding the ability to tell the code where to look for the `.ui` and translation files. One of the major improvements is that we do not need to detect whether it is in development mode or not in the source code. The locations are hardcoded automatically depending on whether we give the `--enable-development` option to the `configure` script or not.

If we did give the option, `PACKAGE_UI_DIR` points to the `src` directory while if we did not, `PACKAGE_UI_DIR` points to the `/usr/share/web-browser` directory. This is done at compile time, so don't forget to omit the `--enable-development` option before building the deployment version.

In order to get the value of `PACKAGE_UI_DIR` accessible from the code, we insert the value into the `config.h` file. And this is how we do it in the `configure` script:

```
AC_SUBST(PACKAGE_UI_DIR)
AH_TEMPLATE([PACKAGE_UI_DIR], [Location of the .ui file])
AC_DEFINE_UNQUOTED([PACKAGE_UI_DIR], ["$PACKAGE_UI_DIR"],
                   [Location of the .ui file])
```

Then, we need to make it accessible from the Vala code by adding this into the `src/config.vapi` file:

```
public const string PACKAGE_UI_DIR;
```

And the variable can then be used as `Config.PACKAGE_UI_DIR`.

The next interesting thing is that we have these lines:

```
PKG_CHECK_MODULES(WEB_BROWSER, [gtk+-3.0 webkitgtk-3.0])
PKG_CHECK_MODULES(TEST_WEB_BROWSER, [gtk+-3.0 ])
```

The first line will export new variables of `WEB_BROWSER_CFLAGS` and `WEB_BROWSER_LIBS` automatically, while the second one will export the `TEST_WEB_BROWSER_CFLAGS` and `TEST_WEB_BROWSER_LIBS` variables. We use the first variable in `src/Makefile.am` to compile the application, as shown in the following snippets:

```
AM_CPPFLAGS = \
    -DPACKAGE_LOCALE_DIR=\""$(localedir)"\" \
    -DPACKAGE_SRC_DIR=\""$(srcdir)"\" \
    -DPACKAGE_DATA_DIR=\""$(pkgdatadir)"\" \
    $(WEB_BROWSER_CFLAGS)
```

and

```
web_browser_LDADD = $(WEB_BROWSER_LIBS)
```

It means that the build system picks up the flags and header files needed for compilation as well as the library names required for linking the application. All of these are required to make the stub compilation successful.

We have the `webkit.vala` code to stub the WebKit to make unit testing easier to carry out. As we can see from `tests/Makefile.am`, we compile the test files with `TEST_WEB_BROWSER_LIBS` to exclude the original WebKit library being linked into our unit test. With this, we are sure that our source code in `src` will be compiled with WebKit, and the source code in the `tests` directory will be compiled with our stub.

However, in our unit test, we still use `WEB_BROWSER_CFLAGS` and not `TEST_WEB_BROWSER_CFLAGS` in order to use the original WebKit header files. The original header is needed to compile the generated C source code.

Now, let's move on to the i18n part.

We put our Vala code, which is `src/web_browser.vala` and the `.ui` file, into the translatable files by putting them into `po/POTFILES.in`. We don't need to add all files, but only hand picked selected files which contain translatable text. Next, we add all generated C code into `po/POTFILES.skip` to mark them as non-translatable. This is to avoid double translation.

The rest is pretty straightforward, so let's move on to the meat.

Time for action – finishing up

Now we are going to complete the implementation by following the user interaction design that we have discussed. Make sure you have `src/web_browser.vala`, which is distributed in this book.

1. Fill in `tests/test_web_browser.vala` with these lines:

```vala
using Gtk;

public class TestWebBrowser {

  static void process_events ()
  {
    while (Gtk.events_pending ()) {
      Gtk.main_iteration_do (true);
    }
  }

  static void test_initial_state ()
  {
    var web = new WebBrowser ();
    process_events ();
    assert (web.state == WebBrowser.State.IDLE);
  }

  static void test_typing_url ()
  {
    var web = new WebBrowser ();
    var window = web.builder.get_object ("window") as Window;
    window.show_now ();
    web.url_entry.show_now ();

    assert (web.btn_go.visible == false);

    var entry_w = web.url_entry.get_window ();
    web.url_entry.focus (0);
```

```
        assert (web.state == WebBrowser.State.IDLE);
        Gdk.test_simulate_key (entry_w, 5, 5, Gdk.Key.a, 0, Gdk.
EventType.KEY_PRESS);
        Gdk.test_simulate_key (entry_w, 5, 5, Gdk.Key.a, 0, Gdk.
EventType.KEY_RELEASE);

        process_events ();
        assert (web.state == WebBrowser.State.TYPING_URL);
        assert (web.btn_go.visible == true);

        var btn_w = web.btn_go.get_window ();
        web.btn_go.focus(0);
        Gdk.test_simulate_key (btn_w, 5, 5, Gdk.Key.Return, 0, Gdk.
EventType.KEY_PRESS);
        Gdk.test_simulate_key (btn_w, 5, 5, Gdk.Key.Return, 0, Gdk.
EventType.KEY_RELEASE);

        process_events ();
        assert (web.state == WebBrowser.State.LOADING);

    }
    static int main (string[] args)
    {
      Gtk.test_init (ref args);

      Test.add_func ("/test-initial-state", test_initial_state);
      Test.add_func ("/test-typing-url", test_typing_url);

      Idle.add (() => {
        Test.run ();
        Gtk.main_quit ();
        return true;
      });

      Gtk.main ();

      return 0;
    }
}
```

2. Open the `tests/webkit.vala` stub file and use this code:

```
using Gtk;

[CCode (lower_case_cprefix = "webkit_")]
namespace WebKit {

  [CCode (cheader_filename="webkit/webkit.h")]
  public class WebFrame : Object {
```

```
    }

  [CCode (cheader_filename="webkit/webkit.h")]
  public class WebView : Viewport {
    public bool _can_go_back;
    public bool _can_go_forward;
    public signal void load_started (WebFrame frame);
    public signal void load_finished (WebFrame frame);
    WebFrame frame;

    public WebView () {
      frame = new WebFrame ();
    }

    [CCode (cname="webkit_web_view_can_go_back")]
    public bool can_go_back() {
      return _can_go_back;
    }

    [CCode (cname="webkit_web_view_can_go_forward")]
    public bool can_go_forward() {
      return _can_go_forward;
    }

    [CCode (cname="webkit_web_view_go_back")]
    public void go_back () {
    }

    [CCode (cname="webkit_web_view_go_forward")]
    public void go_forward () {
    }

    [CCode (cname="webkit_web_view_load_uri")]
    public void load_uri (string uri) {
      load_started (frame);
    }

    [CCode (cname="webkit_web_view_load_string")]
    public void load_string (string content, string mime, string
encoding, string base_uri) {
    }

    [CCode (cname="webkit_web_view_stop_loading")]
    public void stop_loading () {
    }

    [CCode (cname="webkit_web_view_reload")]
    public void reload () {
    }
  }
}
```

3. Build and run the application.

What just happened?

As we already have our infrastructure set up, we can concentrate on what this project is really about. Let's open this with the WebBrowser object.

```
const string UI_FILE = Config.PACKAGE_UI_DIR + "/" + "web_browser.
ui";
```

In this line, we just get the exact location of the `.ui` file by getting the `Config.PACKAGE_UI_DIR` value, appended with the filename. Because the location is already hardcoded in the build system, we don't need to put an extra `if` branch code to check whether this is in development mode or not, like we did in *Chapter 11, Making Our Applications Go International*.

```
internal Button btn_back = null;
internal Button btn_forward = null;
internal Button btn_go = null;
internal Button btn_refresh = null;
internal Entry url_entry = null;
```

Those are the navigation buttons and our URL entry widget. We mark them as internal in order to be able to access them from our unit test.

```
internal enum State {
    IDLE,
    TYPING_URL,
    LOADING
}
```

These are the states that we have discussed earlier. One state is missing, which is the clicking link state. We explicitly remove the state from the `enum` loop because the clicking is handled directly within WebKit, while the other states we handle by ourselves. So, in order to avoid cluttering, the `enum` value which we will not use, will not be put in.

However, it is not a good practice to just remove the value. It is better to put some comments in the code explaining the rationale of the removal.

First, we initialize the initial state to be in idle state.

```
internal State state = State.IDLE;
```

Then we have the function which will be called whenever the state has changed. In this function, we will update the appearance or any other properties of the affected components.

```
void update_state ()
```

The following code is to make sure that the `builder` object exists:

```
if (builder == null) {
    return;
}
```

In the idle state, we hide the go button and we use the refresh icon and label for the refresh button.

```
switch (state) {
  case State.IDLE:
    btn_go.hide ();
    btn_refresh.label = "gtk-refresh";
    break;
```

When we type the URL, we show the go button.

```
case State.TYPING_URL:
    btn_go.show ();
    break;
```

In the loading state, we simply hide the go button again and change the refresh button to a stop button.

```
case State.LOADING:
  btn_go.hide ();
  btn_refresh.label = "gtk-stop";
  break;
```

Then, depending on whether we can go forward or not, we set the forward button to be enabled or disabled.

```
if (view.can_go_forward ()) {
  btn_forward.sensitive = true;
} else {
  btn_forward.sensitive = false;
}
```

Similarly, depending on whether we can go backward or not, we set the back button to be enabled or disabled.

```
if (view.can_go_back ()) {
  btn_back.sensitive = true;
} else {
  btn_back.sensitive = false;
}
```

Then, let's see the constructor where we set up the whole interaction of the components.

```
public WebBrowser ()
```

Here, we use the image for the buttons rather than text only.

```
Gtk.Settings.get_default ().gtk_button_images = true;
```

In the following code, we simply open the `.ui` file and insert it into the `builder` object:

```
builder = new Builder ();
builder.add_from_file (UI_FILE);
```

The following snippet shows where we instantiate the web view and display the **Welcome** text. We enclose the text with underscore function of `gettext` to make it translatable. We skip the translation of the HTML heading markup because it's not relevant. We are only interested in the actual text which is displayed rather than the formatting itself.

```
view = new WebView ();
view.load_string("<h1>" + _("Welcome") + "</h1>", "text/html",
  "UTF-8", "/");
```

Then, we connect the `load_started` signal of the view. This is actually called when a link is clicked, which maps to the clicking link state. But just after this is called, the state is moved into loading state. We then update the appearance of the UI by calling the `update_state` function.

```
view.load_started.connect(() => {
    state = State.LOADING;
    update_state();
});
```

However, note that this is also called whenever any other resource is loaded from the Internet such as images, scripts, and any other files.

The `load_finished` signal is called whenever the loading has finished. In this case, we return back to the idle state.

```
view.load_finished.connect(() => {
    state = State.IDLE;
    update_state();
});
```

Here, we handle the key press event in the URL entry. As we designed earlier, whenever we type something, we will update the state to the typing url state. So this is the place we do that.

```
url_entry = builder.get_object ("url_entry") as Entry;
url_entry.key_press_event.connect(() => {
    state = State.TYPING_URL;
    update_state();
    return false;
});
```

The following code simply inserts the view into the container that we prepared in the `.ui` file:

```
var box = builder.get_object ("webhost") as Container;
box.add(view);
```

Then, we handle the click signal of the back button. When the button is clicked, we ask the view to go back by one page.

```
btn_back = builder.get_object ("btn_back") as Button;
btn_back.clicked.connect(() => {
    view.go_back ();
});
```

And the same for the forward button.

```
btn_forward = builder.get_object ("btn_forward") as Button;
btn_forward.clicked.connect(() => {
  view.go_forward ();
});
```

Our refresh button has dual functionalities, so here we check first whether it is in refresh role or stop role. We call `reload` on the view if it is the former role and `stop_loading` if it is the latter role.

```
btn_refresh = builder.get_object ("btn_refresh") as Button;
btn_refresh.clicked.connect(() => {
  if (btn_refresh.label == "gtk-refresh") {
    view.reload ();
  } else {
    view.stop_loading ();
  }
});
```

The go button needs to be clicked or activated (by pressing *Enter*). Both actions lead to the loading of the address typed in the URL entry.

```
btn_go = builder.get_object ("btn_go") as Button;
btn_go.activate.connect(() => {
  view.load_uri (url_entry.text);
});

btn_go.clicked.connect(() => {
  view.load_uri (url_entry.text);
});
```

This simply shows the window:

```
var window = builder.get_object ("window") as Window;
window.show_all ();
```

And as usual, this will exit the application whenever the window is closed:

```
window.destroy.connect(() => {
  Gtk.main_quit();
});
```

We call `update_state` to initialize the state:

```
update_state();
```

The code is quite simple, isn't it? What we are going to do next is test the `update_state` function in our unit test and prepare a stub of the view. Let's take a look at the test first. Here, we declare all tests inside the `TestWebBrowser` class.

```
public class TestWebBrowser {
```

The first function is the `process_events` function. This function is exactly the same as we had in *Chapter 12, Quality Made Easy*. It simply processes all pending events in the queue and explicitly waits until all are done.

```
static void process_events ()
{
  while (Gtk.events_pending ()) {
    Gtk.main_iteration_do(true);
  }
}
```

Then we test the initial state of the browser in this test function. We simply create the `WebBrowser` object and check whether the state is really in idle state. Next, we test the typing url state.

```
static void test_initial_state ()
{
  var web = new WebBrowser();
  process_events();
  assert (web.state == WebBrowser.State.IDLE);
}
```

In this function, we create the `WebBrowser` object and immediately show the window as well as the URL entry with `show_all`. This is to ensure that the widgets can be used immediately.

```
static void test_typing_url ()
{
  var web = new WebBrowser();
  var window = web.builder.get_object ("window") as Window;
  window.show_now ();
  web.url_entry.show_now ();
```

Then, we check whether the go button is visible or not. It must be hidden as we designed.

```
  assert (web.btn_go.visible == false);
```

Here, we prepare the URL entry by putting the mouse focus into it, so that we can type in it.

```
  var entry_w = web.url_entry.get_window ();
  web.url_entry.focus(0);
```

Before checking anything, we make sure that it is in idle state.

```
assert (web.state == WebBrowser.State.IDLE);
```

Then we simulate the pressing (and releasing) of the a key:

```
Gdk.test_simulate_key (entry_w, 5, 5, Gdk.Key.a, 0, Gdk.EventType.
KEY_PRESS);
Gdk.test_simulate_key (entry_w, 5, 5, Gdk.Key.a, 0, Gdk.EventType.
KEY_RELEASE);
```

Note that we must call this earlier on to make sure that the events are really sent to the widget and the handlers are properly called.

```
process_events ();
```

Here, we check that the state now must be in the typing url state:

```
assert (web.state == WebBrowser.State.TYPING_URL);
```

Also we check that the go button must be now visible.

```
assert (web.btn_go.visible == true);
```

Then, after typing, we move the focus to the go button.

```
var btn_w = web.btn_go.get_window ();
web.btn_go.focus(0);
```

And we press the Enter key on the button.

```
Gdk.test_simulate_key (btn_w, 5, 5, Gdk.Key.Return, 0, Gdk.
EventType.KEY_PRESS);
Gdk.test_simulate_key (btn_w, 5, 5, Gdk.Key.Return, 0, Gdk.
EventType.KEY_RELEASE);

process_events ();
```

The state should now change to loading state, because now the web view is loading the page.

```
assert (web.state == WebBrowser.State.LOADING);
```

So far, we have two tests. And it is time to see the main function. Here, we initialize the test suite framework:

```
static int main (string[] args)
{
  Gtk.test_init (ref args);
```

And we register the two tests that map to the functions defined previously:

```
Test.add_func ("/test-initial-state", test_initial_state);
Test.add_func ("/test-typing-url", test_typing_url);
```

After that, we set up the idle handler so the test can be run just after we call `Gtk.main`. We immediately quit the application after running all the tests:

```
Idle.add (() => {
  Test.run ();
  Gtk.main_quit ();
  return true;
});
```

Here, we start the event loop and hand it over to GTK.

```
Gtk.main ();
```

Note that we don't use any network connection to run the test. As we talked about this earlier, we don't even use the WebKit. Instead, we use our own stub to take WebKit's place during the testing.

In our stub, we must use exactly the same name of the object that we want to stub. Here, we also declare the `WebKit` namespace so that we can use the `using WebKit;` clause in our code. We ask Vala to generate the C code with the `webkit_` prefix. Without this, Vala will generate the `web_kit_` prefix (note the underscore in between the words).

```
[CCode (lower_case_cprefix = "webkit_")]
namespace WebKit {
```

This is a helper class that is used in the `load_started` and `load_finished` signals.

```
[CCode (cheader_filename="webkit/webkit.h")]
public class WebFrame : Object {
}
```

Then we declare the variables and the signals.

```
[CCode (cheader_filename="webkit/webkit.h")]
public class WebView : Viewport {
  public bool _can_go_back;
  public bool _can_go_forward;
  public signal void load_started (WebFrame frame);
  public signal void load_finished (WebFrame frame);
  WebFrame frame;
```

Here, we simply initialize the `frame` object.

```
public WebView() {
   frame = new WebFrame ();
}
```

The rest are pretty straightforward and do not require a detailed discussion as we already talked about this in *Chapter 12, Quality Made Easy*. They are only empty functions while in the stub, we only define functions which are really used in the implementation code.

Have a go hero – creating more tests

As you have noticed, we only tested two functionalities. We did not test all of the possible states. Now, please go ahead and craft more tests!

Part II – A Twitter client

Now let's move on to the next project, a twitter client. The feature of this application is to display a stream of tweets with the text that we search for. This is simpler than the web browser, as we are going to use Seed to develop it.

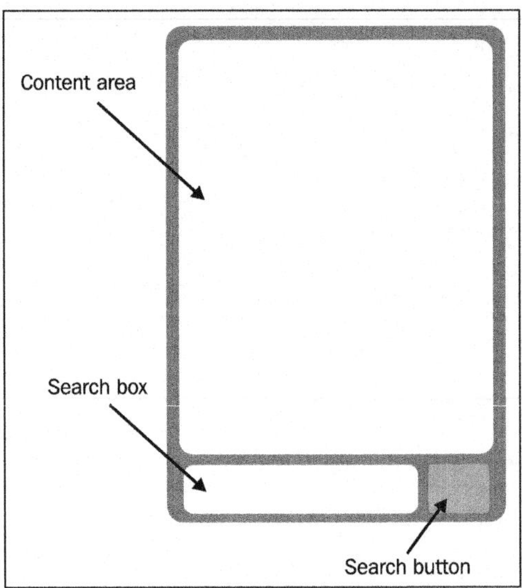

The UI is once again not complex. We basically have two parts of the screen—the Content area and the search area. The search area is divided into two parts, the Search box and the Search button. Whenever we click on the button, the Content area is updated with a stream of tweets with the search text.

Time for action – implementing the Twitter client

We will have three Seed scripts and we need to put them in a directory. Don't forget that we need an Internet connection to run the application.

1. Create a new script called `tweet-feed.js` and fill it with this code:

```
#!/usr/bin/env seed

Gtk = imports.gi.Gtk;
Gdk = imports.gi.Gdk;
GObject = imports.gi.GObject;

f = imports.feedEntry;
t = imports.twitter;

var twitter = new t.Twitter();

Gtk.init(Seed.argv);
var window = new Gtk.Window();
window.resize(400,400);
window.title = "Tweet Feed";
var box = new Gtk.Box({orientation: Gtk.Orientation.VERTICAL});
window.add(box);

var scroll = new Gtk.ScrolledWindow();
var viewport = new Gtk.Viewport();
box.pack_start(scroll, true, true);

var search_box = new Gtk.Box({orientation: Gtk.Orientation.
HORIZONTAL});
var entry = new Gtk.Entry();
entry.placeholder_text = "Enter your search topic";

search_box.pack_start(entry, true, true);
var search_button = new Gtk.Button({label: "gtk-find"});
search_button.use_stock = true;
search_button.signal.clicked.connect(function() {
  twitter.search(entry.text);
});
search_box.pack_start(search_button, false, false);

box.pack_start(search_box, false, false);

var entries = new Gtk.Box({orientation: Gtk.Orientation.
VERTICAL});
scroll.add(viewport);
viewport.add(entries);
```

```
window.show_all();

twitter.signal.connect("data-available", function(object) {
  entries.foreach(function(content) {
    entries.remove(content);
  });
  for (var i = 0; i < twitter.data.results.length; i ++) {
    var entry = new f.FeedEntry(twitter.data.results[i]);
    entries.pack_start(entry, false, false);

  }
});

Gtk.main();
```

2. Add a new file called `feedEntry.js` and use this code:

```
Gtk = imports.gi.Gtk;
Gdk = imports.gi.Gdk;
GObject = imports.gi.GObject;

FeedEntry = new GType({
  parent: Gtk.TextView.type,
  name: "FeedEntry",
  properties: [
    {
      name: 'from_user_name',
      type: GObject.TYPE_STRING,
      default_value: "",
      flags: (GObject.ParamFlags.CONSTRUCT
        | GObject.ParamFlags.READABLE
        | GObject.ParamFlags.WRITABLE),
    }

    , {
      name: 'from_user',
      type: GObject.TYPE_STRING,
      default_value: "",
      flags: (GObject.ParamFlags.CONSTRUCT
        | GObject.ParamFlags.READABLE
        | GObject.ParamFlags.WRITABLE),
    }
    , {
      name: 'text',
      type: GObject.TYPE_STRING,
      default_value: "",
```

```
        flags: (GObject.ParamFlags.CONSTRUCT
            | GObject.ParamFlags.READABLE
            | GObject.ParamFlags.WRITABLE),
      }
    ],

    class_init: function(klass, prototype) {
      prototype.update_data = function() {
        var writer_tag = new Gtk.TextTag({
          name: "writer",
          size_points: 12,
          weight: 700,
          style: 3,
          foreground:"#000000"});
        this.buffer.tag_table.add(writer_tag);

        var user_tag = new Gtk.TextTag({
          name: „user",
          style: 0,
          foreground:"#888888"});
        this.buffer.tag_table.add(user_tag);

        var content_tag = new Gtk.TextTag({
          name: „content",
          size_points: 12,
          style: 0,
          weight: 400,
          foreground: „#000000"
          });
        this.buffer.tag_table.add(content_tag);

        this.buffer.insert_at_cursor (this.text + „\n", -1);
        var start_iter = this.buffer.get_start_iter ();
        var end_iter = this.buffer.get_end_iter ();
        this.buffer.apply_tag_by_name („content", start_iter.iter,
end_iter.iter);

        var cursor_pos = this.buffer.cursor_position;
        this.buffer.insert_at_cursor (this.from_user_name + " ",
-1);
        var start_iter = this.buffer.get_iter_at_offset(cursor_pos);
        var end_iter = this.buffer.get_end_iter ();
        this.buffer.apply_tag_by_name ("writer", start_iter.iter,
end_iter.iter);
```

```
        var cursor_pos = this.buffer.cursor_position;
        this.buffer.insert_at_cursor ("@" + this.from_user + "\n",
-1);
        var start_iter = this.buffer.get_iter_at_offset(cursor_pos);
        var end_iter = this.buffer.get_end_iter ();
        this.buffer.apply_tag_by_name ("user", start_iter.iter, end_
iter.iter);
      }
    },
    init: function(self) {
      self.wrap_mode = Gtk.WrapMode.WORD;
      self.editable = false;
      self.update_data();
      self.show_all();
    }
  });
```

3. Add another new file called `twitter.js` and fill it with this code:

```
Gio = imports.gi.Gio;
GObject = imports.gi.GObject;

Twitter = new GType({
  parent: GObject.Object.type,
  name: "Twitter",
  signals: [
    {
      name: "data-available",
      parameters: []
    }
  ],
  class_init: function(klass, prototype) {
    prototype.search = function(keyword) {
      var url = "http://search.twitter.com/search.json?q=" +
keyword;
      var data_source = Gio.file_new_for_uri (url);
      var self = this;
      data_source.read_async(0, null,
        function(source, result) {
          var input = source.read_finish(result);
          var stream = new Gio.DataInputStream.c_new(input);
          self.data = JSON.parse(stream.read_until("", 0));
          self.signal["data-available"].emit();
        }
```

```
      );


    }
  },

  init: function(self) {
    this.data = {};
  }
});
```

4. Give executable permission on the `tweet-feed.js` file, for example, by typing the following command in the shell:

```
chmod +x tweet-feed.js
```

5. Run it, type any search text, and press the **Find** button.

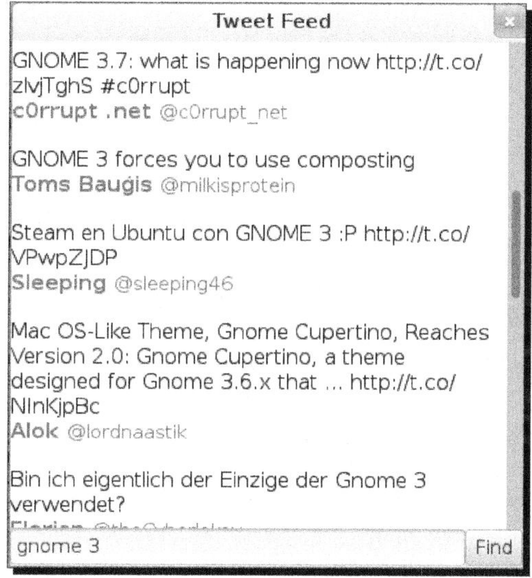

What just happened?

Here, we employ the knowledge of reading a resource from the network as well as the skill of extending an existing widget. We also learn how to develop a Seed application with multiple scripts to modularize and simplify the development.

We divide the application into three modules. The first one is for the main application, another one for reading the twitter data, and the last one is for the newly derived widget to display the tweets.

Let's start from the last one, that is, the `FeedEntry` widget. First, we derive a new widget from the `TextView` widget:

```
FeedEntry = new GType({
    parent: Gtk.TextView.type,
    name: "FeedEntry",
```

This is because we want the text wrapping functionality, which is available in `TextView`. Here, we define some properties with the names that exactly follow the data that comes from the Twitter API.

```
    properties: [
        {
            name: 'from_user_name',
            type: GObject.TYPE_STRING,
            default_value: "",
            flags: (GObject.ParamFlags.CONSTRUCT
                | GObject.ParamFlags.READABLE
                | GObject.ParamFlags.WRITABLE),
        }
```

In the API, we have `from_user_name`, `from_user` and `text` which contains the full name of the **tweep** (the person who posted the tweet), the username, and the tweet itself. So we just use a direct map between the Twitter API and the properties in our new widget.

Then, we define the `update_data` function in the prototype. It means that the function is available in the class.

```
    class_init: function(klass, prototype) {
        prototype.update_data = function() {
```

Then, we define a few tags. The tags are used to style text that we enter into the text buffer.

```
        var writer_tag = new Gtk.TextTag({
            name: "writer",
            size_points: 12,
            weight: 700,
            style: 3,
            foreground:"#000000"});
        this.buffer.tag_table.add(writer_tag);
```

We want to use a normal style for the tweet, bold style for the name of the tweep, and a lighter one for the twitter user ID. But before using the tags, we need to add them into the tag table and we do this for all tags. Then, we insert the tweet first, followed by a newline.

```
        this.buffer.insert_at_cursor (this.text + "\n", -1);
```

Here, we remember the start location of the text by getting the `Iter` object. The `Iter` object is used to point to a certain place in the text buffer. We can think of this with an analogy of text selection.

```
var start_iter = this.buffer.get_start_iter ();
```

And here, we mark the end of the text selection:

```
var end_iter = this.buffer.get_end_iter ();
```

Then, we apply the tag with the specified name to the text which is covered by the start and end `iters`.

```
this.buffer.apply_tag_by_name ("content", start_iter.iter, end_
iter.iter);
```

Back to the selection analogy, we can think of this like giving a formatting style to the selected text in a text document.

Here, we can no longer use the `get_start_iter` function to get the start of the `Iter` object.

```
var cursor_pos = this.buffer.cursor_position;
```

Instead, we get the current cursor position to mark as the start of the text which will be inserted below.

Then, we get the start iter by pointing the cursor position that we recorded earlier.

```
this.buffer.insert_at_cursor (this.from_user_name + " ", -1);
var start_iter = this.buffer.get_iter_at_offset(cursor_pos);
```

This one is the same as the previous one; we just get the end of the text to get the end iter.

```
var end_iter = this.buffer.get_end_iter ();
```

Then we apply the tag into the text in between the `iter` parameters.

```
this.buffer.apply_tag_by_name ("writer", start_iter.iter, end_
iter.iter);
```

Naturally, `TextView` is for editing text, but here, we disable the editing during the instantiation of the object:

```
init: function(self) {
  self.wrap_mode = Gtk.WrapMode.WORD;
  self.editable = false;
```

During initialization, we immediately update the data which in turns renders the data.

```
self.update_data();
self.show_all();
```

That's it. Now let's take a look at the `twitter.js` file which functions as the data source.

Here we define our `Twitter` object as a simple `GObject` object.

```
Twitter = new GType({
  parent: GObject.Object.type,
  name: "Twitter",
```

We have a signal called `data-available` and it is called without any parameters.

```
signals: [
  {
    name: "data-available",
    parameters: []
  }
],
```

The signal is called whenever we have new data in the JSON format coming from the Twitter API. This is the `search` function which we make available in the class. What it does is it simply gets the stream from the mentioned URL, and appends it with the keyword. We use `Gio` to open the stream.

```
class_init: function(klass, prototype) {
  prototype.search = function(keyword) {
    var url = "http://search.twitter.com/search.json?q=" + keyword;
    var data_source = Gio.file_new_for_uri(url);
    var self = this;
```

Then, we read the stream asynchronously so it will not disturb the UI while loading the data from the Internet. When the data is ready, we enter a function which we put as a closure at the end of the `read_async` function. There, the stream is converted into a `DataInputStream` instance and we parse the data into a JavaScript object. When everything is ready, we emit the `data-available` signal.

```
data_source.read_async(0, null,
  function(source, result) {
    var input = source.read_finish(result);
    var stream = new Gio.DataInputStream.c_new(input);
    self.data = JSON.parse(stream.read_until("", 0));
    self.signal["data-available"].emit();
  }
);
```

Our initialization function is as simple as this. It just initializes the `data` member as an empty object.

```
init: function(self) {
   this.data = {};
}
```

Then let's see the main application code in `tweet-feed.js`. Here, we import the other two scripts and make them accessible from the `f` and `t` variables:

```
f = imports.feedEntry;
t = imports.twitter;
```

This could become one of the bad examples when the code base gets larger. Something like `feedEntryScript` or `twitterScript` could be a better name to use.

In the following line, we instantiate a `Twitter` object:

```
var twitter = new t.Twitter();
```

Then we initialize `Gtk` and create the window. We set the initial size and we give it a title:

```
Gtk.init(Seed.argv);
var window = new Gtk.Window();
window.resize(400,400);
window.title = "Tweet Feed";
```

We have a `Box` object to be used as a layout and we put it in the window.

```
var box = new Gtk.Box({orientation: Gtk.Orientation.VERTICAL});
window.add(box);
```

Now, we can add more than one widget into it.

Here, we have a new `ScrolledWindow` object called `scroll`, created together with `viewport`. This is required so that we can scroll the tweets when they overflow the size of the window.

```
var scroll = new Gtk.ScrolledWindow();
var viewport = new Gtk.Viewport();
box.pack_start(scroll, true, true);
```

Then, we add a new horizontal box to be put at the bottom of the screen. This would be the place of the text entry and the search button.

```
var search_box = new Gtk.Box({orientation: Gtk.Orientation.
HORIZONTAL});
```

Here, we create the text entry for the user to type the search text into. We use a place holder text as a hint to the user to tell him or her what to do. Then we pack the entry into the horizontal box.

```
var entry = new Gtk.Entry();
entry.placeholder_text = "Enter your search topic";
search_box.pack_start(entry, true, true);
```

Here, we create the search button. It is a simple button with a stock item, so we don't need to create a label ourselves. Then we connect the clicked signal by calling the `twitter.search` function and initiating the stream downloading.

```
var search_button = new Gtk.Button({label: "gtk-find"});
search_button.use_stock = true;
search_button.signal.clicked.connect(function() {
    twitter.search(entry.text);
});
search_box.pack_start(search_button, false, false);
```

Furthermore, we create a vertical box to host all the incoming tweets. The box is then put into the viewport, which is inside the scrolled window.

```
var entries = new Gtk.Box({orientation: Gtk.Orientation.VERTICAL});
scroll.add(viewport);
viewport.add(entries);
```

This is the `data-available` signal handler. As we discussed earlier, the signal is emitted when we receive the entire Twitter stream.

```
twitter.signal.connect("data-available", function(object) {
    entries.foreach(function(content) {
        entries.remove(content);
    });
    for (var i = 0; i < twitter.data.results.length; i ++) {
        var entry = new f.FeedEntry(twitter.data.results[i]);
        entries.pack_start(entry, false, false);

    }
});
```

So what we do here is we first remove existing entries, if any. Then we iterate all the tweets we have in the `twitter.data.results` array. For each tweet, we simply create a `FeedEntry` object. We pass the entry structure directly as the members of the structure are already mapped in the `FeedEntry` class. Then, we add the entry object inside the `entries` array.

Summary

Now, we have two real applications on our hands. However, there are still missing pieces here and there. And they are waiting for you to fix them.

In our first project, we learnt a new trick to avoid making code to check whether it is now in development mode or not, by hardcoding the path directly from the `configure` script. We discussed how to load a web page and interact with the rest of chrome.

Later on, in our second project, we learnt how to extend a widget and a multiple-scripts application. This is important to know as in the real world, our application would resemble this situation.

Then in both projects, we discussed the logic and UI building separation by putting the non-UI code in a dedicated class. This way, we can easily add more complex business processes and not get confused because it got mixed with the UI codes.

Congratulations, you have reached the end of this book! But, what's next?

After reading this book, of course, we still need to dig the details of the skin of knowledge we read so far. However, as we already get the essentials, it would be easy for you to learn those details. One thing which is important to remember is that the GNOME platform is an open source project. Like any other project, it is awesome because of the contributions of hackers around the world. Now, you are more than capable of doing the same!

Pop Quiz Answers

Chapter 2, Preparing Our Weapons

Pop quiz – naming a signal

Q1   A. `server_on_connection_started`. This is because the first word refers to the class (server) and the rest followed by `on` means that there is some kind of event happening.

Chapter 3, Programming Languages

Pop quiz – how to fix this?

Q1   A. `public`, because we want to access it from `Main` class which is outside the `Book` class.

Pop quiz – what is the value now?

Q1   A. JavaScript will think this is an error because we try to access `.length` from an undefined value. This is because JavaScript can't get a property value from an undefined value.

Pop quiz – can you see the difference now?

Q1   A. `Circle` is a class because it has the definition, and `circle` is an object, instantiated from the `Circle` class.

Pop quiz – how to make it global

Q1   A. Just add `printAuthor` in the `Book` class prototype, and then all objects created from `Book` will have the function. If we put the method in every instantiated object, it would be too cumbersome to do it, while having it on prototype guarantees that the method is always created.

Chapter 4, Using GNOME Core Libraries

Pop quiz – why the value of zero is printed out

Q1   A. Both answers are right. The default value is set in the construction phase.

Chapter 5, Building Graphical User Interface Applications

Pop quiz

Q1   A. Slightly to the left.

This is because 0.3 is less than 0.5. The value of 0.0 means the alignment is totally on the left.

Q2   A. None of the provided answers is right, the correct one is slightly to the top

This is because 0.3 vertically means it is closer to the top which has the value of 0.0.

Chapter 10, Desktop Integration

Pop quiz – a good example application

Q1	A. A battery system tray applet. This is because the data are posted all the time meaning it is good for monitoring applications such as the system tray applet. A battery checker usually just polls the data once or when needed, not all the time.

Index

library
  creating 152-156
  widgets, maintaining 151-156
link_filtered function 167
locale
  about 254
  adding, to system 256, 257
  installing 270
  obtaining 255
  output, obtaining with 257
locale data 255
locale-gen command 257
locale parameters
  exploring 256
localization process 271, 272
loosely typed language 47

M

member access specifiers
  about 65
  defining 65, 67
messages 26
mockup
  about 35
  implementing 109-115
  implementing, raw GTK+ programming used
      117-121
  implementing, with Clutter 121-128
Model-View-Controller (MVC) 180
modularization 61
MPEG codecs 159
multimedia
  third-party library 159, 160
multimedia capabilities 159
multimedia libraries, GNOME
  GStreamer 11

N

navigation
  between tabs 27, 28
network
  accessing, GIO used 97-101
new operator 56
notifications
  sending 249, 251
notification system 249

O

object
  about 56
  constructing 54, 55
  prototypes, modifying 59, 60
object-oriented programming. *See* **OOP**
Ogg demultiplexer 171
OOP
  with JavaScript 52
openSUSE 12
  about 15
  GNOME, installing 15, 17
  SDK, installing 15, 17
outputs
  obtaining, with locales 257
override keyword 143

P

packages
  marking 14
pads 161
pallete 34
Pango 11
passwords
  storing, securely 243-248
Portable Operating System Interface. *See* **POSIX**
POSIX 254
printCounter function 82
private bus 225
program
  modularizing 61, 62
  running, Seed used 45-47
project
  Gee library, adding 71, 72
project tool 26
properties, GLib
  about 86
  accessing 86-90
prototype
  modifying, of object 59, 60
  using 56-58
Python 43

Thank you for buying
GNOME 3 Application Development Beginner's Guide

About Packt Publishing

Packt, pronounced 'packed', published its first book "*Mastering phpMyAdmin for Effective MySQL Management*" in April 2004 and subsequently continued to specialize in publishing highly focused books on specific technologies and solutions.

Our books and publications share the experiences of your fellow IT professionals in adapting and customizing today's systems, applications, and frameworks. Our solution based books give you the knowledge and power to customize the software and technologies you're using to get the job done. Packt books are more specific and less general than the IT books you have seen in the past. Our unique business model allows us to bring you more focused information, giving you more of what you need to know, and less of what you don't.

Packt is a modern, yet unique publishing company, which focuses on producing quality, cutting-edge books for communities of developers, administrators, and newbies alike. For more information, please visit our website: www.packtpub.com.

About Packt Open Source

In 2010, Packt launched two new brands, Packt Open Source and Packt Enterprise, in order to continue its focus on specialization. This book is part of the Packt Open Source brand, home to books published on software built around Open Source licenses, and offering information to anybody from advanced developers to budding web designers. The Open Source brand also runs Packt's Open Source Royalty Scheme, by which Packt gives a royalty to each Open Source project about whose software a book is sold.

Writing for Packt

We welcome all inquiries from people who are interested in authoring. Book proposals should be sent to author@packtpub.com. If your book idea is still at an early stage and you would like to discuss it first before writing a formal book proposal, contact us; one of our commissioning editors will get in touch with you.

We're not just looking for published authors; if you have strong technical skills but no writing experience, our experienced editors can help you develop a writing career, or simply get some additional reward for your expertise.

VMware View 5 Desktop Virtualization Solutions

ISBN: 978-1-84968-112-4   Paperback: 288 pages

A complete guide to planning and designing solutions based on VMware View 5

1. Written by VMware experts Jason Langone and Andre Leibovici, this book is a complete guide to planning and designing a solution based on VMware View 5

2. Secure your Visual Desktop Infrastructure (VDI) by having firewalls, antivirus, virtual enclaves, USB redirection and filtering and smart card authentication

3. Analyze the strategies and techniques used to migrate a user population from a physical desktop environment to a virtual desktop solution

LiveCode Mobile Development Beginner's Guide

ISBN: 978-1-84969-248-9   Paperback: 246 pages

Create fun-filled, rich apps for Android and iOS with LiveCode

1. Create fun, interactive apps with rich media features of LiveCode

2. Step by step instructions for creating apps and interfaces

3. Dive headfirst into mobile application development using LiveCode backed with clear explanations enriched with ample screenshots

Please check **www.PacktPub.com** for information on our titles

Printed in Dunstable, United Kingdom